To: Esmera

ALWAYS.

keep. shining.

I loved meeting you! Here's my number so we could mermaid one day! 305-303-5935

A Memoir

Anaregina Frias

& IG: anaregina.frias

Everyone's name has been changed to the name of a character from a number of my favorite books, movies, or T.V. shows. So, while I protect people's identity you can find out who we both like! …Or don't. Heh.

ISBN-13: 978-0-578-57893-4

Cover design by: Victoria Zabulanes (@victoria.zabulanes) and
Odysseus Mourtzouchos (www.odysseusm-design.com)
Photo of Anaregina Frias by: Julio Colón (@juliocolonphotography)

CONTENTS

"You are destined for greatness."

-Papá

Para ti Papá

P.S. This book is also for you and my 19-year-old self.

PROLOGUE

God, I hoped Jacob wasn't trying to get back with me. Or worse, that he only called for the V. Considering he asked me out on a Thursday in December last year, and I dumped him the following Friday, he never made it to my hallmark "Wall of Flowers," the wall in my room where I paint a flower representing the guy I last went out with. The flowers all connect in a vine "growing" upwards, and each one symbolizes my ex in some way. It begins with Ponyboy, my first love, who is a red rose because it's my favorite blossom, and red means passion. Sodapop, the gorgeous sophomore I dated during my final months of senior year of high school, is a hot pink hibiscus, because, well, he's hot! Jacob would have been a white daisy for sure, because he's sensitive.

"There's an active shooter at my base," Jacob said, as he glanced up from his phone.

"What does that mean?" I asked. He said this, like someone would say, "Oh, let's go take a walk in the park."

"It means that someone came to our base with a gun ready to shoot at us. Probably ISIS. Yeah, I'm pretty sure it's ISIS." Jacob stretched out his muscular arm, baring an intricate octopus tattoo. His fingertips were close enough to touch my tanned, bare shoulder, but given that we're technically exes, I made a conscious effort not to give any I-want-you-back signals.

"That's, like, really scary. How are you so chill about it?" I asked.

"Ana, as a marine, you really just got to keep things light. If not, you'll go insane." He chuckled, the same familiar dorky chuckle as always.

"Wow. I can only imagine. Well, it's a good thing you're here and not there," I said, taking a bite of the chewy chocolate chip cookie he'd offered—no, lured me with— from Starbucks. An hour earlier, I was peacefully reading in my room, enjoying my own company, when I got an unknown number calling me. I answered, thinking it was Best Western wanting to hire me, because the Universe had decided to grant me with the gift of work. But no, it was Jacob again. It'd been one year since we last saw or spoke to each other. He was back, alive, from his first year of being a marine.

I, on the other hand, had a long, sad story to tell him. So, here we were on a legendary blazing, hot summer day in Miami, outside of Panera Bread, the magnificent bread bakery where people freeze inside, then melt as soon as they exit.

"Yeah, it is a good thing," he smiled dorkily. A short, delicious breeze caressed me, as I fiddled to unknot my black, shoulder-length tendrils. He went on, "I went through some rough shit this year. I was in a prisoner-of-war camp when they sent me to Kittery, Maine. And that was basically to prepare me in case I was ever held captive by…let's say…Russian terrorists."

"No way." I cupped my mouth, my eyes widening in awe.

"Yeah! It was crazy. They locked me up, beat me, and yelled at me in Russian accents. Not going to lie—it was kind of scary."

I smiled at him. Fascinating as this was, I didn't know what to say. Jacob had never exactly stimulated my brain.

"So? It's your turn," he said. "We've only been talking about me since I picked you up. What's gone on with the girl with the blue hat?" He smiled.

I touched the tip of my hat and giggled nervously. I felt more at ease, now that I knew I wasn't just a booty call.

"Let's walk." I stood, feeling comfortable in his company. A flock of black crows squawked behind us. Just kidding, this was Miami. A cluster of grackles chirped annoyingly. Jacob followed me, and I stayed quiet, playing with the impossible knot that clung to my still-wet-from-the-shower curls.

"So, are you gonna start, or what?" Jacob probed my silent bubble.

"I'm just warning you…it's sad. I went through some rough shit this year, too."

"It can't be as rough as mine."

"Eh, that's debatable."

We strolled into Staples, the perfect place to tell a long story. We were old friends catching up. Old friends, that is, until Jacob was hell bent on the two of us going out. "You wanted air conditioning, didn't you?" Jacob stood back to let me walk in first.

"Hyeah," I laughed, "you didn't?"

"No, yeah, I definitely do." Jacob smiled and stretched out his arms, as we relished the cool air, practically skipping into the office supply haven. I took a moment to admire the colorful miniature binders, while Jacob followed me to the best section of Staples—the office chairs.

His large chest puffed up, as he exhaled. "Alright, Ana, you managed to get me to tell you about my ex fiancée, my torture camp, and the whole journey of traveling from Miami to South Carolina, back home to North Carolina, to Twenty-nine Palms, California, back home to Pensacola, to Maine, then Arkansas then back to Miami. What's your story? You're killing me with anticipation!"

"I'm telling, I'm telling!" I smiled, letting myself be engulfed by the comfy, large, leather chair. He sat in a similar one. A young man in a bright, red shirt and black pants put supplies in order, as he stood on a metal ladder across from us. Inching myself closer to Jacob, I took a deep breath.

"You are such a writer." He chuckled; his chocolate-brown eyes glowed with…admiration? Yeah, I'd say admiration. Leaning forward, his shoulders tensed almost imperceptibly. Catching a whiff of his skin, I remembered the way he smelled, and the nostalgia settled in, reminding me of the time when everything was okay in my world.

CHAPTER 1
Cubicle Thirty-Three

"You are going today," my dad said in a stern voice, leaving no room for hesitation or retaliation on my part. I stayed quiet, keeping all thoughts inside. *I don't want to go. I don't want to go.*

"You can't wear that dress, Anaregina. Wear pants, an appropriate shirt, and closed-toed shoes." He stood in my doorway, analyzing me from head to toe.

I gulped. "What do I wear to visit someone in jail?"

A part of me laughed inside, because I never thought, in a billion years, that I would be asking myself that question. But I was, and I chose a black and gray plaid shirt, light blue jeans, and my brown leather combat boots. The boots gave me confidence. I needed courage to visit someone I wasn't ready to see.

Dad leaned against the door frame. "I'm just letting you know now, there's something I have to tell you and your brother." His voice was grim and hollow. Whatever confidence I'd managed to muster up dissipated and was replaced with fear. Fear, that in a couple of moments, I would witness my brother in the light of a criminal, something I knew in my heart he wasn't. Fear that it was so easy for life to lock away someone you loved over such a trivial thing.

My brother, ever the problem-solver, decided to lodge himself in a relationship between the girl he felt he loved and the guy who was ultimately abusing her, a.k.a. her crazy boyfriend. Whatever my dad had to say to the both of us could not have been that bad. Although, the longer he stood there thinking about how to say it, the more I felt the air teeming with uncertainty and anxiety.

It was still early enough in the afternoon for birds to be chirping, as we left my house and stepped into my dad's white Volkswagen, en route to visit Adam at Miami-Dade's Correctional Detention Center. Outside the window, the scenery shifted from popular restaurants and clothing stores, like Chili's and Old Navy, to the familiar area of Doral with neatly-trimmed plants decorating modern building complexes. We took a street littered with potholes lined by tall trees and vivid green shrubs resembling a forest. The outside world looked wild and poorly maintained. To our left, a bit of land was under construction, and as we approached our destination, a man-made lake sparkled next to us.

I texted my friend, Phoebe, telling her my situation. During our senior year of high school, we became close. We could tell each other everything.

I'm trying so hard not to cry, it's taking everything in me to not cry.

I hit send and continued to endure the pressure that made its home in my chest. As I waited for her reply, I squirmed in my seat until my dad finally broke the bubble of silence between us.

"I went to the doctor a while back…" he began. Already, the pressure in my chest tightened into a knot. "Because I was having some pain when I would pee. It turns out I have a tumor in my bladder."

I turned to face him. Every cell in my body lit on fire. "You mean you have cancer?"

He shrugged. "There's a chance it's malignant," he said, then entered his own cloud of silence.

I couldn't believe it. It was so much to take in, I felt like the news folded itself into a neat little package and tucked itself away into some hidden compartment in my mind labeled: Deal With Later.

We arrived at a large cement building with tiny slits for windows surrounded by a tall silver fence topped with barbed wire strangling the edge. Slowly, I stepped out of the passenger seat and took in my new surroundings like a frightened animal.

"Does Adam know?" I asked Dad, as we walked towards the entrance.

"Not yet. I'm going to tell him now," he said.

As my dad opened the hideous, olive green doors, I took a deep breath, held it, and exhaled. How would Adam digest the news I couldn't even fathom to face? The scent of trees and Miami's legendary humidity disappeared as soon as I stepped inside. When I saw the security guard dressed in a dark green uniform asking me for my ID, I started trembling. She scanned my outfit to deem whether or not I could see Adam. God forbid I should show half an inch of cleavage to go see my own brother or worse, open-toed shoes. The guard asked my dad for Adam's cell number. My dad had already memorized it and recited it in the same stern, monotone voice he used with me earlier.

A thick glass separated us from the silver slot to exchange IDs. I was beginning to wonder if I was in a nightmare, but the hollowness in my stomach made it clear that this was real. I scanned the faces of the people gathered in the small waiting room who all had the same expressionless looks on their faces, as if they'd been waiting for hours. Except for the blonde girl sitting towards the back who looked my age. I sat next to her.

"Hi," I said, crossing my legs and folding my arms together.

"Hi." She turned to look at me. Her eyes were brown and big and filled with anticipation. Like mine probably were.

"This is my first time ever visiting someone in jail. It's kind of nerve-wracking." I mumbled.

"It gets better with time, trust me. Who are you visiting?"

"My brother," I said, expecting her to ask me why he was there.

But she didn't. Maybe it was an unspoken code not to ask. "I'm seeing my boyfriend. Hopefully, he'll get out soon. It's been a while."

I began wringing my hands, as if they were made out of malleable clay. Before I could answer her, they called her boyfriend's last name, and she shot up from her seat, eager to go through the door to see him. She smiled at me sympathetically, and I tried to smile back. I wanted to hear her sweet, soothing voice again and imagined myself telling her exactly why my brother was here. That whole thing about confessing to a stranger making you feel better.

And what exactly had happened to my brother? Well, apparently, his ex-girlfriend was trying to escape her physically abusive ex-boyfriend's home (they were living together…don't ask), and she was too afraid to take their dog, which she felt righteously belonged to her, so she called Adam for his help.

"Would you like a piece of gum?" A man with a black mustache sitting in front of me asked, pulling me out of my thoughts.

"No, thanks," I said, rubbing my arms for warmth. I would like nothing more than to run into Sodapop's arms and hide there, ignoring the fact that our relationship was walking on egg shells, sure the beach day is nice but when the sun goes down its time to leave. My eyes were drawn to the list of rules on the oatmeal colored walls. "Visitors are prohibited from wearing: Clothing that resembles an inmate uniform, such as orange, red, white, colored scrubs." The signs were made of a green metal, and the words were in English, Spanish, and Creole. My dad sat next to me, patiently waiting, staring straight ahead. "Frias. Adam Frias." A different security guard scanned the waiting room. My dad and I rose from our seats and followed him through the door where we were asked to remove any metal that we had on us. I removed my silver necklace, earrings, and boots, gathering everything with my ID together on the wooden table next to the metal detector. It's like an airport but worse. My dad removed his belt and shoes and walked through. There was a loud, annoying buzzing sound, which meant we could pass through the second deteriorating door.

"You're number thirty-three," the guard told us.

The large numbers were painted in orange above the cubicle spaces. We walked towards Cubicle 33 and sat in cold, plastic chairs. I stared at the red phone hung on the wall to my right and reminded myself to breathe. I hated seeing my brother in this place. Biting my nails, I glanced at my dad in his perfect composure.

Finally, my brother arrived, looking forlorn. The sadness on his face shocked me so much, I began to tremble, but there was nothing I could do other than wave at him through the scratched, opaque glass. Prior visitors had tried carving hearts with initials on them, but they came out looking like chicken scratch. He waved and picked up the phone. My dad did the same. Every minute felt like an hour, as my dad told him about his potential cancer. I dug my nails into the skin of my hands, trying everything not to scream or cry. I couldn't hear what my brother was telling my dad, but the pain in his eyes was enough to make me understand why some people cut themselves when they can't handle their reality any longer. To pass the time, I started to count the rings of the red corded phone.

"Do you want to speak to her now?" my dad asked.

My brother nodded. I tried to make out whatever he was saying by reading his lips. The glass barrier was so cloudy, I saw my own goddamn reflection. My dad passed me the phone, and I took it, eyes focused on Adam. In his bright, orange jumpsuit with a white shirt underneath and long black hair, he looked wilder than usual.

"Hey," Adam said.

"Hi," I said. *Be strong, Ana.*

"I'm sorry you have to see me here. I wish you didn't have to." Adam's eyes reflected pain and torment.

I stayed quiet, wanting to ask him why. Why did you have to pick up her phone call and go to her psychotic boyfriend's house and take "their" dog, because she wanted to run away with it? Why didn't you just say no?

I opened my mouth to speak, to tell him what I thought of him, of his "girlfriend," of his stupid actions for such a petty girl. My dad, sensing what was coming, lightly nudged my arm. "Remember you're not allowed to talk about the case," Dad muttered.

I nodded. My words would come one day, when he was out of this forsaken place, they would come. But for now, no words were necessary. He could see my pain.

CHAPTER 2
Test Results Plus a Bruised Heart

The pain did not stop there. In the span of one week, the following series of unfortunate events occurred:

- Day one.

I got hired as a waitress at Don Burrita. Lucky me! (Yay, right?) By the second day, I wanted to cook myself.

It was my first job, even though I don't consider it. I didn't even get an interview; I literally had five connections to the boss and I'm Mexican and speak Spanish. It was a cute, cozy Mexican restaurant close to my house that needed help on the weekends. They served mouth-watering, soul-savoring food, but weekends in the restaurant world translated to hell. I was extremely nervous about working with new people and serving strangers large, hot plates which would burn my fingers every time I picked them up. I hated having to learn everything in Spanish, and the boss lady spoke so fast, it was like she had her own language going, one that everyone else could understand except for me.

I remember the first man whose order I took and his coffee I poured. He had no idea that I wasn't yet a waitress in my eyes, I was simply trying to convey the illusion that I was in order to get by, and like most people, he ate it all up.

"Atiende las mesas, no tengas miedo de la gente." Cute and Possibly Gay Manager ordered me to attend the tables, and not to be afraid of people.

"Sí, claro," I said with a forced smile.

As soon as he shuffled away, I leaned against the mustard yellow wall, feeling the scorching heat emanating from the busy kitchen as I scanned the occupied tables. It was funny to see the customers interact before they ate.

They'd walk in expectant and hangry, and then, as soon as the food arrived, their faces would light up, eyes glowing with love for life again. Every time I ate there (which wasn't too often), I'd get one beast of a pimple on my cheek. I called it "My Don Burrita Pimple." Totally worth it.

Even though I wore light makeup, I could feel it melting off my face, as I went to check on Tables 1, 2, 3, 4, 5, 6, 9, 8, 10, 11, and 12. There was no seven, and after six, the tables were out of order which set my structure-loving mind on fire. No organization in that place! Eventually, I caught on to the language of waitressing which consisted of exchanging silent glances that would say, "clean that table," or a nod that indicated, "put chips for the new customers that just walked in." I'd quickly nod and go get chips and salsa from the kitchen.

My fellow Mexican coworkers were all older, and all possessed the warm, vivacious energy our culture emits, except the girl who was closest to my age. Well, she was nice the first day, but the second day was where shit got deep.

- Day Two.

I woke up with an indescribable empty feeling in my stomach. It's when your gut knows, and I mean knows with its whole heart and soul, that you are going to be losing someone important soon. Sodapop, my boyfriend, was acting distant. You know…three-hour replies, less heart emojis, no "I miss you" back texts. Yeah, well, PLOT TWIST—he wasn't the impending loss that day.

"Where's Mama?" I ask Dad who was still in his plaid blue and red PJ pants and white T-shirt.

"She didn't tell you?" He hesitated when speaking. When I slowly shook my head and raised my eyebrows, he went on, "She went to take Snoopy to get put down." He paused, letting the information sink in. "I thought she told you."

"No. She did not," I said through gritted teeth. In an absolute fury, I stomped into my room, slammed the door, and threw on a black V-neck shirt and black jeans with black leather stripes on the side. What, the f u c k, Mom. I flew to the bathroom and managed to get ready in less than ten minutes, a huge milestone for a girly girl like me.

"I'll take you to go see him," my dad called out. Thank God for him.

We were on our way to the vet where they were possibly already euthanizing my dalmatian I've had since I was six years old. Dad had surprised me with him for my sixth birthday, an adorable puppy in a box wrapped in Snoopy wrapping paper. As soon as I lifted the lid, he popped out, eager to meet his ecstatic owner and make a mess of the world. Now, twelve years later, arthritis had gotten the best of him, and Snoopy was in pain every day. It was the right thing to do, but still, she could've told me.

Hot, fat tears of grief and boiling frustration raced down my cheeks. "I see exactly why you left Mom," I said, not bothering to hide the revolting bitterness in my tone.

"Anaregina, don't talk about her like her that. She probably didn't tell you because she was afraid you would try and stop her." Ugh, even after divorcing her, he still defended her. Oh. My. God.

"That doesn't give her the right to prevent me from saying goodbye to him!" I angled my body away from him and glued my eyes to the rearview mirror that read, "Objects are closer than they appear." The morning was lead pencil gray and cloudy, cliché death weather.

"I'm sorry," Dad genuinely apologized. He placed his comforting hand on my shoulder. I tried to turn from him as much as possible and gave up on suppressing my uncontrollable sobbing. *You could have said something to her, Dad.*

By the time we arrived at the small veterinarian's office with white walls boasting preventative flea medicine, a short, buff vet greeted us, and I was already embarrassed before even entering the room where Snoopy, The Traitor, and The Traitor's Mother were.

"We're here for Snoopy," my dad told the vet.

"Yes, right over here," Dr. Gonzalez replied, acknowledging me with sad, brown eyes.

The aroma of dog and cat fur wafted into my snot-covered nose. I wiped off the snot and nodded, as the both of us followed him into the back. I already knew that Snoopy was still alive, because I spoke with my mom on the phone while getting ready. I shot her and my grandma a glare before resting my eyes on Snoopy, skinny and quivering with fear on the shiny, metal table. It's obvious my mom was right to make this decision, especially with the pressure my grandma was putting on her to put Snoopy out of his misery. In her eyes she needed to release some kind of suffering in the Frias household, and she wanted to protect me from more pain, the delusional fantasy of every caring mother.

"Poor baby, my Snoopy." I pet his soft, black ear and tried to give him as much comfort and loving energy as I could. I wasn't going to voice my goodbye with two vets in the room, so I settled on thinking it instead. The thin, taller vet was the one putting Snoopy to sleep, and as he did, I focused on Snoopy's puppy brown eyes and continued to caress his spotted forehead and "silently" weep. The shorter "hot" vet gently put his hand on my left shoulder for a moment, and I felt guilty for finding him attractive at a grave moment such as this.

You'll always be my puppy, Snoopy, I thought, holding onto him as long as I could, until they pulled him out from under my grasp.

An hour and a half later, I was on my way to work, and my face was redder than a chili pepper. It was still early in my shift, and no one wanted

Mexican food at four in the afternoon, so I sat next to my coworker, Priscilla, the two of us folding napkins in kitchen utensils.

"Why are you so slow?" Priscilla asked in the most condescending tone of all CondescendingTone-Landia. I put down my half-ass kitchen-utensil-napkin arrangement and looked her in the eye. Wisps of frizzy hair framed her round, plain face.

"My dog just died," I said, half-expecting her to understand, half-expecting her to sympathize. Instead, she just glued her eyes to her unwrapped silverware and made some weird sort of grunting sound. Even a fake sympathetic smile would've been better. To make matters worse, the chick proceeded to tell me how she overheard Boss Lady telling Cute But Possibly Gay Manager how much she disliked how long I took to eat lunch with my boyfriend and his mom when they unexpectedly walked in after they went to do their nails together. Or as Sodapop said, "Buff his nails, because businessmen do it."

"I asked her if it was okay for me to eat with them, and she said yes. She said there were no customers to attend to," I countered. It was true.

"Well..." She clucked her tongue. "I'm just telling you what I heard."

Okay, so she's nice yesterday and a PMSing bitch today? Cool.

The rest of the day consisted of greeting people with the biggest, fake smile possible plastered on my face, listening to upbeat Latin music fused with the soccer game on TV while a thunderstorm rumbled outside. I rushed to place menus, silverware, chips and salsa on the tables, took orders, answered the phone and took more phone orders, cleaned the floor and tables, went to the store to pick up whatever the kitchen was missing, made drinks, and basically acted nice to extremely rude, self-entitled people (those are the ones who stuck out the most). Breaking three martini glasses, I picked them up with hands burned from the hot, heavy plates I could barely carry, and—oh, yes—I also made 3,456 mistakes and was held accountable for each and every single one of them.

By the end of the shift, I was so stressed and hungry, I could barely remember that a quarter was worth twenty-five cents. After every mistake, my evil mind would remind me, Oh, and Snoopy died today.

During the hectic dinner wave, I remembered that SpongeBob episode where all SpongeBob knew was fine dining and breathing. I sympathized one-hundred percent and was reminded of the feeling of taking the SAT, that feeling like your entire life becomes that test for those four hours. Well, that was being a waitress for me at Don Burrita. The only solace I found that day was receiving an eight-dollar tip from a guy who told me, "Keep it for yourself."

So generous.

- Day Three.

Needless to say, my third day was my last day, but at least by then the customers no longer made me nervous, some would even compliment me and ask me where I was from. Boss Lady said she would call me for my next shift, but never did. Thank the Lord.

- Day Four.

I wore my black Harlem pants and a rose-printed crop top with a black sheath around the shoulders and collarbone area. I had to look good, as my dad was driving me to Florida International University today. The sky faltered between gray and bright blue, the upper atmosphere full of sunshine and cumulus clouds. The Mamas & the Papas were softly playing on the radio. I mentioned to my dad how I was anticipating running into people that I knew at my orientation. Subtext: I wonder if I'm going to run into my first love or not.

All morning, I hadn't eaten anything, because I chose a face full of makeup over breakfast, but Dad got me covered with seven bucks. By the time we arrived on campus, the sky had settled on a dull and light drizzle. I turned to my dad. "Adiós, Papá, te quiero mucho."

He told me he loved me too and wished me luck. Really, he needed the luck, not me. Today was the long-awaited day of finding out whether or not the tumor living in his bladder was either cancer or a bitch that needed to move the fuck out. By the time orientation was over, I would know, and the fate of my college schedule would be made.

Butterflies in my stomach reproduced faster than sexually repressed mice, but I thought to myself, He's going to be okay, it's not going to be cancer, don't worry. Mind you, for about ten days, I felt like I couldn't even breathe the same. When I arrived at the gorgeous giant ballroom, I sat in the back corner riiiiight next to the pasta, cookies, and brownies. YES, comfort food! I listened to the speakers and simultaneously scanned the room for cute college boys—nobody really stuck out—and finally, I waited in a long line to be able to create my schedule with a friendly brunette woman.

"Do you want to have morning classes Mondays, Wednesdays, and leave early on Fridays?" she asked.

"Uh, I mean, like, sure. I guess that's okay," I stuttered, biting the inside of my lower lip. Fate was happening as we spoke.

"Do you want Speech or Intro to Philosophy?"

"Intro to Philosophy," I said, wondering what my dad was doing right now. Were they giving him good news or bad? "Oh, and nothing before ten AM" She nodded understandingly. Whenever I speak to people, my voice gets instantly twice as high, and I sound extra sweet. I don't know why, but I was aware of it right at that moment.

She handed me a pamphlet about FIU and Miami-Dade's Dual Admission Program, and I accepted it with a smile. She also told me I would also have a Miami-Dade advisor. I saw a couple of people from

TERRA Environmental Research Institute, my old high school, and we exchanged that awkward I'm-going-to-be-decent-enough-to-acknowledge-your-presence glance that forms on your lips, creating some type of face lift that might be classified as a smile. Suddenly, I was back in the outside world again, admiring the abstract sculptures littered all over FIU's modernesque campus. The humidity clung to my mane, and the heat made my face all greasy.

As I patiently waited until 5 pm to make the call, here were my thoughts at 4:57 PM:

Wow, I'm going to be here two years from now.

Look at that couple over there. I wonder if they're in love. They look so cute.

Hmm, but she could be faking it, or maybe he cheated on her last night, and she has no idea. Maybe I should go over there and tell her.

I've always liked to attach make-believe stories to people and situations I know nothing about for entertainment purposes. Finally, it's 5 PM, and I went to my recent contacts on my phone to call my dad, a.k.a. Rogelio. As soon as he answered, I made the split decision to ask him about the results later when I'd be in the car with him. My stomach, dissatisfied with the decision, knotted itself even tighter. Sitting on a smooth bench, I waited for my dad's white Volkswagen to pull up by the Gold Garage parking lot. He was poker-faced, as was I.

"Hola." We both greeted each other at the same time, as I slid into the passenger seat, making an effort to gently close the car door.

"How was it?" he asked.

Okay, so we're starting with me. Not a good sign. "It was really good…I liked it a lot. I got free food and have my schedule already. I'm taking ENC1102 since I passed AP English at TERRA, College Algebra, Intro to Philosophy, and some computer class we're required to take."

"Sounds good, sounds good. I'm proud of you. Are you excited?" His eyes were pasted to the road, as his hands firmly gripped the wheel.

"What is there to be proud about?" I laughed nervously. "It's just school. But yes, especially for my philosophy class." I began to play with the air vent, and finally faced it away from me. The longer I could pretend my life was normal, the better.

"You made it, you're going to college," he said with a smile on his face. My dad's short salt-and-pepper hair with thick matching eyebrows and stubble around his chin gave him a handsome face.

"Yeah." Finally, the white elephant in the car took a giant shit, and it became so unbearable that I needed to acknowledge it, because God only knew that if I didn't ask my dad now, he might not ever tell me. "So, what were the test results of the tumor?"

His jaw tightened before speaking. "It's malignant. It's bladder cancer."

I heard what he said, but I cracked my knuckles and refused to let it sink in. He turned to look at me. I could feel his eyes burning into my cheek, but I could feel nothing.

My eyes fixated themselves on the black grackles that congregated on the phone lines (why on the phone lines?) every day around twilight. For some reason, they had a deep fascination for Kendall Drive. The word "cancer" in my dad's voice entered in one ear and slithered right through the other, but then it looped around, and did the same to the other ear. It was the beginning of my own emotional cancer, and I didn't know it then.

"You're going to beat it, Papi," I said with the utmost confidence.

Cancer, cancer, cancer. The word looped and looped around like a freaking merry-go-round of insanity. Who was I to tell him he would beat it? Still, it seemed like the right thing to say.

"Well, I sure hope so," he said, hands tightly gripping the wheel. "I am definitely going to try my hardest."

"What stage is it in?" I asked.

"Four," Dad muttered. Suddenly, it dawned on me how little I knew about cancer.

"Is that…is that, like, the last stage?"

"Yes," Dad answered, and a cloud of silence engulfed us in the car.

My stomach became a pretzel and remained that way the rest of the night. You would think that I would've cried, bitched, screamed, shouted, exhibited a normal human being emotional reaction. But I felt…n o t h i n g. I texted Phoebe about it, and she apologized and invited me over to digest the news, telling me I could vent and scream if I wanted to, and she'd listen. I declined, instead going out with my two best friends, Monica and Rachel, their boyfriends, and our friend, Tim. I didn't even feel like telling my other two guy best friends about it. Ted and Barney. They were brothers to me.

"Where's your kid?" Ross, Rachel's boyfriend, teased. It took me a moment to realize he was talking to me.

"My boyfriend is busy serving people fro-yo," I answered with annoyance drizzling in my tone. I checked my Galaxy S III for no reason, opening up Snapchat to see if datsexythang sent me a snap. Nada. Whatever.

"I think your dad will be okay." Rachel's long caramel curls spoke. I couldn't see her face, she was in the passenger seat facing the dashboard, her curls bouncing out her empathy.

"I think so, too. But like, I just, I…just…still…can't…believe it."

"I think that's normal," she said. "Right, Ross? Denial is one of the first stages of grief?"

"Yes, it is."

The bass sounds in the car reverberated house music, putting Ross in a good mood after almost getting in a fight with some guy who checked out

Rachel's "fat ass," as the Latin swine called it. We were leaving Coconut Grove, sober and a little bit hungry for more fun and food, when Monica, and her boyfriend Chandler, and Tim all deviated from the group. I forced myself to shrug it off, but really the cancer merry-go-round was still going on in my head.

Just stay light, Ana, and you'll be sane. I couldn't believe one of my biggest fears was happening to me. Supposedly. I still hadn't accepted it yet. The tension between Rachel and Ross was palpable, and I internally groaned, bracing myself for one of their iconic, soap opera fights.

"Here we go again with your drama," Ross poked at Rachel.

"Ross, we talked about this. You're seriously gonna disrespect me like that?"

"Don't be so sensitive. Chill bro," a douche chuckle ensued.

"No, Ross, you know I don't like that shit!"

Little did they know their fight would be published in a memoir four years later. I could make a lame popcorn joke here, but all I could think about was my dad has cancer in his bladder, Snoopy died, and my brother is sitting in jail for a reason I still don't even completely understand. After their tears, screams, and finally, declaration of love—Rachel and Ross didn't hold back, even with a friend in the car—I was finally being dropped off at home, sweet home. I still felt nothing, except now I had a throbbing, headache to accompany my pretzel of a stomach.

- Day Five.

I think you and I should talk.

I read the text over and over again, anxious, as though it were going to suddenly transform into a fire-breathing dragon and eat me alive. I waited a whole day after getting it, then finally asked Sodapop about it, but by that time he said to forget it. Ha, boys and their texts. If they could understand their texted words' uncanny ability to stick in a girl's brain, I think—well, hope—that they'd think twice. Forget about it. Okay Sodapop, okay.

Sodapop was a year and a half younger than me—insert cougar joke here—six foot, four inches tall with a swimmer-water-polo-hockey-player-god-like body. He captivated me with his emerald green eyes, uhhhdorable smile, friendliness towards everyone, and subtle American accent. We'd been on the same water polo team, which was how I got to know him and that was great for me, because one word: Speedo.

The phone rang, and it was—you guessed it—Sodapop. "Hey, Ana," he said sweetly. I paused for a moment to cradle my phone with both hands. I was standing in front of European Wax Center, because I'd just gotten my vagin—whatever, that's beside the point.

"Hey, Sodapop." In my head, I'd planned on sounding stern with a hint of bitchy, but instead, pure sweetness sugared my tone. Ugh.

"What's up, baby?" he asked in that sweet voice. I cringed. I freaking loved being called baby.

"Nothing. Just got out of waxing. You?"

"Ooo," he giggled, "Did it hurt?" Oh sure, now you're attentive, but when my dog died you poofed into thin air the whole day.

"Not really." I heard a video game in the background. "If you want to call me later when you're free, go ahead."

Six seconds later… "No, no, no, it's fine, baby. I want to talk to you," he cooed.

So, we talked and laughed and smiled. Typical boyfriend-girlfriend shit. Then, I mentioned how much I suck at waitressing, and he told me how maybe now isn't a good time to be working, and that I should spend as much time as possible with my dad.

And everything came to a halt.

Advice to all friends and/or girlfriends/boyfriends/significant others/cousins/friends with benefits/exes who still have a thing/co-workers/aliens/whatever you are: Do NOT. And I repeat, NOT tell the person who just found out their loved one has cancer to "spend as much time as possible with that person." It's like you already prophesied that the person with cancer isn't even going to make it, and I HATED THAT.

I clucked my tongue. "Actually, Sodapop, my dad told me to treat him exactly as I would if he didn't have cancer," I said, even though I was already disobeying my father by buying him a red velvet cupcake from Sweet Times. Just because.

"Okay, well that's good, too." The electronic noises of the video game continued on. So much for sounding sweet on the phone.

"Yeah, so when will you be free to talk?"

"We're talking right now," he said.

"You know what I mean." I laughed nervously without a trace of humor. I'd already made my decision about us in my head, and Sodapop could probably sense it. You know what? Maybe it was easier this way.

"I'll let you know in a little while." I heard Sodapop's smile fade away, along with his desire to put any effort into this. "I'll see you later."

"Okay. Well, bye, Sodapop."

"Bye, Ana." He clicked off.

Wow, I hated having to break up with someone. I'd rather get waxed down there three times in a row, but hopefully it would be over soon. My dad picked me up, and I told him about my decision to break up with Sodapop. As usual, he supported me by telling me it was my choice, and I should do whatever I want. My dad was freakin' awesome.

I got home and changed into my break-up outfit, which probably had black in it, and three hours later, Sodapop was at my front door, as attractive as ever in a white cut tank showing off his tanned arms. We walked to his greenish-gray van, and he opened the door for me, as we small talk*ed* as if absolutely nothing was going on for the first five minutes of the car ride.

"Ana, there's so much tension, I could cut it into little pieces and serve you a slice." He used an invisible knife to serve me our tension slices on invisible plates. I cracked up, feeling my whole body ease, which was nice. Sodapop smiled, as I pretended to devour a slice of tension pie, making him giggle.

"I wish I was mature enough for you," Sodapop sighed.

I opened my mouth to speak, but nothing came out. The glow of the green light dripped over the dashboard onto Sodapop's face and arms. He turned left, and before we knew it, there we were breaking up in the parking lot of Best Buy. In retrospect, that was the Best break-up I'd ever had. Sodapop understood that he couldn't be halfway in the relationship. It was either completely in our completely out, and he felt really bad, and so did I. Like, I cried, okay. Then, he offered me a milkshake (a milkshake, people!), but I declined.

After that, I drove his car home. For some reason I can't remember, Sodapop ended up having to floor it, as I screamed, because the car seat was broken, and I was too short to reach the wheel. I clung onto it for dear life. He took a picture of me. We couldn't stop laughing. Then we started to make out at red lights, which led him to drive us to a dimly lit neighborhood by my old high school.

I'm sure I don't have to tell you the rest—we bowm-chicka-wow-wowed. Fornicated. Got lain—which by the way, is the correct grammatical term for "getting laid" in past tense after breaking up with a guy. Just as when I was having second thoughts about our break-up, I checked his phone to glance at the picture he took of me driving, and there was a photo of some girl's naked ass staring at me.

"Nice." I handed him back his phone.

"That was sent to me in a group message. My friends are weird, okay? They all send nudes to each other. I didn't cheat on you, okay?" He defended himself in vain, as he stared at his phone. Well, that's my sign. My cue to go. The drive back was sad and bleh and miserable. I cried a little bit more, and Sodapop told me how it was going to take him a long time to forget me, and I told him that I was going to miss his foot fetish a lot, and to remember that having one isn't weird.

(Actually, it was very odd at first, but then I ended up loving it!)

The ironic part was the last thing he said before he dropped me off: "If you ever need to talk, you could talk to me, okay?"

I was like, really dude, that's all I wanted this whole time. I agreed, and we embraced for the last time as boyfriend and girlfriend in our four-month relationship. I shut the door, took one long last look at my water polo god, then texted the whole story to Phoebe, my insta-therapist. Then, I crawled into my room and cried for what I'd lost. Or maybe for what we never had. A couple of days later I texted my first love, Ponyboy and saw him after seven months of not uttering a word to each other. After seven months of ignoring his monthly "hey" texts.

If I were to say, "Day Six," I'd be lying, because this actually happened about one week after breaking up with Sodapop. I was in Boca Raton, vicariously living through Lily, one of my best friend's life as a go-away-college student. My other best friend, Robin, was with us as well. The feeling of independence was absolutely magnificent. It had only been about an hour since Lily's mom had dropped us off at Florida Atlantic University, and finally seeing Lily's beautifully decorated dorm was awesome! It was excruciatingly tiny with Lady Gaga posters e v e r y w h e r e, and had a beachy, earthy touch to it. That was Lily alright. The walls were painted egg-shell white, and she had a beige desk beneath her bunk bed where the first "bunk bed" would be. After Robin and I scavenged her cubbies for food, we settled with mouthwatering Nutella and peanut butter sandwiches and Nutri-Grain bars. Climbing up to her new comfy bed, Lily followed us, yelling, "Don't leave any crumbs up there, guys!" Her voice was serene and very girly.

Robin and I laughed, scarfing down our delicacies. "Okay, so you guys remember how I said I wasn't going to reply to Ponyboy's texts anymore?" I said, savoring the last bite of fruit bar.

"Yes!" Lily chirped. Her huge hazel eyes suspiciously smiled at me.

"Oh, God, here we go again with Ponyboy," Robin groaned.

"Okay, well I lost willpower and texted him back three days ago," I confessed.

"Why?" Robin asked. "You were doing so well not talking to him!"

"Let her finish her story!" Lily interjected.

"I don't know, one night I just couldn't stop thinking about him, and I just said fuck it, and I replied, and he was all, 'I thought you got abducted by aliens or something!' I almost regretted it, but I was like, you know what? I'm just going to tell him to stop texting me and that'll be it."

"Which, of course, didn't happen," Robin guessed.

"Well, not exactly. It was so weird…I had a dream that night that he wanted me back, so he took me to a fancy restaurant where he said, 'Just get whatever you want.' Then, he surprised me with a cake and a really sweet, meaningful card, and I was like, 'Of course, yeah,' and then I woke up feeling depressed as fuck, because none of it was reality, but then in real life, we continued to text until the connection got all crappy, and I called him thinking I was going to sound all stern and affirmative, but hearing his voice kind of made the anger melt away."

"Yeah," Lily nodded. Robin rolled her eyes.

I shoved her knee before continuing. "But I told him, 'Ponyboy, I'm done with the vicious cycle we have going on. It's like, we text, then we hang out and end up hooking up, and I'm left wanting more, and I'm back to square one of moving on. No, I'm done with that. So please stop texting me. And he was all like, 'It's not a cycle…blah blah blah…it could be different this time.'"

"Oh, my God, boys I swear," Lily muttered.

"But then, you saw him, didn't you?" Robin asked. Sheepishly, I smiled, staring at the green-leaf print bedspread.

"Wait, I'm not there yet!" I giggled. "So then, he texted me something like, 'Alright, fine,' and we basically fought for a little bit, until I just stopped replying. But while I was painting Sodapop's flower on my wall (I decided to paint him as a hot pink hibiscus), I just got two looong texts from him. I couldn't freakin' believe what he was telling me!"

"Why, what did he say??" Lily demanded to know.

"He was all like, look, when I last talked to you, I was still caught up on Piper (which was my Pre-K best friend, by the way) we had just broken up, and I wasn't sure what I wanted. The reason why I said you and I only had a physical connection is because I knew I didn't want a relationship at that time. Now, I'm actually open to it. And c'mon, ever since eighth grade I've always come back. If that isn't an emotional connection, I don't know what is." So of course, after that, I told him about the dream and how crazy it all was, and he joked around about coming over with a cake. Which almost ended up happening! Except it was too late at night to buy one, so he ended up showing up at my house around 1 AM with a jar of mini chocolate chip cookies!"

The girls laughed, so I went on.

"I snuck out of my house. I was soo nervous, and then we talked in his car for about two hours, which felt amazing. It felt just like eighth grade all over again. Then, at one point, he asked me what I wanted, and I just leaned over and kissed him. We were about to leave to drive to my park, when Jodie showed up wagging her tail right in front of his car! Like if he hadn't looked, he would have ran her over."

"Jodie?" Robin's jaw fell open. She was about to crack up, her broad swimmer's shoulders shaking up and down.

"Yeah, I guess she wanted to be part of the adventure too," I laughed, "because I opened the car door, and she just hopped in without any hesitation."

"She escaped, too?" Lily asked.

If you hadn't guessed it yet, Jodie was my other dog, otherwise known as the real love of my life.

"Yeah, and so we drove with her underneath my feet to my park, and we started making out in the back seat when suddenly

(I'msorryifanyofmyfamilymembersreadthis), my dog…literally saw us doing it doggy style."

The three of us laughed so hard that Lily farted, and I could not stop snorting, making Robin practically pee from laughter. I'd love to tell you that after that, Ponyboy and I made sweet, passionate love, and we took each other back with open arms, as he was there for me throughout the most difficult time of my life, but you can read Nicholas Sparks' The Last Song for that kind of story (I recommend it too!). This was real life, and the passionate fire that burned that night eventually died out over the next couple of days, just as I had predicted it would.

But anyway, next story—My First Ticket.

SO. Sometime in May, I'd gotten my driver's license, and the night it happened was June 30th, 2014, if I remember correctly, a year ago as I write this. One of cancer's worst enemies is fever, because fever can lead to riskier health situations, like getting an infection. Sadly, the diseased body is much more receptive to any sickness, because of the weakened immune system (because of detrimental, life-saving chemo sessions). So, getting a silly cough could turn into a vicious fever in less than forty-eight hours, which was exactly what happened to my dad that late afternoon. My mom, maternal grandma, and I accompanied him to Baptist Hospital, even though they all insisted I stay home because I'd be bored, and it would be hours of waiting.

"I don't care if I wait the whole night," I protested, standing my ground with Phoebe's book in my hand. The hospital's exterior was cold but beautiful with pineapple statues and art everywhere. Peachy pink walls with Greco-Roman architecture (I learned that in my Humanities class), and inside, the walls were egg-shell white with soft lighting, giving the atmosphere a pleasant ambiance. We checked into the emergency room with a pretty brunette who took pictures of our faces with a little security camera, then handed us red stickers featuring our faces, and this was our visitor pass. Needless to say, the photo was very unflattering. I was not amused by how much I looked like a blotchy blob, but regardless, I stuck it to my blue, flower-printed romper anyway.

"You really don't have to stay here, Anaregina. It's going to be hours. Who knows when they'll admit me," my dad said, but there was no way I was leaving him.

"Papi, I…don't…care. I really don't mind." I shook my head and planted myself on the seat next to him. In front of us was a young couple with tired, grief-stricken looks on their faces. Everyone around us looked somber, sleep-deprived, or sick. I opened Phoebe's book, A Long Way Gone, by Ishmael Beah, and began reading the most depressing memoir I'd ever read in my eighteen years of living. I utilized it as a distraction and a way of putting me in perspective of my situation. I used that book, and frankly, I was unintentionally using boys as a distraction too.

Why are you in the hospital?? came Ponyboy's text.

Because my dad has a fever, which really isn't good when you have cancer I replied after having finished reading the last paragraph on the page of my book.

Ohh, i see i see. That suucks, he answered.

Damn, not even a " /: " face? Okay. I continued to read and text. At one point, I was texting Ponyboy, Sodapop, and Ron. Ron was the new guy I was sort of talking to who I'd met in my English class back at TERRA. Also, I was probably sending Phoebe goofy snaps, like we did every day.

"How long has it been?" my dad asked, looking at his watch. For having Stage 4 cancer, a fever, a son in jail, an ex-wife (my mom) who hadn't gotten over him, at fifty-seven years old, my dad looked great. He went to the gym religiously, groomed himself daily, and always ate really, really healthy. He never even drank nor smoked. Occasionally, he'd have a glass of wine at dinner parties, but otherwise, he was super healthy. In fact, he was the one who sparked my love for working out.

"Let's see," I glanced at the time on my phone, "we got here around six, and it's now 10:30. It's been like…" I counted my fingers on my right hand. "Four and a half hours by now." Math wasn't my greatest subject.

He groaned. He was wearing his favorite light navy blue sweater.

I leaned my head against his cozy shoulder and closed my eyes. "We could have made it to Orlando by now," I said with a light chuckle. I was getting tired and hungry, but I didn't want to show it. Finally, a nurse with a clipboard called out, "Frias, Rogelio Frias," and my dad was up faster than I was.

I grabbed my black sweater and accompanied him to the nurse. My mom and grandma had already gone to our house, and I knew deep down my dad was glad that I'd stayed with him. The nurse led us through a heavy door with a small rectangular window in it and into a small white room with two blue chairs, a metal scale, and another nurse facing a computer screen in front of beige cabinets surrounding her. She was on a swivel chair, and the bags under her eyes could probably carry baby kangaroos.

"Hi, my name is Karen. I'm just going to be asking you a couple of questions before we get your room okay?" she said drowsily.

"Nice to meet you, Karen." My dad smiled, as he sat on the chair closest to her. She began to ask him typical questions like why he was here and what he was feeling, and she typed away while I took a moment to reflect on the feeling lingering between my hunger and fatigue—fear. I asked if I could weigh myself, and she said "sure" in a why-are-you-even-asking way. As soon as she was out of sight, we were led to another room, deeper into the maze of the emergency ward, and I asked my dad what he thought of her.

"I liked her." He shrugged.

"I didn't. She had this 'I don't want to be here' attitude."

"I think she was just tired. These nurses work late shifts." My dad, defending people again.

Instantly, I took back my judgment and felt sympathy for her. I observed the temporary room we were in with deep fascination. Aside from the white, hospital bed my dad was resting on, everything else was a wonder to me. The monitor hooked to the bed had three different colored cables connected to it, each representing a different bodily function, like heart rate. A doctor came in and assured us that he would be moved to another room later, and that he may even be discharged tonight because the fever was going away.

This made me really happy, but by the time it was almost 4 AM, my dad suggested I go home and get some sleep. At this point, I agreed, as a wave of adrenaline washed over me because, Oh my God, I've never driven alone so far from home before! He handed me his keys with a little hesitation and told me to call Mom to let her know. I agreed, as Dad gave me directions on how to get home. I still didn't know streets of Miami, (I still don't really know) but it's okay because that's what a GPS is for!

"Call me as soon as you get home, okay?"

"Sí, Papi," I replied, bending over to give him a kiss on the cheek.

"And if they discharge me earlier, then I'll call you to come and pick me up." I couldn't believe he trusted me with his own car to drive alone! I eagerly nodded. "Please drive carefully, okay? Especially at this time."

"Okay, Papi," I said confidently. Holding his keys felt like I was holding a winning lottery ticket.

"Really…call me. Okay, well, bye. I love you, thank you for being here with me all this time. I'm sorry it was such a long wait."

"Papi, I don't mind. I sleep all day for a reason. Bye, love you too." I dashed off towards the main lobby with a little skip in my step. I know he wanted me to stay, I thought. The closer I approached his shiny white Volkswagen, the more nervous and excited I got. *Okay, Ana, you got this, you're okay, it's 4 AM the streets are basically empty right now.*

Getting in the car, I nearly forgot to turn my lights on, but I did and then found myself ecstatically giggling the moment I was out cruising on the road with my phone's GPS telling me where to go. *I'm doing this, oh my God, I'm actually driving alone, by m y s e l f!* Did I know where I was? No, but that didn't matter. Soon, I recognized the shops on 104th Street and felt at ease. Three cops passed me by, and I practically peed myself each time, because I wasn't insured on the car, and that was the reason my mom refused to let me drive it. When I reached my humble abode, I turned the car off, and the first thing I did was call Ron to tell him of my phenomenal personal achievement!

"Ron, Ron, Ron, guess what? I'm ALIVE!"

"Good, I would hope so. I'm glad you made it okay. I told you, you would be fine."

"Oh, my God, that felt so…so…liberating. I don't know. I just feel so independent, you know? Like wow, I could actually drive a good distance and make it on my own okay. I feel like such an adult!"

"Yeah, I know what you mean," Ron chuckled, feeding off my excitement. Then his voice got cut off for a second, and I glanced at my phone screen.

"Wait, hold on, I'll call you back later, okay? My dad's calling," I whispered thinking my mom might be asleep. "Ha-lo?" I answered.

"Guess what, Anaregina? They're going to discharge me now, so you're going to have to come pick me up."

"That's funny, I just got home. But I got home fine, so yes, I'll go pick you up. It's noooo problem," I said, confidence booming in my voice. Suddenly, my mom emerged from the darkness like a panther lurking in the bushes. *Oh, shit!* I jumped.

"What's going on?" she muttered. I told my dad I was on my way before hanging up and responding to my PJ-dressed mother.

"He's getting discharged, so I'm going to go back and pick him up."

"No, you're not, Anaregina. Look at the time. It's past 4 AM I'll go."

"No, Mom! Trust me, it's fine, I'll go. Go back to sleep." Why did she have to insist on stealing my thunder? I was an adult. With a car!

"Anaregina…" Mom hesitated, then sighed.

Wait, had I won? Yet something deep inside me told me I should let my mom go and stay home, but I ignored this gut feeling, of course. After telling my beloved baby Jodie goodbye, she wagged her tail at me, and I watched her, as I slid out of our garage. I closed the automatic fence and felt my surge of energy lift as the GPS asked me where I wanted to go. My tight grip on the leather wheel, me feeling one with the car, plus gliding with complete control was invigorating. It was just Ana and the empty streets.

Nothing was going to happen to me!

And then. My phone died. GPS could no longer assist me, and I wasn't completely sure how to get there. Maybe if I'd paid attention to my surroundings the first time, but I hadn't, and now my nerves began to rattle my clouded brain. I plugged my phone into the car charger, and guess what? It wasn't turning on. I tried not to panic, but my wicked mind loved to remind me: *Also, you're driving without insurance, you're driving without insurance. Yup, noooo insurance, Ana. I'm not sure where I'm going. Just drive forward, yeah, that seems right. Wait, a second, why is there a cop parked in the middle of the street? And why does he have his car door open?*

"Okay, this was not in the driving manual," I said aloud to myself, gripping the wheel tighter until my knuckles turned white. *What do I do? What do I do?* Then, the Universe showed me exactly what to do. Some small white car just went right around the cop car, so I proceeded to do exactly the same. Not as smooth as the car in front of me, but the same nonetheless, and at the speed limit too. Phew, okay! Okay. I'm good.

I continued to glide through Kendall Drive. Bright red and blue headlights shone on my left rear-view mirror, but I dismissed it. Now, there was blaring police sirens splitting my ears, as the car approached me from behind. That cannot be for me. I didn't do a n y t h i n g wrong. Suddenly, there was a fat, white-haired policeman hanging out of his mirror, yelling at me to pull over. His huge, clear blue eyes were going to pop right out of his eye sockets!

You have got to be kidding me. Not remembering this from the driving manual either, I did not "PULL OVER IMMEDIATELY TO THE RIGHT," and instead, I continued to drive about half a block until there was an entrance to some neighborhood condominium. And this is how the rest of my police encounter went:

Angry Cop: "EXCUSE ME, DID YOU NOT SEE THE LIGHTS AND HEAR THE SIRENS? YOU NEARLY BLEW MY CAR DOOR OFF!"

Me (angry and nervous but keeping calm): "I'm sorry, officer, this is only my second time driving alone. I'm just going to pick up my dad from the hospital."

Pig-nosed Police: "AND YOU'RE SUPPOSED TO PULL OVER IMMEDIATELY TO THE RIGHT! HOW AM I SUPPOSED TO KNOW YOU'RE NOT PULLING OUT A GUN OR ANY OTHER WEAPON?"

Me: *Really? Me? A gun? I'm like a harmless, little girl, but okay.* "I'm sorry, I didn't know."

Po-Po (shakes his head disapprovingly): "Let me see your license, registration, and insurance card."

Almost crying me (gulps): "Yes, officer." Slowly, I pulled out my registration and license, then handed it all over.

The Heat: "And your insurance card?"

Trying so hard not to cry me: "I…I don't have insurance on this car yet. It's my dad's. I was just picking him up from the hospital, and that's it."

The Law (very dickish tone): "Alright, so one of three of these things is going to happen to you. One…you will go to traffic school, two…pay the civil penalty and the price of your insurance goes up, or three…by the request of me, Officer Dickhead (at least I think that was his name), you will make an appearance in court and plead guilty."

Crying me (tries to hide signs of weakness by wiping away tears and slightly turning head away from him): "Y-y-es, officer."

Officer Friendly: "I'll be back with your ticket, miss."

Ana's Thoughts Meanwhile: *I can't believe this is happening to me! Oh, my God, he probably doesn't even believe that I'm actually driving to the hospital.* I can hear him talking to another officer about me. *He definitely doesn't believe me! Everything happens for a reason, Ana. Ugh, but this is so unfair! I did nothing wrong! Wow, this is probably what my brother went through, except he actually got arrested. What the hell is taking him so long? Why does my phone STILL refuse to turn on despite being plugged into the car charger? Still…still…oh wow, would you look at that? The little bitch still doesn't turn on!*

The blue and red lights swarming the scene instilled a sense of paranoia in me. I clenched the steering wheel with my clammy hands, taking deep breaths, but I wanted to step out of the car and just yell, "EXCUSE ME, I HAVE A SICK, TIRED DAD WITH CANCER IN THE HOSPITAL WHO'S WAITING FOR ME TO PICK HIM UP, WHO DOESN'T EVEN KNOW I'M STUCK HERE!!!"

But judging from the movies and TV shows I'd seen, I knew it was best to remain in the car. Tears of frustration meandered down my hot cheeks, and finally, after about literally twenty minutes, the policeman returned with my yellow ticket, license, and registration. My mind and body couldn't hold it in anymore, and there before this man I'd never met, I exploded like a river whose dam just violently broke. His entire demeanor morphed into a sympathetic human being, as his shoulders dropped, and his entire expression softened.

"Look, I'm just trying to do my job and protect the streets. We wouldn't want anything to happen. I understand this is your second time driving, and you didn't know. So, you can take the option of going to court and pleading "not guilty," and you will not be guilty. Alright? Drive safe, young lady." He handed me my ticket and left with a sorry expression on his wrinkly face. *So, I'm not guilty, and I'm still getting the ticket? Okay.*

I rolled the window up and sobbed incessantly. The cop remained parked behind me for about five minutes until he left. Finally, my phone turned on. I managed to leave my dad a voicemail that I was a little late, but I was going to make it, and I'd explain later. And because luck was not on my side tonight, my phone died again. *Damn battery!* My weeping stopped, and sense of logic returned. I would not let this night beat me. I drove in circles until I recognized my friend Robin's neighborhood and headed straight home from there (it's funny how well I know the route to the hospital now, a year later). As soon as I arrived home and told my mom what happened, she bitched at me, saying that was why she didn't want me driving in the first place. She called my dad and headed straight to the hospital. It was close to 5 AM at this point. I was in Mom's room facing my startled grandma, Alba, when suddenly, it all became very clear, very vivid. Suddenly, it sank in and felt a lot like a snake's fangs piercing my heart, and the poison was making my entire body shake.

"HE HAS CANCER! MY DAD HAS CANCER! WHY? WHY IS THIS HAPPENING, ABUELA? AND MY BROTHER IS IN J-JAIL OVER A STUPID GIRL FOR WHO KNOWS HOW LONG! AND SNOOPY D-DIED, AND I L-LOST MY FIRST JOB, AND I HAD TO B-B-BREAK UP WITH MY B-BOYFRIEND BECAUSE HE DIDN'T WANT A RELATIONSHIP-P WITH ME ANYM-M-MORE, AND NOW MOM IS M-MAD AT ME, A-A-AND I GOT A TICKET I DIDN'T EVEN DESERVE, AND PONYBOY PROBABLY DOESN'T EVEN L-L-LOVE ME ANYMORE! WHY STAGE FOUR C-CANCER, WHY!!?!?!! I DON'T UNDERSTAND WHY THIS IS HAPPENING ABUELA!?!?!? AND…AND THIS IS-SS-S-S HURTING M-MOM S-SO MUCH.

For the longest time, I wailed, feeling sorry for myself but grateful that my grandma was there for me at that moment. She hugged me, and the both of us cried together. Like an angel from some unearthly place, she absorbed most of my pain.

But not all of it.

CHAPTER 3
Chemo Plus "Equality" in the R Justice Building

If you've ever taken a close relative to get chemotherapy treatment, I want you to know that I have so much respect and admiration for you. That was one of the hardest things I ever had to do in my whole entire eighteen years of living. I literally got about three hours of sleep the night before, because the only thought that would run through my mind was, *he has bladder cancer. He's getting chemo tomorrow. I'm eighteen, and I'm taking my fifty-seven-year-old dad to get chemotherapy, which is poison to all cells. What if he doesn't make it? No, no, no! Don't think that, Ana! Think positive, c'mon. But still what if…*

Repeat about 1,956 times.

It was a forty-five-minute drive to the chemotherapy session. My best friend, Ted Mosby, was driving the family red Prius, while I rested on the gray passenger seat, and my dad was sitting in the back seat. My dad was told that chemo might make you feel faint right after, so it's best to have someone drive you back home, ergo Ted driving. We pulled up to a round driveway in front of a pale-yellow building. Dad opened the door for me, and we strolled right in while Ted parked the car. It might've been my imagination, but the scent of urine wafted into my nose, and seeing the old, bald sick people made my stomach drop to the gray, tiled floor. We were greeted by a sweet, warm lady with crazy, curly hair and an enigmatic smile, as my dad signed himself in. Of course, we were both hiding our true emotions, as evidenced by neither one of us exchanging words to the other.

"Do you want a cup of water?" I asked Dad.

"No, thank you," he said.

I got a white Styrofoam cup and filled it up to the top. We sat next to each other in silence, me sipping my water like a baby might suck on a pacifier for comfort. Three sips of H2O later, I asked, "How do you feel?"

"Ay, Anaregina, I just want to get this over with. I admit I'm a little scared, but I know I'll be okay. What about you?"

Out of habit or maybe anxiety, I bit the top of the cup, creating little upside-down arcs all along the edge. "I'm okay. Just tired. It wasn't exactly easy falling asleep last night." It was true, my exhaustion was slowly consuming any emotion or worry left in me to feel. It was like 8 AM in the morning or something. After about ten minutes of silent waiting, someone called, "Rogelio Frias!" By then, Ted was with us. My dad said goodbye to us at the entrance door and reminded me to come back around noon with lunch for him. We agreed to call each other, and then parted ways.

Ted and I set out to adventure, as adventurous as one could feel after dropping their father off at chemotherapy. We found ourselves in a shopping center where we hit a busy Starbucks full of business people. When we overstayed our welcome at Starbucks, we headed to Publix, a wildlife aquarium store that had a hot pink jellyfish, and finally, after a three-hour nap in the car, we hit good ol' Subway.

"I'm so over Sodapop," I muttered, as I scanned his Twitter feed. I didn't even like Twitter.

"Yes, I can see that." Ted, Prince of Sarcasm. "What makes you say that, Ana?" He finished off his sub with a monstrous bite.

"He called another girl 'B', and 'B' was our thing, like we didn't call each other 'babe' or 'bae.' It was always just 'B.' And look…" I showed him my phone, and he leaned in to read the stupid post. "He called another girl 'B'!" Ferociously, I chewed a bite of my delicious tuna sub.

"Well, with all due respect, Ana, you did go back to Ponyboy, just a tad bit."

"Well, that's different! Actually…yeah, you're right. Let's not talk about that." I forced a small smile and sighed, and suddenly, the weight of the world was on my shoulders. Yeah, one of those sighs.

"What's wrong?"

"It's just...I don't know, this is all really hard, Ted. Like, really, really hard. I mean, just seeing that place, I don't know, like, it's not something I've ever seen before. I still can't believe it, that's all."

Ted sighed sympathetically, his whole upper body shifting to look more assertive. "I know it's hard, but you're going to get through this fine. You're strong, and you know it, and your dad knows it, and I'm sure he really appreciates you being there for him. And remember I'm always here for you, no matter what. No. Matter. What. Ana."

"I know," I said softly. "Thanks." I checked the time on my phone. It was a couple minutes before noon.

"You ready to head out?" he asked.

"Mmm-hm," I nodded. We cleared our pine-green trays, and I grabbed the bag containing my dad's lunch, then walked towards the Prius. On the drive back, I started fantasizing about vacationing in Cancun, Mexico, with my cousins like I did last summer, and before I knew it, we were back at the chemo place. This time, we were going in past the entrance door. My stomach was not having it, and this was the first of many times my face became a mask for my dad's sake.

"Just make your way through the hallway, and it will be on your left." The curly-haired receptionist guided us. I felt like I floated over there. The open room resembled a beauty salon, but instead of the people having their hair dried or nails painted, they had tubes inserted in their wrists connected to IV bags. The moment I saw my dad having chemo injected in him, two things happened. The first, my stomach involuntarily clenched itself so hard, I had steel abs for a moment, and the second…the image of Walter White receiving his chemotherapy bled into mind. *So, this is the real thing*, I thought.

"Hey, guys," Dad greeted. He looked perfectly fine. Calm, even. The nurse probably greeted us too, but I was too busy staring at my father looking perfectly chill. I'm pretty sure I was holding my breath unconsciously the whole time.

"Hello," Ted said.

I handed Dad his Subway bag and smiled.

"Thank you, Anaregina," Dad said, elated. I smiled. The nurse smiled. Everyone smiled. These were different kinds of smiles, though. I don't know how to describe it. It was as if smiling was all you could do to hide the pain. "Well, as it turns out," my father said, "the session is going to last about two-and-a half more hours. Sorry, but you guys will have to keep waiting. Just go wherever you want, and I'll keep in touch with you."

"That's not a problem at all. I'm glad it's going well," Ted said. His blue-green eyes twinkled through his glasses.

"Okay, see you later, Papi," I mumbled, floating after Ted out of there, until finally, I took my first real breath in the urine-scented waiting room (I've got strong lungs, I swam for four years on TERRA's swim team).

"Oh, my God," I whispered. "I almost couldn't breathe in there."

Ted put his comforting arm around my shoulder, and I slightly leaned on him, as we headed for the car. I Googled "bladder cancer" on my phone, but I couldn't absorb what I was reading. The words jumbled up and made no sense, and I found myself reading the same sentence over and over again. So instead, we ended up watching Friends on Netflix until the agonizing wait was over.

It was July 17th, 2014, 9:00 in the morning.

I was nervous, but honestly, I didn't have much hope that there'd be justice in the courtroom that day. It was Adam's hearing, and we were there with one goal in mind: to get Adam on house arrest until the next court date. It didn't exactly help that on April 7th, just a day after his 22nd birthday, he got arrested for possession of heroin. The charges were dropped the next day when the police officer failed to provide proof of the heroin. Adam was just drunk and high off pot at the wrong time and place. He got lucky he was home the next day. Now, his luck was really pressed.

"Please rise. The Court of the Second Judicial Circuit, Criminal Division, is now in session. The Honorable Judge, Looks-Just-Like-My-Junior-Year-English-Teacher presiding," the plump bailiff boomed (obviously, he said her actual name). My dad, mom, best friends, Rachel and Barney, the rest of the people in the courtroom, and I all rose. Standing there, I took in my surroundings. Everything was shit brown. Brown walls, brown floor, brown seats, brown desks, a brown sign that read: We Who Labor Here Seek Only The Truth. All fake, diarrhea brown wood! The judge smoothed her shiny brown hair, and the blurry memory went as follows: "Everyone but the jury may be seated. Mr. Balding Bailiff, please swear in the jury," Judge Pretty Face commanded.

"Please raise your right hand. Do you solemnly swear or affirm that you will truly listen to this case and render a true verdict and a fair sentence as to this defendant?"

They said, "I do."

"You may be seated."

The way the judge looked at my brother was despicable. And seeing Adam in his orange jail suit and his hands in handcuffs made me teary-eyed. How could I make the judge see him the way I did? As a stupid big brother who always made me laugh and had never had a cruel bone in his body? At one point, Rachel, Barney, and I all took deep breaths at the same exact time. They shared my massive knot of anticipation. Halfway through the prissy prosecutor accusing Adam of threatening to kill the abusive boyfriend of his ex—which was not true—a very unexpected thing happened.

We all heard a strange sound coming from next to me. It was my dad, breaking down and crying, his head hung low. It became even more surreal after that. It was uncharacteristic of him to show emotion in the first place, but I was sure that having my brother twenty feet away from us, and not being allowed to run up to him and hug him was a stab in the heart. Here were these strangers judging my brother's character and having such a profound impact on our family when they had no idea what the fuck we were going through, and who Adam really was—it felt like our lives were a suspense movie at that point.

"Your Honor, I've been in this job for over thirty years, and I know what fits the profile of a criminal, and Adam Frias does not fit that description…" the detective trailed. Finally, some hope. From then on, my hope would blossom and do cartwheels anytime I would hear Adam's lawyer, Alicia, speak. She defended my brother with such conviction and eloquence, I truly admired her and wanted to hug her for it. Her character was as fierce as her brilliant red hair and bad-ass-lawyer-way-with-words-ness.

I tried to absorb every word, but it was similar to the time Dad told me about his cancer. In one ear, spinning around the other, like a merry-go-round of madness. Instead, I fixated my focus onto the judge. You know when you just know, woman to woman, when a chick is on her period? Okay, well, I knew this woman was on her period! I. Could. Detect. It. Alright, so I had no concrete proof of my mental accusation, but I swore by the way she was acting, that she was giving off I'm-On-My-Period signals. It seemed to me that she was genuinely annoyed to be dealing with his case and would speak of Adam as if he were worse than vermin that needed to be guarded from civilians (as Jacob calls people). All this while pouting her thin, glossy pink lips. I imagined myself bursting in a fit of tears, claiming to be insane, as I deliberately broke the courtroom rules and ran as fast as I could towards my brother to get the hug we both deserved—no, needed—from each other. That was the real me, I decided. This version of myself, the one calmly sitting here, was just a human playing the role of a sane, society member pretending this whole thing was not a violation of human rights. To love. To love in a desperate time of need for it.

Needless to say, she judged that Adam would remain in jail until further notice and would not be going home today.

So much for equality.

The rest of my summer went by like a blur. I hung out a lot with Ted, and Barney (we called ourselves "The Tremendous Trio"). I ended things with Ron, although he also gave me advice that changed my perspective forever on getting over someone, which was something about a cup and putting it to wash, and the connection never being lost. No, wait. That wasn't it. Hold on, here we go: "The connection that you shared with that person is still at the bottom of the cup you were once drinking from. It's up to you whether you want to keep on drinking or whether you think it's finally time to stop and put the cup to wash."

Now comes a story I like to call, "The First Time I Kissed a Total Stranger." Mm-kay, so he wasn't a total stranger, he was the younger brother of the guy that Robin was hooking up with. But…this was the first night I met him. It was July 2014. And boy, I wanted him.

- PART ONE

"Who is that boy?" I asked Robin, Margo, and Dayanara (Robin's

German cousin). The night was young, beaming with promise that it could be remembered. Even through the dim light and the glass between us, this boy was the epitome of gorgeous, as he stood in front of his house, facing the minivan we were huddled in.

"That's Emmett," Robin said, a smile creeping over her thick lips.

"That's Jasper's little brother," Margo giggled.

"The one whose Instagram we were stalking earlier, remember?" Dayanara added.

"That's him?" I asked, my jaw falling to the floor. So that's the guy they were fawning over while Robin waxed my happy trail. "He's pretty cute," I emphasized 'pretty' only a bit. He walked back into his house, probably to get Jasper, and my gaze followed. Cutest butt I've ever seen on a guy, hands down.

"Yeah, well, he's a football player at Columbus, and he's had a girlfriend for over a year, but I heard he's cheated on her with two other girls. Plus, I think he was in an orgy too or something," Robin said. It was like opening your fridge expecting to eat your favorite dessert only to discover it was way past expired and so rotten you throw up in your mouth a little bit.

"We're coming now!" Jasper called. Jasper was handsome too, but he was Robin's dessert. Emmett followed him. Ugh. Look at him. With his big, brown hazel eyes and adorable smile, of course he plays football at Columbus and is a cold, cocky cheater. *No, I don't want to look at him!* But he moved to the back seat of the car and leaned over to talk to Robin and me, and I could feel his "guyness," that aura of a hot boy being near you so close, you can smell him. Now, I had to look at him. He talked about beer, how he was a linebacker, and he mentioned that he played the drums in Jasper's band, Sound Glass.

"How old are you?" I asked. Also, I'm not falling for any of this, you jerk. Jock, whatever.

"Sixteen," he said in a sweet voice. His cheeks were like two perfect apples that met his eyes when he smiled.

"You're sixteen?" I blurted.

"Yeah…" He cocked his head, looking a little confused.

"I just…I thought…you look older. You look like you're twenty-one or something," I said, turning away, pretending like the outside world was way more interesting than this boy behind me.

"Yeah, people always think I'm the older one, right, Jasper?"

"Yep, totally true," Jasper said in his monotone voice.

The rest of the car ride, we small-talked, and I became less and less annoyed by how attracted I felt to Jasper's younger sibling, more entranced by the beauty of the location we were about to submerge ourselves in.

"Oh, my God, it's beautiful!" I exclaimed to nobody, as lights shone beneath the massive trees lining the pristine white mansion we were about to party in. "This looks like it belongs in a book or something!"

I followed the group to the intricate black gate, and we entered through enormous chestnut doors. The split staircase cascading down on both sides, elegant chandelier above us, and whole damn aura of the house screamed "RICH! RICH! RICH!" with every step I took. Walter, the one who lived here and went to TERRA with us, invited us in with such a happy demeanor, I knew right away he was drunk.

"Alright, guys, so the party is right over here. Try not to break anything!" He chuckled. A fuchsia bruise covered three-fourths of his pale neck. I had a feeling he wasn't aware of it. We walked through the living room which had glossy white floors and a plasma screen so large, it could've just been a black wall. A fluffy, persian cat strutted in front of us, as if flaunting the mansion. Even this prissy cat got to live in this beautiful home, and I didn't.

Total crazy, beautiful chaos. Within the first five minutes of being there, Jesse, this really cute basketball player, was dared to jump over the beer pong littered with beer bottles. No way, he's not going to do it.

"JUMP! JUMP! JUMP! JUMP!" The group of intoxicated boys around him egged him on. And guess what? I was wrong. I held my breath and cringed as Jesse's six-foot-three body leaped over the length of the table. The guys let out a collective roar of laughter. The table flipped one hundred and eighty degrees, and then came a thunderously loud crash of the bottles breaking, then the table landed, followed by Jesse. He got up, wincing in pain, as he cupped his right knee, which was bleeding profusely. A shard of broken glass had cut him. Compared to death, I thought he was pretty lucky.

One of his friends, Troy, also a cute basketball player, attended his wound. Beer in hand, I observed the crazy party people, recognizing almost all of them, not by names, but their faces. It was strange seeing them this way instead of really nerdy in TERRA uniforms, green polo shirts tucked into navy blue pants with a belt, and here they were wearing barely any clothes and blithering drunk. A DJ played house music in the corner of the patio, and I found myself catching up with a couple of classmates who were nice and genuine. Occasionally, I took sips of beer and some of Robin's vodka. Every time, I'd pass Emmett, he'd playfully poke my shoulder or back, and I'd glance at him scrunching my nose up, as if to say "Stoppit." At one point, he motioned for me to sit next to him, so I did. We sat observing the partygoers, and the more we talked, the more I realized he didn't know anyone at the party except us. How could such a cute guy not know everyone around him?

After a while, the sea of red cups, dolled-up, sweaty girls, and horny, sweaty boys began to bore me. "Let's go in the pool!" Robin yelled to Emmett and me.

"Can we?" I shouted.

"Why else would Walter have a bunch of towels over there?"

Just like she said, a bunch of towels were strewn across a plastic treasure chest. Excellent deductive reasoning, Robin. We glided over to the towels, and Robin asked Walter if it was okay for us to jump in the pool. After getting the green light, Robin grabbed me by the arm and we practically skipped to the edge of the pool, giggling like we were five. Her drunkenness made me tipsier than I was, and I couldn't stop laughing.

Emmett followed but protested that he was not going in the water.

"What if I get naked?" Robin proposed. "Will you come in then?" She batted her naturally long eyelashes.

Emmett laughed, "I don't have a bathing suit."

All the better, I thought, imagining Emmett in the pool wearing the bathing suit he did not have.

Suddenly, Robin was taking off her crop top and flirtatiously throwing it onto the chair Emmett was leaning on. A group of guys considered popular at TERRA appeared before us like groundhogs checking the weather. Emmett continued to shake his head, laughing. One of the guys asked Robin if she would get completely naked, and she simply looked at me and said, "Yeah, Ana and I are both going to get naked, and then you guys will all go in." Even in the dark, I could see their peering irises dilating.

"Um…no, we're not!" I shouted, laughing nervously.

They lingered to see if maybe I'd change my mind. Meanwhile, Robin was already short-less and nudging me towards the water. I hopped behind Emmett, and he chuckled, revealing the gleam of the metal in his mouth. I promise you he rocked those braces, though. Robin swam away like a mermaid, and I took the opportunity to investigate Mr. Cheatah McCheater.

"So," I said, looking into Emmett's pretty eyes. A faint glow of light from the patio fell on his adorable face by the lights of the pool. Perfect for up-close scrutiny.

"Soo," Emmett cooed. I had to cock my head up to look at him. He was about six-foot-one.

"A little birdy told me that you've had a girlfriend for like ever, and that you've been cheating on her left and right." I put my hands on my hips and narrowed my eyes at him.

"What? That's not true! I did have a girlfriend, but we broke up six months ago."

"And you weren't in a cheating orgy?"

"I wish!" He laughed, shaking his head. "I mean, no. Jasper told you that, didn't he?"

"Well, he told Robin, and then she told me."

"I don't know why he always makes up stuff like that about me. I'm not a cheater," Emmett continued. Ohhh, he's probably jealous that Emmett is the hotter brother. Makes sense, makes sense. Wait, but what if Emmett is lying? He gazed at me with those innocent, sweet, puppy eyes and I knew he meant what he was saying. After all, it made sense. An orgy at sixteen? C'mon. Much later I found out he *was* lying! The long-haired mermaid, Robin, returned, and I tried to mentally tell her the new information I had acquired. Slowly, I dipped my body into the warm water and felt their eyes on me. The water reached up to the top of my thighs, and just when I thought, "Okay, that's it, no more," Robin had stepped up to the top step of the pool and shoved me in with full force.

The water embraced my hot skin up to my torso. Standing on the second step of the stairs leading into the pool, I thought, Fuck it, I'm basically in. I laughed incessantly and accusingly squealed, "Robin!" In the water, I stripped my favorite pair of high-waisted shorts (which made my butt appear big) and threw them by Robin's clothes. Moments later, we both submerged ourselves completely, Robin waving her tanned arms in the air.

I laughed so hard, I felt my chest expanding. After all that had happened in the last few months, it was good to laugh again.

"I knew you'd go in!" Her eyes gleamed with happiness. And it was contagious. So contagious that when we both asked Emmett to join us, he finally agreed and started to strip to his boxers. The power of flirtation times two. Ha, ha. Now, let's put two and two together. Emmett was single and hot, and I was single and freeeee! Of course, we ended up kissing, but there I was flirting with him in Robin's flowy, white crop top, as we kissed for about three-point-four seconds thinking that would be it, when suddenly, he firmly placed his hands on my waist, and a pop kiss turned into one of the hottest, most passionate kisses I'd ever had. I sound like such a girl, but it's true!

My thoughts as it was happening:

This is soooo nice.

I wonder if he likes lip biting…

Okay, yes, he definitely likes that.

This is so crazy! I am making out with Jasper's little brother! This is so fun!

Oh, my God, I barely know anything about him. Woah, woah, your hand is not going there. At least not yet.

Gently, I placed his wandering hand back to the small of my back and could hear the conversation of two guys near us. They were talking about losing their virginities. *Hmm, is Emmett still a virgin?* I highly, doubt it. I ran my hands down his muscular back and chest, pretending I was his personal masseuse. Oh, yes. Oh. *Yes.*

After what felt like an hour and a half, maybe more, he asked me in a low voice, "Are you a virgin?"

"I was wondering the same thing!" I squealed louder than I intended to.

"Are you?"

"Guess," I giggled, flipping the white sheath flowy part of the crop top over my head.

"Well, you're older, and you're pretty, so I don't think you are."

"Correct, and thank you," I smiled. "I'm guessing you aren't either." He sure as hell didn't kiss like he was.

"I am."

"You are? Really?"

"Yep."

"Wow, I wouldn't have thought so, not in a million years."

"I mean, I've done everything else. Just not that yet."

With my hands around his neck like a koala bear, I giggled. Wow, I guess my friends are right. I am a bit of a cougar. I am a cougar bear.

"You're so hot, though! I'm honestly surprised."

"Why? I'm only sixteen."

"I don't know. Why haven't you lost it?"

"I just want to be comfortable with whoever I do it with." I could tell he meant all of his words, and something about his sincerity made me want him even more. We continued to kiss for a while, turning everything hotter.

"Do you want to go to the bathroom, and…you know?"

"Nope." I glanced at the corner of the mansion where the bathroom was, and my eyes glued themselves back to adorable Emmett. Everyone and everything else melted away. Emmett didn't even flinch at my response, but I could tell he was thinking about it.

"Look, I have a rule," I explained. "I don't have sex with a guy unless I know for sure it's going somewhere, or he's already my boyfriend."

"Okay, that's fine." Emmett smiled warmly. His lips were soft and plump. And everything was wet. And I do mean everything. After hours of making out, my hands had familiarized themselves with his body, and our lips had become the best of friends. At one point, Emmett grabbed me by the waist and switched us around, so that now I was facing the mansion, and he was facing the bushes. The sound of a loud engine revving up made me jump. We pulled away from each other, and I watched a truck full of drunk teenagers speed their way through the large front yard. I prayed for the cat I saw earlier, hoping they wouldn't crash the truck and murder anything. For a few minutes, they continued on like this, and I muttered, "Oh, my God, they want to get themselves killed."

Then, the truck was out of sight, and I heard no dying cat noises, so I sighed in relief. At around 4:00 AM, I couldn't feel any more young, alive, and free in that moment, as Emmett and the stars smiled at me. I registered everything around me as if to crystallize the memory. The vines of maroon flowers that romantically crawled down the white balcony of the second floor of the Victorian mansion, the glow of the moon over the sculpture of a woman in the water fountain, the soft sounds of splashing whenever we moved—all of it relaxed me, and I felt truly happy.

If only for one night.

If my mom knew I was here, and not sleeping over Margo's house like I'd told her, she would've probably killed me, and knowing that just made me relish the moment even more.

- PART TWO

"Wait, your mom doesn't know I'm here?" I whisper-shouted to Emmett. I instantly imagined her walking in on us butt naked on this warm August night, her face a cocktail of shock and disappointment.

"No, she's asleep." He grinned. "So, we have to be quiet." Emmett grabbed my phone, which I made sure was on vibrate in case my parents called. He plugged it into the charger by his dark blue wall and placed it over his wooden drawer cluttered with football trophies, clothes, and school supplies. My parents thought I was at Margo's house. Which I was. Earlier. Just not at the very moment.

"Is she a heavy sleeper?"

"Yes," he reassured me. Okay, good. A shuffling noise ensued, as if someone had just risen from their bed. Emmett threw his soft covers over me and like a tiger, he leaped from his twin bed to his door, shutting his lights off. Oh, goodie. Please don't come. Please don't come. Pleasepleaseplease.

Moments later, he announced. "We're clear, it was just Jasper."

"Oh, okay," I whispered, as he switched the lights back on. His shirt was off, and his abs were like an unwrapped Christmas present. He was wearing Family Guy themed PJ pants which I thought were cute. Cuter off, though. Was I considering breaking my own rule?

"Do you want the lights off?" he asked.

"Uh, huh, and these too." I tugged the top of his pants and tickled his irresistibly smooth skin. All of his body felt like a baby's ass really. In one swift movement, he got up, turned them off, and grabbed me like I was his teddy bear, snuggling next to me on his cozy bed. We cuddled until it became really hot, and I had no other choice than to take off my shirt as well. The heat, you know. He had the pleasure of carefully peeling off my denim shorts, and I basically clawed off his pants, like the cougar I was.

In between the covers, Emmett pulled my face toward him, grabbing fistfuls of hair, as he kissed me with more and more pressure, until I was tugging on his thick lower lip with my teeth, and his tongue kept exploring the inside of my mouth. He smelled like aftershave, Old Spice. I dug my nails into his wide back, then ran them down his bulging biceps, as he squeezed me like a fresh lemon.

I suppressed a moan, as he unclipped my brassiere. I relished the sound of our heavy, uneven breathing, as I planted gentle pecks around his neck and down to his very happy, happy trail.

Ana's Thoughts During the Non-PG-13 Event:

WOW, he tastes like water! I wouldn't mind going on forever.

But seriously, what time is it?

I bet it's been like twenty minutes… So, it's probably like twelve, unless it's already twelve thirty, and it just doesn't feel like it…

But my parents would have called or texted.

So why haven't they called?

A sudden knock on the door set my heart into a frenzy, pre-cardiac arrest. I was still registering that we might have just been caught by his mom when Emmett was already back in his pants, at the door muttering words to Jasper. Relief flooded over my nervous system.

"What happened?" I asked, still shaken.

"Jasper said that Margo says that your parents have been calling her, so you better pick up your phone."

Oh. My. God. Shitshitshit!

"Crap. Okay, get dressed. We gotta go now." I jumped to my feet and began shuffling around, searching for my things like a spy on a secret mission on the verge of being caught.

He pulled a white T-shirt over himself and handed me my phone. Six missed calls and three text messages from my mom and Margo. Each. My mom called again, and I answered while trying to pull my shirt over my head. A lie was already cooking in my mouth. I patted down my mane, trying to look like I hadn't spent the entire night making out with Emmett.

Mom: "Anaregina!" *bitch* *bitch* *bitch*

vs.

Ana: "I know, Mama, I'm sorry, we were watching a movie, and there was no service in her house and… (Mom interrupts to bitch some more) Yes, yes, I know, I'm sorry."

vs.

Mom: *Bitching* *Bitching* *Stiiiiiilllll bitching*

vs.

Ana: "Yes, I'm at her house! Where else would I be? *shits pants a little*

vs.

Mom: *Incessant bitching while I finish getting dressed and hop into Emmett's car* "Oh, really? I don't believe you, Anaregina, you sound like you're lying."

vs.

Ana: (In the most confident voice) "I'm not lying, Mom, I have no reason to. I'm on my way, okay?"

vs.

Mom: "Well, turn back around, Anaregina, because I'm already on my way to pick you up at Margo's house."

vs.

Ana: "Okay." *clicks*

"Emmett. DRIVE TO MARGO'S HOUSE!!! We have to get there before my mom does!!!!!" I whisper-shouted.

"Alright," he muttered. His expression turned seriously concentrated, like the road was his football field. The boy floored it, like my life depended on it, which it did. My mom didn't even know this guy, a *must* in a Hispanic household. And probably everywhere else, actually. Luckily, we weren't too far from Margo's house. Emmett made a sharp turn, and my body swung to the left like I was riding Crazy Mouse at the Youth Fair. I clung to the edge of the tanned, leather passenger seat with both hands. Nonchalantly, I tilted my head to my left armpit and smelled rotten asparagus. I hoped Emmett couldn't smell my disgusting nervous sweat scent.

"Emmett, please slow down, the last thing we need is to be pulled over by a cop."

"Okay, sorry."

"It's okay," I said, clutching my phone, going to my recent calls, and pressing Margo's name. She picked up on the second ring.

M: "Ana! Why weren't you picking up your phone?"

A: "It was on silent, even though I could have sworn I had it on vibrate, but anyway look—"

M: "Your mom kept calling me! I didn't know what to do, so I just didn't answer."

A: "I know, I know. Thank you so much for letting me know. Totally saved me through Jasper. Here's the thing, though, my mom doesn't believe I'm at your house, so Emmett is dropping me off right now. Is that okay?"

M: "Yeah, it's fine. You're so dumb, Ana."

A: "Shut up. Thank you. I love you."

M: "I love you too. Text me when you're at the front door. Actually, I'll just leave it open, but be really quiet cause my mom is sleeping."

A: "Okay, bye." *clicks*

So close. So close. Just a couple of blocks away. Down that street, we turned left into her neighborhood, and finally after about seven minutes, we arrived. Yes! We made it! Yes! Yes! Yes! Then, I got a phone call I wasn't expecting at all. It was my dad. I cringed before answering, and every nerve in my body was on high alert. Emmett put a reassuring hand over my bare knee, as we faced the entrance of Margo's dimly lit townhouse. The air was warm and thick, perfect weather for blood sucking mosquitos.

Guilty Daughter: "Hello?"

Pissed Off Father: "Anaregina. WHERE ARE YOU?"

Tiny Voice: "Papá, I'm in front of Margo's house."

Very Very Very VERY VERY Furious Father: "ANAREGINA, IT IS 1:30 IN THE MORNING! YOU SAID YOU WERE GOING TO BE HERE AT 12:30! WHY AREN'T YOU HERE, ANAREGINA? DON'T YOU UNDERSTAND THAT YOUR MOM AND I ARE TIRED? AND MAMÁ GETS WORRIED ABOUT YOU, WHICH KEEPS ME UP. AND NOW SHE'S TELLING ME THAT SHE DOESN'T EVEN THINK YOU ARE WHERE YOU ARE SAYING YOU ARE! WHAT IS THE MATTER WITH YOU? GIVE ME A BREAK, ANAREGINA! THINGS ARE DIFFERENT NOW, WHEN I'M ASKING YOU TO BE HOME EARLIER IT'S NOT BECAUSE I WANT TO BOTHER YOU, IT'S BECAUSE I AM SICK, I HAVE CANCER, AND I'M TIRED! DO YOU UNDERSTAND THAT?"

Guilt consumed me. My father was battling for his life, and here I was, traipsing around town with some guy I just met, making him worry for no reason. What was wrong with me?

Holding Back Tears: "Yes."

Dad: "Okay, Mama should be there any minute now. And please, Anaregina, for the love of God, answer your phone and do not keep her waiting."

Ana: "Okay, I won't. Bye, Papá, I'm really, really sorry."

Dad: "I'll see you when you get home. Bye, Anaregina."

Ana: "B-bye."

Dad: *hangs up*

At that moment, I was one-hundred-and-twenty pounds of guilt. I was used to dealing with my mom bitching at me for stuff like this. But my dad? That was the first time in almost three years that he was actually a dad-dad to me. And with real emotion too. I could hear the exasperation and stress in his voice.

Emmett raised his eyebrows. "Do I leave?"

I nodded at him. Because he thought I was still on the phone with my dad, he mouthed, "Are you okay?"

I nodded again. Thank God it was still dark. I waved him off with a forced, grateful-for-you-getting-me-back-here-on-time smile. He drove away, and I stood there with the disappointed night and starless sky above. A frog croaked nearby, as though telling me I was a terrible daughter. As promised, the front door was unlocked, and I tiptoed inside Margo's house. Now I was one-hundred-and-twenty pounds of anxiety.

Margo appeared in the foyer. "Are you okay?" She hugged me, easing off the edge I was feeling.

"Not really, my mom bitched at me, which okay, that's nothing I couldn't handle, but then my dad called and like…he just went off. Talking about how he has cancer, and I'm keeping him awake, and he's tired, and now I just feel really bad."

"Aw, I'm sorry, baby." Margo strolled to the kitchen, like she could read my mind, because I was hungrier than a rhino, and this was the location of the famous Quaker's Oats Granola Bars! Yes! Comfort food.

Sitting at the kitchen table, I stared at my cracked Galaxy S III screen, checking the volume and making sure it was on low. Margo reached into her wooden pantry and threw me a granola bar with chocolate chips. I caught it and devoured it in two-point-six seconds. I went to get another one and scarfed that one down too.

"SO. Emmett. Did you fuck him?"

"No, I didn't." I unwrapped the third granola bar. "We were just making out and stuff when Jasper walked in with the message."

"Oh, my God, Ana, you're so lucky I messaged him, and he followed through."

"Dude," I bit my pointer finger, "I know, I keep on thinking about that."

"Your phone isn't on silent now, is it?"

I checked again. "No, it's not, my mom should be here any second. So, just to review, I told her that you and I were watching 'the movie' in your living room where there was no service, and that's why neither of us picked up. If she asks you what movie we saw, we could say that we saw…hmm…" I took a bite of the chewy bar and mumbled, "Mean Girls 2!"

"I hate that movie."

"Me too, but just say it. Dude…" I checked my phone again. "Why isn't she here yet? It's making me so anxious, like I'm starting to get anxiety, Margo."

"Relax, you're good, you're already here, dummy."

"I know, but…but still. I'm still so shaky from everything." I couldn't take the anxiety anymore and started to do what I always did whenever I felt this way. "One." I squatted. "Two." I squatted.

"Ana, why are you doing squats right now?"

"Three." I squatted. "Four…"

"It's…" I panted. "The only thing that could calm me…" I exhaled. "Down right now."

Margo laughed. "Oh, my God, bitch, no wonder you're so fit!"

I squatted until I got to twenty-four, and then I smiled, as my heart rate increased. "I'm going to get to one hundred. Want to…do them…with…me?"

"Not really," she said, biting into a granola bar. We were pretty much done with the whole box by this point. By the time I got to seventy-two, my annoying ass ringtone went off. I took a deep, calming breath before answering.

Mom: "I'm outside."

vs.

Ana: "I'm going." *click*

I hugged Margo and told her goodbye and thanks, and she wished me luck. Opening the door, I stepped in the Prius where a very angry mother made no eye contact with me and didn't say one syllable to me the whole way home. It was like she wasn't even breathing. Ah, the silent bitch treatment of the caring, overprotective mom. Rare, but useful and rightly deserved. I angled my face away from her, trying to force my lips to stop forming the huge victory smile I had welling up inside me.

A silent mother was better than a bitching one.

CHAPTER 4
"La vida es un script." - Mom

August approached itself, unannounced and unnoticed like a creature sneaking up on you.

"Mamá, what are you doing?" I asked.

She plucked her eyebrows. "What are you talking about?" She knew exactly what I was talking about.

"Papá!"

"What about him?"

"You're just going to let him stay here without any regards to the fact that you guys split up?"

"He is here, because his doctors and surgeon are much closer to him here than in Hollywood, and it's much easier to resolve all the legal issues with Adam with the lawyers with him staying here."

"Until when is he staying?"

"We haven't really discussed that," she sighed.

"Yeah, and you're probably not going to unless you say something." All the inexplicable resentment I had fermenting inside me towards my father seemed to bubble up to the surface. Even though I adored him, I experienced what my parents' separation had done to my mom, and I didn't want to go through that madness again. Ever. Mom stayed quiet, because she knew I was right. "Mamá, we just, I mean we finally, I mean, YOU just got over the separation a couple of months ago. This isn't going to help you at all. I just…I don't want to go through what we went through two years ago again. It wasn't exactly easy, Mamá. Really, really, really far from easy."

She plucked and plucked, until she finally plucked out her words to say to me. "Anaregina, honestly, what else do you want me to do? Do you want me to tell him to go home and have zero contact with him the way some ex-wives would? He is sick, and Adam is not even here to help you take care of him. You would have to do that all by yourself. You would take him to all of his appointments, to the hospital, you would have to drive an hour to go visit him and take care of him if he needs it. Is that really what you want, Anaregina?"

"Okay, I understand that. I get it. I just, I don't know…" *He's going to leave again, and then I'm going to be here holding up an "I told you so, Mom" sign.* I played with the tips of my frizzy curls. "Until when is he going to stay here?"

I could feel my mom's trepidation through the invisible umbilical cord that attached us together. Mixed with confusion and anxiety, and unrequited love, I felt a whole cocktail of emotions stirring inside her. I felt split in half again. Like two separate children. My dad's adoring, loving little girl and my mom's loyal, headstrong daughter. The two of them couldn't be in the same room though because their love for their parents fought each other to a bloody massacre. I just want to avoid as much blood as possible. Stitching a heart together isn't easy. It takes time and patience. And more time, and more patience. It's insane how many pieces it can break into. Witnessing a divorce is like constantly having two songs play in your head, one over the other. The harmony all fucked up.

"Hmm?" I persisted.

"Ay, Anaregina! I don't have an exact date okay? We haven't made the time to talk about it, but I'll make sure the very first thing I do is make sure you are okay with the arrangements, since you get to decide that, apparently." Her voice was heavy with sarcasm.

"Mom, you don't need to be so dramatic, I just want to know." *I just don't want to go through divorce round two. This isn't The Parent Trap.* I felt my blood boil just a bit.

"Anaregina! For all we know, he won't even have the chance of making it, and he'll leave all of us again, this time through death!"

OH MY GOOOODDD, THIS IS EXACLTY WHAT I MEAN ABOUT BEING SO DRAMATIC!!!

I paused and thought about her words. Why did she have to be so blunt? Why drive that nail home for me? Why? "Okay, Mom. Wonderful, well, I'm going to go to sleep now. Thank you for the head's up. It was really helpful. Goodnight," I smiled sardonically, biting back tears that lurked in the back of my throat.

It wasn't that I didn't want my dad to be with us here again, I just didn't want my mom to go through the pain, and the fear of losing him again, and frankly, neither did I. Sometimes I wished I could control people's feelings. I went to bed, reciting my "rap" until the anger simmered down and was replaced with anxiety and excitement for tomorrow.

Preface for the next story…

A couple of days ago I was walking around school, heading towards the library, when some chick with a hoop nose piercing was like, "Do you have a minute for gay rights?" And that led me to landing a successful interview to work for the Gay Rights Campaign.

- First Day of Work at the Gay Rights Campaign Story! September 13th, 2014

I don't know if I want to work here or not. I'm still not even sure how this works. Canvassing? It sounds like I'm going to be painting pictures all the time. Ugh, I really hope I like this. Please, Universe, please, let me like this job.

I crept to the front door that proudly displayed a navy-blue sign with a mustard yellow equality sign on it and opened it. Inside were a couple of blue chairs with smiling people sitting in them, reciting the rap and more equality stuff decorating the walls, such as a rainbow flag. There were tables along the sides, but none of that stuff mattered to my curious eyes. Instead, I zeroed in on the tall, green-yellow-eyed stranger with jet-black hair and a gleaming white smile. His sharp jawline was outlined with a five o'clock shadow.

I love my job. I love it so much.

"Hey! Welcome to GRC, I'm Edward." The beautiful stranger extended his arm. I smiled giddily and shook it. He looked older, like twenty-two maybe.

"I'm Anaregina."

"Nice to meet you. Here, why don't you take a seat and we'll practice the rap, so you've got it down for today."

"Y-yeah," I said shyly, as I sat on the chair he pulled out for me. He smiled at me, and all I could do was giggle. I can't believe I get to work with him!

"Alright guys, so let's just start from the top again, so we're all together."

Oh right, there were other people in this group. I introduced myself, and they all genuinely smiled and introduced themselves back.

"Anaregina, you want to try?"

"Sure," I tried so hard to suppress my giggle.

"Alright, so I'm going to go first, and then just repeat after me."

"Okay," I said softly.

"Great. What's your name?"

"Anaregina." We shook hands again. A chorus of suppressed giggles erupted. Damn it!

"Nice to meet you, Anaregina." He grinned. "My name is Edward, and

I'm working on behalf of the Gay Rights Campaign. We're the nation's largest LGBT civil rights group, and we're out here today signing up members, so thank you for stopping." He said the last sentence so slow, it gave me a chance to cherish the sound of his deep voice and actually listen to what the heck he was saying. "Okay, your turn."

"Okay." I smiled. "Great. What's your name?"

"Edward." I shook his hand, and for a second, forgot what to say next. "Nice to meet you, Edward. My name is Anaregina, and I'm working on behalf of the Gay Rights Campaign. We're the nation's largest LGBT civil rights group, and we're out here today…" Dammit, I forgot.

"Signing up members…" whispered dazzling Edward.

"Signing up members." I felt my cheeks turn every shade of beet red. "So, thank you for stopping." One could fry eggs on my face at times like these.

Would you like an omelet?

Oh, sure!

No problem let me just crack some eggs on Ana's blushing cheeks right now! It'll be twice as fast as on a frying pan!

I explained to him that I smile and laugh a lot whenever I'm nervous and that I was nervous right now. Nervous about what? About having to give this rap to strangers today. Just nervous about the rap. Not him, just the rap. The rap was exactly one minute long and encompassed saying who we were as a political campaign, speaking of the issue…

In twenty-nine states, people are at risk of being fired for being gay. (Side note: Yes, there are actually anti-gay groups who strive to continue discrimination across the country and support the horrible oppression that gay people have to face daily, and yes, the year was 2015).

My mission was to help sign up members who'd pay small contributions a month to lobbyists and lawyers who fight these cases in the big courts. It turned out I was becoming a part of something that was a pretty big deal and pretty freaking awesome if I do say so myself. It was glorious, and scary, and nerve-wracking, and incredibly fulfilling to be asking complete strangers if they had a minute to support gay rights, on only two hours of sleep in front of burning hot Kendall Chipotle with a confident, quirky woman by my side who I totally thought was Edward's girlfriend at first, but it turned out she was a lesbian!

There was some hope for single me. But contrary to what you have probably assumed by now, I never made my relationship status a priority. There were more important matters at hand that involved letting the number one most important man in my life know that I was one-hundred percent A-okay with his sexual orientation, even if he wasn't.

The plot twist in my memoir goes as follows.

Plot twist!?!?

What do you mean a plot twist? This is a memoir. Memoirs can't have plot twists?

.....Can they?

Oh…but they can.

I paced around the living room of my house like a mad scientist on the precipice of her next creation, unsure of what words were going to come out of my mouth.

"Dad." Finally, I took a seat on a black, wooden stool that faced our small, gray kitchen. Mom was at work. He turned, appearing caught off guard by the tone of my voice. Little did he know how nervous I was.

"Yes?" he asked curiously.

"I work at the nation's largest LGBT civil rights group…" I trailed off, letting my words hang in the air like gnats when it's rainy outside. Oh, God no, that was a terrible simile. They don't "hang," they freaking fly into your eye. Every. Time.

He seemed relieved. "God job on landing that job." He smiled, but his mind was elsewhere. His brown eyes were vacant and hollow. I always called this look of his "tree mode."

I bit my thumbnail.

Ana's Thoughts:

Just do it. Just say it, Ana. C'mon!

But I don't know what to say…

Yes, you do.

Okay, but what if he reacts angrily like he did last time?

Things are different now, he won't react that way.

Or worse…what if he doesn't react at all?

Then the words all spilled out of me, as if the Universe had planted them inside my soul billions of years ago when the "Big Bang" occurred. I inhaled a deep breath and exhaled:

"Papá, like I said, I'm working for the lesbian, gay, bisexual, transgender civil rights group, where I'm asking literally hundreds of strangers a week to support gay rights and end discrimination. You know…stop workplace equality. Like, I'm invested in this, I actually want people to stop firing other people for being gay or bisexual or whatever. It matters to me a lot. And when Mary, my boss, asked me why I wanted the job, I told her about you."

I waited for a sign from him. Anything.

He only kept his eyes on the paper he was pretending to read, so I went on.

"I told her that I felt like this was the best way I knew to show my support towards you being gay or bisexual, or whatever you consider yourself to be." Please, please don't be angry.

My dad looked up, folded his paper, took a deep breath, then left to sit down on the couch in the living room. My gaze followed him. I watched the hollowness in his expression being stripped away to something real, a fragile emotion that had been guarded for decades. He was motionless, but at least he wasn't mad.

I continued, "I work with so many gay people, Papá, and you know I hadn't really been around too many gay people before, so honestly, at first it felt a little weird for me. But getting to know them, I think they're some of the greatest, coolest people I've ever met. They're characters. They know discrimination all too well. Like I have this one co-worker, Leslie, who got kicked off the dance team in middle school just because she kissed a girl, and she is a dancer, Papá. It's hard to be who you really are in a society that condemns you for it. Especially with the stereotypical family view that society holds of a married man and woman with children. I understand. Like, you have this horrible disease now, and I don't think you should waste another minute not being who you really are."

His eyes were now glazed, gleaming with admiration and gratitude, and I knew all at once he was taking this exactly as I wanted. So, now for the hardest part.

"Look, Mom told me about the sex addiction you had, and whatever…I mean, Adam was addicted to heroin; I've had obsessive thoughts over things. So, I guess addiction is just a thing that runs in our family. It runs in a lot of families, I'm sure. Depression and all that. I want you to know that it's okay. Okay?" I sat down next to him and looked into his eyes. "I'm more than fine with you being gay or bi. I accept it. I couldn't possibly accept it any more than I do. So, if one day you wanted to have your friend, or boyfriend, or whoever he is to you come over for dinner, that's perfectly fine by me."

The last sentence tasted funny in my mouth. I never thought I would be saying that to my dad. I could feel something fragile breaking in me too, as the next sentence entered in my mind. I saved it there, because I could see all the emotions welling up in my father who loved me so much. He didn't need to say anything. I leaned over and hugged him. As he embraced me, I heard the muffled tears break through the person my dad had pretended to be for the longest time.

"Thank you," he said softly. I nodded and smiled, getting a little teary-eyed myself. "You are such a smart, capable, and empathetic woman, Anaregina. You really are destined for greatness, and I know this by the way you perceive things that aren't exactly easy to comprehend, but you take them with such a mature and graceful manner that I'm blown away. Thank you."

"Of course, Papi," I said, flattered, so happy to be his daughter at that moment. He stood from the couch and strolled to the dining room. I followed him, leaving the dead shell of what was once a façade in that living room. He was no longer an emotionless tree in that moment, but a human being. My father. Rogelio Frias, to be exact. A mystery to me, since the days I was able to perceive the world as a young woman, instead of a little girl.

"It wasn't easy," he said. "It was like living in two different worlds."

"Yeah, I always had a feeling, Papá," I admitted. His bushy salt-n-pepper eyebrows raised up in surprise. "I remember a couple of months ago when I was watching Breaking Bad, I really started to think about Walter White and how much he reminded me of you."

"Really?" My dad chuckled. "How so?"

"Well, I remember one time after we watched a movie and went to Anthony's Pizza, you were speaking as if you were living a completely different reality somewhere else, just like Walter White. I remember asking you if you secretly cooked meth or had a meth lab that you weren't telling us about. More than once I asked you! Remember?"

"I remember that." My dad cracked up, as the memory replayed in his head, and I used the levity of the atmosphere to finally say the last thing I had to say on the me-coming-out-for-my-dad topic. "Y-you know," I stammered, "if what you truly, truly want is to be with your friend instead of over here with Mama, me, and Adam—well, when Adam comes back—that's okay. I want you to do whatever makes you happy. I think that would even benefit your health. No, I'm sure that would benefit your health," I said with confidence.

I twirled the tips of my hair, hoping I was saying the right things.

"I don't know. I've been asking myself the same thing. He's been really great, and he would be extremely supportive, but he also has a lot of financial issues, some emotional too. Of course, we all do, but I also don't want to leave here again," he said, "I've been stressing about this over a while."

Even though I'd never been a bi dad of two children and an ex-husband to an incredible, loving woman (though my mom could be a crazy, pain in the ass sometimes), I felt like I understood the inner turmoil. I simply nodded.

"Well, I still love you Dad." And the visible stress that clung to his face like a small child clings to her mother melted off just a teeny bit.

Whew, glad that was over.

CHAPTER 5
Truth or Dare

Screaming into my pillow for hours became the norm. Between wondering when the hell my brother was going to get out of jail, a new merry-go-round formed in my head. It went like this: "My dad's going to die, my dad's going to die…" I pushed that merry-go-round to the deepest part of my brain as possible, and at school I focused on being bubbly, s t u d i o u s Ana, that is until fate brought me back to a familiar face.

"I should really go back to the math lab," I told Harry. His enormous brown eyes blinked at me, pleading with me to stay with him and all his charm.

"Just stay an hour more. You've been there all day. C'mon, you basically live there," Harry said. We both knew I was definitely going to ditch the math lab to continue playing the "college version" of Truth or Dare.

"Okay, fine, but I'm going back like at…" I glanced at the time on my Galaxy. "Six-thirty. Latest seven!"

"Alright, alright," Harry smiled. A boy could always get me with his smile, and this boy did exactly that two years ago when we met after a swim practice at Tamiami Pool. For about ten minutes, until we went our separate ways.

"What are the odds that you and I would find each other again at Dade two years later?" I exclaimed. I couldn't peel my eyes off of him. It wasn't even that he was incredibly handsome or something, it was the vibe he gave off, so effulgent, so vibrant. I was a total magnet for this guy.

"Kendall is a small world." He chuckled. His laugh could probably make Hitler smile. Wow, I liked him. Like like-like. "Alright, so what are the odds…" He paused to think, as his gaze followed the people who roamed the campus. "That you'll go to where the palm trees are, you know right there, right where the people are, and you'll just start dancing like a crazy person." He flashed me a huge grin, finishing his dare proposal.

Psssh, I could do that. It's not like I have to sing to them too.

"Umm," I melted into a fit of giggles, debating my odds of carrying out the dare into action. "One to five." I squeezed my eyes shut, the number already in my head.

"Okay. Okay." His thin lips curled up, "do you have your number ready?"

"Yes, I do."

"Then on three. One…two…three."

"FOUR!" We both shouted unanimously. "Dammit! Fuck! Really four?" I exclaimed. I was so sure he wouldn't have guessed it.

"Alright then. Go show them your best moves." He urged, leaning into my face, absolutely teasing me. The air was sticky with humidity, but I didn't care. I felt pretty, and the birds were chirping rhythmically, while the sun said its last goodbyes.

"I will," I said confidently. I raised my shoulder to my chin flirtatiously. I could feel his eyes glued to me, as I gracefully propped myself up on the square where the palm trees were in plain sight of the students. Quickly, I swallowed my pride. Harry cracked up, a couple feet away from me, doubting my ability.

"C'mon!" He whispered.

I literally pretended I was at a club, and that I was on the dance floor, getting low to some beat that had me moving like my hips don't lie, and went on like this, until I felt more than one group of people drill their eyes into me. I started blushing, and jumped off the square, as I laughed and skidded my way back to Harry.

His eyes glazed with pure amusement. I punched him in the shoulder. "Your turn."

"Go." He challenged. From my peripheral vision, I noticed a tall dude on a skateboard, skating his way towards the concrete ramp that was in front of us.

"Okay, see that guy?" I motioned towards him as inconspicuously as possible until Harry nodded. "Go up to him and yell that you love him."

"What? Ana…" He hesitated.

"Go! Go! Go do it!" I said, feeling my stomach all fluttery. The stranger slid right past us, and just as he got on the ramp, Harry trailed behind him and shrieked, "I LOVE YOU!" The skateboarder turned around in bewilderment, then skated away, his face a perfect combination of confusion and disregard.

"Oh, my God, you're great!" I smiled. "We didn't even do the number thing!"

"Yeah, I know. You got that one for free," Harry laughed. "His face was priceless!"

"I know, I know." As we were laughing, I stole a glance at his lips. His awesome, inviting lips.

What are the odds that you'll let me kiss you?

Zero to Nothing, he would say.

Then, we'd have our first kiss, and it would be so freaking cute, that I wouldn't shut up about it forever.

"What are you thinking, Ana?" he asked.

That I totally want to kiss you.

"Nothing, nothing." I smiled sheepishly.

"Tell me," he pried. His hair was short, dark brown, his tanned face clean shaven.

"I'm just thinking of the next dare for you," I said, gazing down at my hands. My red nail polish was chipping off after like one day.

"Well, it's your turn," he reminded me.

We went on like this until it was night time, and the math lab closed, so I had to wait for my dad to pick me up in his white Volkswagen with Harry still by my side, the sun in both of his eyes. My dad pulled up, tired, but pleased to see me. I peeled myself off the bench and wrapped my arms around the top of Harry's strong shoulders.

"See you Wednesday?" His voice was a calm, summer day in my ear.

"Yes, at the math lab. My second home," I giggled. I opened the car door and stepped inside, greeting my dad. We pulled out of the student bus drop-off area. I waved goodbye to Harry, and when he waved back, that caught my dad's attention, so even my dad waved at him too. Holy hell. I knew it had only been a couple of days since reconnecting—if you could even call it that—but I felt such a strong connection forming with this guy, it made my heart smile. I even read him the prologue of the story I was writing when I had only shown that to my mom!

"How was your day?" Dad asked. His hair had turned grayer and finer over the last couple of weeks. A bald spot was forming on the crown of his head.

"It was gooood," I sang, not bothering to hide my smile. He was happy I was happy. In fact, I was smiling so much, I felt like I was on top of the world. I had magnificent professors (except my math one, although attendance wasn't necessary, so that was pretty spectacular), I was earning ACTUAL HARD-EARNED MONEY, I re-met Harry at the math lab, of all places, and I was pretty sure he liked me as much as I liked him. Now, to break off with Carlisle…Carlisle sat next to me in homeroom my senior year at TERRA, and we had on and off crushes on each other. We didn't officially start talking-talking until the night before the first day of college, after my adventures with Emmett ended. More than anything he was a close friend first. Or so I thought.

Oh, Carlisle, I knoweth thee wast mine valorous cousin senior year and we wanted to beest with each other so lacking valor, but the truth is I feeleth so guilty being with thee because Phoebe is a valorous cousin to me and the lady loves thee, and the fact that thou smoke weed every day very much turns me off, and now I am totally in like with another fellow. My most humble apology…

Oh, Ana, I completely understandeth, don't worry, thou art still a quite quaint soul to me. If 'tis be true, this sir can treat thee like the queen that thee art then I too, wilt beest joyous that thee art joyous. Farewell, Ana.

Fare thee well, Carlisle, a good wish upon you :)

In reality, I became distant after a small argument until Carlisle had had enough and called me a bitch over text, so then I dropped his ass like a hot potato. Sorry, but I never tolerate insults from anyone, especially a freaking boy who wants to be my boyfriend. And the "relationship" I had with him was incredibly fucked up anyway because Phoebe loved him. Even though I asked Phoebe if it was okay for me to date him and she said yes, I knew deep down she still wanted him, and I was an asshole for going there. Of course, she dumped me as a friend! And that sucked. A lot. I lost my insta-therapist, I lost a good friend during a time in my life when I needed all the good friends I could possibly have.

NOT all is fair in love and war.

Anyway, life moved on. My mom and dad started acting like they were husband and wife which was weird after knowing about my dad's "friend," and Harry and I saw each other that Wednesday at school. He told me he "pineappled me" which translated to "I like you" (that was an insider joke, since he was obsessed with pineapples). He helped me with my math homework and lent me his precious volleyball jacket when I was cold and made me laugh until I snorted like a pig. Everything was going really great between us, and even my friends were all like, "Damn, he's so sweet, definitely a keeper yadda yadda…" But then life threw that boy a very, and I mean very, very, very hideously nasty curveball—death.

No, I don't mean his death. Here's how it went down:

Ahem, it was someone's 19th birthday yesterday
and someone forgot to text someone happy
birthday *mad face emoji*

I'm so sorry Ana, I didn't text you because
last night my best friend got in a
terrible car accident, and I've been with

his family this whole time

Oh my God, no Harry, don't worry
about it at all, I completely understand.
Is he okay??? What happened
exactly? (...Well, I feel like a
douchebag now..)

He was with another one of our friends,
who dared him and another friend to run
across the street and he took the dare,
but a car was coming very fast and hit them,
the friend managed to jump out of the way
and has a couple of broken bones but
my best friend got hit full impact. He has a
couple of broken ribs, a fractured
lung, and he cracked his skull open.

Wow… that's crazy… I'm so sorry to
hear that Harry. I really hope he'll be
okay soon <3

He will, he's a strong kid. He'll
be okay. And thank you Ana.

He died one week later (may he rest in peace eternally).

So, even though Harry faded from my life like an old tattoo, the tragedy that happened to him offered me an entire world of perspective on my mental merry-go-round of death. I learned death was not simply terminal cancer—you have x number of months to live—so enjoy the time you have left. Death is potentially around the corner at any given moment in time. It isn't about spending your time and cherishing your memories with that person with cancer or old age, it's about cherishing and spending time with all the people you love at all times, to the best of your abilities. Because you never know when a best friend, a perfectly healthy young person, even if they're nineteen years old and know better, is going to take a dare to the point of life or death.

CHAPTER 6
Surrender

"Accept that you have no control over it, and that all you can do is be there for your dad."

- JOHANNA CHAVARRY (AN AMAZINGLY AWESOME COWORKER OF MINE WHOSE ADVICE TOUCHED ME TO THE CORE OF MY VERY SPIRIT)

I detested the present that my dad got me for my nineteenth birthday. I scanned the first couple of pages briefly, immediately putting it down and burying it deep in my bookshelves. It was a small book called, *I Wish For You - Gentle Reminders to Follow Your Heart* that contained meaningful messages and inspirational quotes to follow your dreams and heart and all that Hallmark goodness. I felt like he'd walked into Barnes & Noble and went straight to the Father-Dying-Get-Daughter-Her-Last-Gift Section.

There was no way I was reading that piece of crap.

So, for my dad's birthday, I went to Walgreens and bought a black picture frame containing three frames in one. Perfect. There was a black square on it that read in white letters, "Family, around us, beside us, to love and to guide us." A little cheesy, but whatever. Inside the first picture frame I put a picture of him holding me as a baby in Acapulco, Mexico by the sky-high rocks at the beach. In the picture frame next to it, I inserted a photo of us sitting on the same rocks (okay, maybe not the same exact rocks, but the same location). I was sitting in his lap, except this time I was thirteen. And then in the third picture frame, I wrote in the empty white space, "Reserved for when we visit Acapulco, Mexico again. Te quiero muchisisisisisimo, y Feliz Cumpleaños Papá. <3 - Anaregina."

I know he understood the message behind the third empty space, but we didn't speak about it. He simply said, "thank you" and smiled. We ate at Longhorn with my mom, and I passionately told them about the philosophy lessons I'd learned on God, all with a smile on my face. They listened to me, intrigued. We didn't focus on the fact that my brother wasn't there for my dad's 58th birthday, or the grim reaper's carousel, taking my dad away. Quietly, we devoured the chocolate cake my dad let me pick for him.

It was the last birthday celebration I would spend with my dad, and it was one of the best.

***

- Ghosts of Exes Past

All in one day, I saw Augustus, my third boyfriend, the purple tulip with the stigma sticking out, representing the loss of our virginity, Stella (the girl who was my best friend in ninth grade until she basically replaced me with someone else), and Ponyboy (read in annoying tone: "my first looove"). It was a hell of a day canvassing at Florida International University. Not easy concentrating on gay rights when I was acting like a meth addict on a paranoia wave. Half of everyone I've ever known went there. That same night, I met the fifth flower on my wall—Will. He hated pickles and thought canvassers were a n n o y i n g.

"So…if you were to pass by me, and I asked if you had a minute for gay rights, you would just say no for no good reason?" I asked. I sat across from him in Barney's dorm at FIU criss-cross applesauce in a flower print dress from Forever 21.

"Yes, and then I would move out of the way," he said calmly, crossing his hands on his lap. A silver chain hung from his neck, and he wore a black, fleece long-sleeved shirt and black leather pants with black combat boots. A monochromatic Cuban, white guy. He wore a smug smile on his perfectly symmetrical face. "Yeah, I'm a dick. My name is Will by the way, nice to meet you." He chuckled softly.

He is a dick!

Paradoxically enough, that turned me on. I still can't explain why. Disapprovingly, I shook my head and filled him in on workplace inequality.

"...which means in twenty-nine states, gay people can get fired without any say in court, because they don't have that right, say the way women do.

If I were to get fired for being a woman, then I could take it to court and win fair and square because I have that right. Gay people don't," I sighed, exasperated, eager to change his mind. I had to explain that to at least twenty-five people in one day. It would be so much easier if I could just publish a book for everyone to read.

"Shit, really?" he said. "Damn, I didn't know that."

"So, now would you say yes to me?" I clutched Barney's fleece Hollister sweater, draping it over my freezing body.

"I'd think twice about it this time." He wore a toothy smile. This guy knew he was good-looking for sure. Most good-looking dicks knew. Then, he stood up and left, and I realized how incredibly short he was. He's like two or three inches taller than me, I thought, and I'm five-one-and three-quarter inches tall. I remember one night telling Barney and Ted that after experiencing Sodapop's gorgeous gigantism, I'd never date a short guy again. But yet there I was wanting him.

"Hey, we're going to have some best friend time, so leave us alone," Barney called out to Will, who was in and out of Barney' dorm room with their other best friend, Saul. I started to spill all my thoughts and feelings to Ted and Barney who were some of the best listeners in the entire world, because as you could tell, I was a detail freak when it came to storytelling.

"...so, then about two hours after I saw Stella, I ran into Ponyboy who was walking towards me while I was canvassing with this guy who was flirting with me, asking me for my number and shit, and I was trying to be like, 'No, I'm just trying to do my job here.' Then out of the corner of my eye, I see him. I recognize him and thought about telling flirt-guy, 'Also, if you look right over there, I haven't been able to get over that guy since eighth grade, so you're wasting your time."

Barney laughed. "Oh, God."

And Ted asked, "How did you feel seeing him?"

I opened my mouth to speak but then closed it to find the right words. On one hand, words were forming in one language from my heart and in another from my mind. Then, Will popped out of the hallway—shirtless, I might add—and glided over to where we were seated at the small kitchen table to offer a piece of gum.

"Sure," I said, flashing him a smile, glancing at his toned torso. He handed me the piece of gum and left the room, but man did he totally do that to show off his body! And it worked!

"Did you see those muscles?" Ted gushed. Ted was straight by the way.

"Yes, I did!" I gushed even more. "And he has a tattoo on his bicep." Bicep tattoos for me were like big, beautiful boobs to a guy. Or a lesbian.

"So…go on…you'd just seen Ponyboy," Barney reined us back to the topic.

"Right. So anyway…I felt nervous, confused, happy...confident. We had like a twenty-six second conversation that went, 'What are you doing here?' 'Me? Oh, working.' 'Nice, well I have to go study for a test.' 'Good luck.' 'Thanks.'" I gave them the entire breakdown of that scintillating conversation.

Whenever I spoke as if I were Ponyboy, I used this funny, deep douchebag voice just because it always made my friends laugh. "Whatever, I know I looked cute today!" I burst with joy. Because there was nothing like looking cute when you run into a ghost of ex's past. "And, I'm still not going to text him!" Although, deep down inside of me, a part of me burned with desire to do so. And Ted and Barney could see right through it.

Whatever, it didn't matter. I was brimming with excitement about Will now, feeling the beginning of a crush brewing inside of me. I kept wondering what the shaded, triangular tattoo was on his bicep. "Whatever makes you happy, Ana," Ted said, as I stood up.

"I know, I know." I shrugged. "Hey, are we going to watch a movie or what? I'm exhausted from talking." *Not really, I just want to see Will.*

Ted shot me a look, as we walked into Barney's tiny bedroom, that best friend, I-know-what-you're-thinking look. I smirked at him. But unfortunately, we didn't watch a movie like I wanted to. Instead, we all started watching dumb videos of some immature, animated character whose name I can't remember. Will came in too.

Barney and Saul were laughing their balls off, while I stretched out on the bed, as Ted gave me cosquillitas on my arm. That's part of the friendship contract when people sign on to become my friend. In small print, it says, and from now on, you will be Ana's Cosquillitas Slave. Whenever she stretches her arm out, you are obliged to tickle her until fatigue sets in your own arm.

I relished the relaxation of being among friends, not having a single worry about my dad, my brother, or my crazy stressed-out Mom. Or school. Or work. I just enjoyed our conversation about the Everglades, falling in love with the sound of Will's deep, confident voice, laughing at all the silly things he said and ogling over those biceps!

"Dude, we should totally go to the Everglades at night," Saul suggested. He wore glasses and had a blanket of acne over his face. I know you might be thinking nerd, but he was actually really cool.

"On Halloween," Barney chimed in. Barney was shirtless, because Barney liked to live his life without being confined by any clothing on his upper body. Not that I was complaining.

"What about human trafficking?" Hank, another of their friends added. When I first saw Hank, I had a weird first impression. I don't even know how to describe it—it was like he was a co-collaborator on a Tim Burton movie or something.

"I know." Will brought his gaze towards me. "We'll sell her to human trafficking. We'll get good money for what she's worth."

I gasped. The nerve of this guy (though I secretly liked him)!

"Wow, really?" I said, annoyed. I wanted to punch him in the face. With my lips.

"Yes," he laughed, amused with himself.

"What's your tattoo about?" I asked moments later. I pointed to his bicep. It bared a triangle with an intricate realistic eye in the middle.

"Do you want the short version or the long version?"

"Long," I paused, "always the long version," I smiled.

"Alright well, you've seen this before, right? The all-seeing eye?" he pointed to the symbol in the pyramid.

"Yeah," I said, "It's on the dollar bill."

"Cool. So, it represents a company I want to start where we decide on a set location where people from all over the community can come together and share ideas without any prejudice, and as a way of bettering ourselves as a whole society. It's just free talking space, that encompasses all kinds of people, and all kinds of ideas,"

"That sounds really cool," I said, "What's the short version?"

He shrugged. "I just tell people I want to be a musician and that will usually shut them up,"

"Yeah, and how about a human trafficker?" I poked.

"I also write poetry," he smiled.

"Oh, I'm sure you do."

"I do, it's part of being a lyricist."

"I'm sure that goes really nice with your illegal reputation and evil joking."

"Why would I joke about the truth? With a face like that, you would make me rich."

"You're a terrible person!"

"You like it."

And we went on like this, taking jabs at each other all night until Barney butted in and said that we already fought like an old married couple. We were both taken aback, because in that pivotal moment, Barney's premonition might not actually be that far off.

***

So, here's how Ana's planet works in the relationship Universe. It would be much easier to draw a diagram for you, but I'll try my best with words. I dated my first love, Ponyboy, right? We were young, innocent, all we did was care for each other… (yes, those are the lyrics to Lean On by Major Lazer). I fell in love with him at fourteen. He cheated on me, we got back together, and then he cheated on me again, then we broke up again. I wasn't that heartbroken though, because I thought, "Oh, we'll get back together for sure. He just has to change, and that's it." Easy as pie, right?

No, that is the stupidest thinking ever.

Instead, what happened was I started a vicious hook-up cycle in which I would completely romanticize us all throughout high school. So, boyfriend number two would end, then I'd go back to Ponyboy. Then boyfriend number three would end, and I'd go back to Ponyboy again. Then, boyfriend number four would end, and I'd go back to Ponyboy again, and guess what? Things never escalated or improved between us. In essence, they'd go NOWHERE. You'd think I'd have learned my lesson at this point but, wait, there's more.

Let me tell you the story…

"I feel bad saying this, Mom, but I think if Harry's best friend hadn't died, Harry and I would probably be together," I said, sprawled on my olive-green couch. She was sitting in the dining room in front of me doing the bills.

"Please." My mom looked up at me. "You just want to be with Harry to forget Ponyboy."

"That's not true, Mom, I actually really liked Harry!" I whined. I really thought he was potentially my soul mate, the love of my life, the father of my future children. Buuut…I also imagined that same scenario for every new guy I liked. The illusion would always wear off after a week.

"You're just trying to forget Ponyboy, and you're not going to by dating Harry," she pressed. What blasphemy. Ponyboy was forgotten to me! Sort of, kind of, okay, fine no, not really. I thought of him every day. "You need to let him go, you're both in college now. The healthy thing would be to move on from each other," she preached. This was new for my mom to be telling me this, considering she used to think he and I were soul mates. She even once said we had some unresolved shit in our past lives.

"You're right, Mom. I am going to let go of him completely."

And then, speak of the devil, my phone vibrated. I swear it was right after I said that. Like he knew. I stared at the ten numbers in shock. Reading them again, just to make sure it was really him.

"Mom…" I murmured. "He texted me right now."

She sighed. "Of course, he did! Ay, that boy knows when you want to cut him off!" My mom is a therapist, but she's also spiritual as heck. That there was her hippy side. An idea popped into my head at that moment.

"I'm going to call him," I muttered. Yes, that was my big plan. "And he isn't going to answer, and that will be that."

Ponyboy had this idea that talking on the phone was forbidden, texting was allowed. So, I went to my room, called him, and to my surprise, he actually picked up the phone. He was a little drunk too, I might add. Moments later, I was getting ready to see him. So much for forgetting him!

My excitement was uncontainable. I glanced at myself in the mirror, my eyes dilated, as if I were on cocaine (I've never done cocaine, for the record, but this was how my eyes would look like for sure…two giant black circles). I deliberately wore a conservative outfit, and only a light coat of mascara. I wasn't going to show any hint of sexual invitation this time. When he called me to tell me he was almost here, my heart started beating like a rabbit's about to get slaughtered. My mind raced with a thousand thoughts, the nervous energy making me so giddy that by the time he pulled up to the front of my house and jokingly pretended to speed off when I opened the door, I was laughing like a crazy hyena. The smile on his face was so huge, I must've passed for one cute hyena.

"Dick!" I clucked my tongue, narrowing my eyes at him. Ponyboy wasn't cute, or hot, or handsome by normal standards, or any other standards that describe aesthetic beauty. He was just Ponyboy. His looks could just be described as: Just Ponyboy. His smile probably knocked the socks off some girls, but to me it was just Ponyboy's smile, Ponyboy's hair, Ponyboy's ears.

When he finally parked and got out, he gave me a quick hug, laughed his deep, hearty chuckle, and asked me where I wanted to go. Then we spent the next hour driving around aimlessly trying to pick a place to go (clearly, a metaphor of our "relationship").

"Do you want to smoke? Or wait…actually I remember you don't smoke," he said. He brushed his hand against mine for a moment, and I felt like I got electrocuted with desire to touch more. We were parked in front of Barnes & Noble, where we always hung out when we were thirteen and fourteen.

"No, I don't." I giggled. I put my hand away, not wanting to betray my no-touching rule. Just to save you the annoyance of repetition, I giggled nonstop throughout my entire time with him. If there was a Nonstop Giggling Championship, I would've taken the gold crown for that. We took turns yelling out suggestions of where to go or what to do, and then we rejected them all right after. It became like a game.

"Okay, fine, I'll smoke with you!" I exclaimed, exasperated. I just wanted to do something. Living in Kendall was getting boring after a few years.

"What? Really?" he asked, surprised. There was Ponyboy's smile. Glittering straight teeth, thin lips.

"Yes." Smoking with Ponyboy...very unlike me, but very appealing right now. I remembered when he used to be so against weed, and now look at him.

"I don't want you to feel like I peer-pressured you," he replied.

"What? No. I just decided this."

"Are you sure?" His thick brown eyebrows creased with concern.

"Y-yes." I hesitated. Wait, now I wasn't so sure. I'd only smoked weed twice before, and I swore I'd never do it again.

"No!" He blurted out. "You're not going to smoke with me!"

"What?" I laughed, confused. "I thought I just said I would."

"I'm peer pressuring you into not smoking with me, and I am not taking yes for an answer!"

"Okay, okay!" I agreed. I glanced down at my body and saw I was completely angled towards him. I admit that my body wanted to have sex with him, but I, Anaregina Frias Diez de Sollano, did not.

We ended up driving to "my lake," which was a street away from my house. It was my happy place, perfect for calming crazy thoughts. My church, my little piece of heaven. We sat on a huge limestone rock facing the quiet water. There was a full moon which rendered every feature of the night to be unearthly and beautiful, it felt like crickets were singing songs to it. We reminisced about old memories from eighth grade, and he told me about his "complicated status" with his on-and-off girlfriend, Piper. I felt strange hearing him tell me about her, but it didn't bother me.

I told him about being on the brink of dating Harry, which temporarily disrupted the blissful, nostalgic energy between us. We joked about being caught by a cop for having sex outdoors and explaining to him that we were choosing to remain abstinent this time. After that, Ponyboy gently laid his arm around me, and I felt like I could drink the sweet, irresistibly warm nectar out of that moment forever. It's the blind curse of first love. I loved who I was when I was with him. A confident girl still blossoming into herself. I wanted to crawl underneath his soft skin, soak up all his warmth, and feel exactly how he made me feel before: loved and protected from anything. And by anything, I mean the insufferable pain headed my way because of my dad's debilitating disease and my imprisoned brother.

But Ponyboy was like an indecisive teen girl, when it came to his feelings.

"You know how you feel for me deep down," I said to him lightheartedly. He drilled his eyes into mine for a moment, and then tore his gaze away. I wasn't even sure what I meant by my own words. All I could think was yes, the connection is still there. My elbow happily rested on his sturdy knee, proving my point. The protruding rock poked at my butt, but whatever.

Ponyboy was quiet, but for the first time in five years, his lack of emotional conviction didn't annoy the hell out of me. I simply enjoyed our moment together, and I kept leaning over to his neck to inhale the scent of cologne like it was a narcotic drug and I was its personal junkie. He joked that if I kept leaning over to smell him, he was going to break our rule and kiss me.

Oh, no, how terrible, I thought sarcastically.

After a while, we got up and wandered around the lake where I got a teeny crack of emotion out of him. "I'm trying to remember a word I heard on some lawyer show the other day. It describes how I feel for you, but I can't remember it," he said.

"What does it mean?"

"It means…" He paused to think. "Not being able to express."

***

Hazel Grace. Hazel Grace was an adorable minion bursting with energy from the way she spoke to the way her crazy, curly mane dwarfed her sweet face. If I were a lesbian, and she was a lesbian, my story would have taken a completely different turn right about here. Unfortunately, for me, that is not the case. I met her my junior year at TERRA through a mutual friend but did not speak much to her since we had different friend circles.

However, in college, The Universe decided to cut my life some slack by introducing her back into my life in my algebra class (I don't know what it is about meeting significant people via the classes I detest the most). One day after hell class, she asked me what was wrong, and I, being the open book that I am, revealed to her my dad's cancer and how it was affecting me. She looked into my soul and confessed to me that her mom had passed away from lung cancer two years before, and that no matter what, I was going to be okay. Whatever happened, I would be okay.

In telling me about her mother's illness, Hazel said, "It got to a point where I was the one feeding her, taking care of her. It got to a point where I actually wanted her to die, because that's how bad she was suffering."

Well, that's not going to happen to my dad was my first thought. The weight of her words sank in my stomach like lead. She told me I could reach out to her whenever I wanted, that she rarely reached out herself but that I shouldn't hesitate. She also warned me to not be overly optimistic. All I could do was stomach the pain and accept the gravity of her genuine advice.

So, there I was at lunch with her some weeks later, reaching out to her about boys. We went to Subway, Land of the Sandwich Artists where I gave her an overview of my love life.

"What was his name? I'm sorry, I can't keep up with all of them!" She laughed. It was not the first time one of my friends told me this.

"My first love?" She was asking about the red rose on my wall.

"No, that's Ponyboy," Hazel said. I was surprised she could keep track. "The other one, Harry. What happened with him?"

"Oh, him. Well, after his best friend died, he just dropped me, which is fine. I understand. But it was totally okay because then I met Will!"

"So, let me get this straight. No Harry, yes Ponyboy, now Will, and who was the other one?"

"Blake, but we're not talking. He just gave me his number, because he thought I was cute, but yeah Ponyboy is out of the picture now. Apparently, his girlfriend, who was my Pre-K best friend, told my best friend, Monica, that I needed to 'back the fuck off,' and that I was crazy and what not, so they're back together, and I don't want to get involved in that…" I trailed off, taking a bite out of my meatball sub.

I'd already felt the anger of the entire situation when I ran almost three miles at the gym at an inhumane speed that day.

"No, you don't. That's not a good idea right now," Hazel said.

"So, after that, I went on a rebound date with Emmett, who's the guy I was hooking up with in the summer."

"The hot football player?"

"Yeah, that's him," I smiled, thinking back to Emmett's perfect tall form and dazzling smile. Sigh. "But he's too young, and I don't want anything serious with him. Blake is cute and all, but who I'm really interested in is Will."

"Who you met at FIU through your friend, Barney?"

"Yes, him, I find him sooo interesting."

In fact, let's stop the chit chat with Hazel right here, so you could truly understand how interesting I found this guy. It was a Thursday night, there was a full moon, and as always, I needed a ride to get from work to my house to my very first drum circle in Miami Beach. My coworker, Charlotte (who I feel is the lesbian version of myself), dropped me off and gave me a huge hug before I entered what was going to be the stripping of my emotions, because alas, I was alone with only my thoughts, and only my feelings, with the pillows in my living room to drown out my demon-sounding screams. I had had a great day at work, even though I didn't make quota (which I usually surpassed), because I was surrounded by so much love. So much spectacular, gay love. But that love wasn't enough to pacify what I was really feeling, because if my dogs could speak, they would tell you: She is literally going insane.

I had so much energy pent up inside me. In fact, here is exactly what I wrote that night:

I feel like there are blockades on every orifice of my body trying so hard to desperately keep it in. I feel like every smile I smile is a smile that takes form the shape of a knife that stabs me in the back because it betrays the very center of what I'm feeling which is raw, livid fear. Fear dressed as anger. Or anger dressed as fear, I'm too insane right now to even tell the goddamn difference. If you could swim inside my mind right now you would be swimming in deep waters, where the water goes from black to crystal blue, from a fucking whirlpool to a fucking calm bay. Being inside my shoes is like constantly being on a roller coaster, or the way you feel like when you get back from a cruise and the floor feels like it is constantly shifting beneath your feet. One moment I am hanging by a thread, the next I'm smiling from the genuine happiness I feel for that fleeting moment and then it is back to the anger, and the pain, and the frustration. I know that I am rambling, and rambling, but there is a current hurricane inside my brain, and this is the only way that I could tame every thought flying inside there. I know I am going crazy because I am so fucking calm right now yet one moment ago, I was screaming into my pillow as if someone was about to kill me. Yet not one tear escapes my eyes. It's like I'm in three different bodies, it's like I have three different minds, it's like I am always experiencing three different emotions at once, and I don't know how the hell I'm not literally crazy yet. It feels like I have bricks that have been embedded in my back and I have a stack of them on my shoulders. It feels like someone tied a tight knot from my neck to my chest and is constantly playing tug-of-war with me. It feels like I want to stab myself with something sharp just to feel a different kind of pain, but it also feels like I'm swimming through crystal clear waters. You see, I already know what it's like to be on the other side. I already know what it is like to go crazy, and I have no intention of ever going back again. Because I know that if I could get through it once, then I could get through it all fucking over again.

I wasn't kidding about the last part. I had gone crazy in the summer of 2011 when I bottled up a year's worth of emotions. I went from not eating, to not sleeping, to bam! Full blown manic episode, but that is another story in and of itself. In this story, as soon as I finished typing the last line, Will was waiting outside for me in his black Passat. I scarfed down a banana and reassured my dogs I was going to be okay. Jodie just wagged her tail at me, like saying, "I know you are. Go have fun now!" And then my rat terrier, Tuti, just stared at me with her giant, beady eyes, like saying, "Stop worrying about your dad so much. It's a good thing he's getting taken care of at the hospital."

These dogs, I swear. So smart.

I entered the car and immediately felt myself morph into a shy, quiet, giggly girl. Will's friends, Brian and Saul, were in the car along with two other girls I'd never met before, as well as sleep-deprived Barney. We exchanged hellos, and I smiled at Will who smiled back, with a cool "hey," and finally happiness had found its way back into my system. Until a minute later when I heard his music play. There was no room for me to sit, so I sat on Barney's lap in the back seat.

Oh, my God, please shut this off. Why are we listening to this? The dude is screaming! This is not music. This feels like my mind in sounds. This is giving me anxiety. I tried not to focus on it so much, tried having a normal conversation with Barney, who was on day two of no sleep. Maybe three.

"Did you just sneeze?" he asked. His jittery energy made me nervous.

"No," I paused, turning to face him, "I asked if you knew who sings this."

"It's them!"

"Them?" I asked, confused.

"This is our band," Will announced from the driver's seat. I could hear his smile through all the screaming.

So, this mass of nervous screeching was his band?

"What's it called?"

"Quantum Waves," he said.

I may not have dug his music so much, but I did dig boys in a band. As soon as we got out of the car and onto the sand of Miami Beach, my body naturally gravitated towards walking right next to him, and he appeared to have no problem with that. I felt uncharacteristically shy, awkward, and pent up. How was he supposed to get to know me like this?

"I just feel like going crazy tonight," I told him.

"Crazy?" His eyebrows flew up. "Like how? You're going to drink or something?"

"I…I don't know. My mom doesn't know I'm here. She thinks I'm at the FIU dorm watching a movie with you guys."

"You are such a goody two-shoes, aren't you?"

"I guess you could say that," I said. Honestly, I didn't know which side of me I was right now. I studied his face and the manner in which he walked. Such a manly, confident demeanor. Carrying himself with an "I have it all together" vibe. Where could I get some of that?

Eventually, we deviated from the group and the alluring fire breathers. As much as I loved watching people fearlessly juggle balls of fire, I wanted to be away from the crowd and feel the shore kiss my body, as sounds of waves calmed me. I wanted Will next to me. Instantly, I regretted eating that banana as soon as he sat next to me and wished I could magically make my breath minty fresh.

"So, what's your thing, other than fighting for the gays, or whatever?" He sat in the sand and stretched his legs out.

"I write." I scooped up some sand and dumped it on my legs. "I'm actually writing a book right now." I smiled and sexily rubbed my legs together. My body always knew exactly how to flirt.

"Really? No way, that's awesome. What's it about?"

I continued to play with the sand a little before answering. "It's a first love story."

"Elaborate," he urged. The distant ambiance of the people dancing and banging instruments reached my toes, making them wiggle.

"It's about a girl who's been trying to get over this guy for years, the story of how they met and all that," I said. There, that should satisfy him. Hopefully.

"Tell me more." So much for that.

"Tell me about your music," I said, flipping the script around. It wasn't that I didn't want to talk about me tonight, but…I didn't want to talk about me. "Which sounds sort of crazy if I do say so myself."

"I know why you say that. But the song is actually written very much like a book. It's divided into four sections where initially in Aspire the guy, who's an astronaut, wants to shoot for the stars, because he feels like that's where his dreams are, then in Power he starts to become corrupt with societies' influence on him, leading him to collapse where he loses all his power and his mind. There he hallucinates a man of light guiding him through and out of his psychosis."

"So, what I heard in the car was the man of light trying to help him out?"

"Yes, he was trying to tell him that it's all in his head even though he was just in his head too."

"Is he crazy?"

"He's extremely depressed and feels like there's nobody who shares his point of view."

"Does he end up achieving his dreams?"

"Yes, that's in Enlightenment when he realizes that it was his entire fault for his madness and he already has everything he's looking for, but tell me about your story." I guess neither one of us wanted to dwell on our own lives.

I shrugged, and while my body wanted to kiss him, I was going to wait more time. Get to know him a little more. A salty breeze doused my nose. "I don't know if you've seen the movie Blue Valentine, but it's structured like that, so it begins with the older character, Rachel, finally getting over her first love and goes back and forth to when she meets him in sixth grade until twelfth grade."

He looked at me in an almost invasive way, without actually invading anything. His gaze pierced right into my soul. "She's obviously you," he said, brown eyes smiling.

"Well, that astronaut guy is obviously you as well," I said, adding a knowing smile because I knew I was right, "Damn, and I thought I was crazy."

"I am definitely crazier than you."

We continued to talk about our art, sharing stories, while occasionally throwing sand at each other like we were five years old. I like him, I like him, I like him! Then, he started talking about how he felt like he had an angry alter ego, one which he called "The Reptile." He said it wasn't until recently that he let the negative energy all go.

Oh, baby. From artist to artist, I was so hooked. Until....

"The thing is, I've had depression since I was eight years old." He cradled his knees in his arms. "And I've been battling it ever since." The crowd dispersed away concluding the night of my first drum circle.

I listened intently, but something strange happened. As he rambled on about the things his depression made him do, his macho, confident, put-together, I've-got-it-all-figured-out demeanor faded away like a veil being stripped off and magically removed. Suddenly, I saw a scared little boy staring back at me.

***

"There's only one, little problem with Will," I told Hazel the next day.

"What?"

"He's interesting and all, but he's a bit depressed."

She hesitated before answering, but Hazel was the type of person who would tell you exactly how it was even if you didn't want to hear it. "Ana, I have a cousin who went out with a girl who was depressed, and it was okay at first, but after a couple of months, it got really, really draining. I don't recommend you go out with him. You're already going to be on a rollercoaster of emotions, trust me. Last thing you need is to have to take care of someone else."

She must have sensed my apprehension, because then she said, "But you will get through it, you will do well in school, you're smart, you have your family, and friends—hello, me!—and to top it off, you're pretty."

I smiled. Her reassurance and the confidence it gave me had never felt so good as in that moment. Hazel was mature, wise, experienced at life, and she'd just become my number one role model. And Will…

Well, I always wanted to date a Will.

CHAPTER 7
Delicious Dead Bird

Will Grayson instantly became my therapist—my therapist who I had sex with very frequently. I wasn't allowed to have a boyfriend in my room with the door closed, nor did I have a car I could use as a traveling sex motel. We had something better though. His black Passat, the vessel on wheels of all our fears, all our secrets, and occasionally our bodily fluids (I'm strictly referring to my tears here). It was two days before Thanksgiving, and the underlying current of unease I'd been feeling for a while could no longer contain itself.

"What's wrong?" Will asked. I didn't have to show any signal of distress for him to know there was something not okay with me. Nine Inch Nails was probably playing in the background.

"It's Thanksgiving on Thursday," I said. Tears began forming in my eyes, though I didn't know why.

"Okay, what about it?"

I was quiet, as I always was when something wasn't right with me. My mind drifted back to many Thanksgivings ago, when I was little, and we were a typical, happy family. Me, my dad, my mom, and Adam.

"Perdy is eating the turkey, Papi. Perdy is eating the turkey!" I squealed. She was my childhood pet.

"What? Okay, I'll be right there, give me a moment," Dad called from the shower.

I couldn't help but laugh, as I stared at our Dalmatian standing on her hind legs as she passionately licked the prepared turkey we were supposed to be saving for later tonight.

"Perdy, get off!" I said. She didn't listen. I guess she thought she deserved some turkey too. My dad arrived in the kitchen moments later, towel around his waist, and had to forcefully peel Perdy off our main dish, while the dog fought with all her might. Dad scolded her, and she walked away on all fours looking sheepish with her tail between her legs. He and I stared at each other for a suspended moment until we both cracked up at the same time.

"We can't eat it now!" Picky-little-me insisted. "It's got dog cooties all over it!"

"Of course, we can," Dad said, grabbing a carving knife and removing the contaminated areas, feeding them to our guilty dog. He made some joke about rewarding bad behavior, and my Mom, brother, and I joined in laughter when we realized how stupid we all were for leaving it out on display right on the edge of the kitchen counter.

Will may have been excellent at picking up emotional cues, but the boy was not a mind reader, so I said, "I'm angry with my dad." That came out of nowhere. I didn't even know that I felt that way.

"Why?"

"Oh, God, that sounds so terrible right now, but it's true. I can't believe I feel that way."

"Ana, it's okay to feel that way. Don't judge how you feel. Why are you angry at him?"

"Because Will, he was with us my whole life, and then two years ago, he left, and it was horrible getting used to it, especially with how hard my mom was taking it, she was so stressed and detached, yet juggling everything on her own." I slowed down to take a breath. "But he was my dad, and I adored him, so I tried not to feel bad about it. It wasn't until last year that things were finally calming down, and we were all getting used to it, and I accepted things for what they were. You know like, I go spend some time with him and Adam, and then Adam and I spend some time with my mom." The tears fell at such a fierce rate, there was no time to save them.

Will grabbed my hand, but I turned away from him.

"And now…and now he's just back?" I said into the car window. "Just like that, he's back in our lives as if nothing happened? It was hell to go through that, and I do not want to go through that again. Like what the hell are we? All of a sudden a family again just for the holidays? I'm so confused. I don't want to feel this way. I hate that I feel this way towards him."

"Ana, look, I really don't want to sound like an asshole for saying this, but you know I'm going to be blunt with you, and I know you can take it. Okay?"

"Okay." I still couldn't turn around to look at him. Talking about this and admitting it to myself was hard enough without facing someone else.

"Your dad has cancer, and while yes, he's getting treated and hopefully, and most likely will get better, there isn't...you know." He hesitated. "A guarantee. So, if I were in your shoes, I would talk to him, tell him how you feel. That way you can have a genuine relationship with him from here on out. Really, I think your mom and him and you should talk and get out a loooot of shit you guys have been holding back for some while. It would be good for the three of you."

I agreed and was glad for the advice, even though it would be easier said than done. Then we hugged and kissed, and the wave of sexual tension that followed emotional turmoil rolled over me and thrashed me around, but it was easy and swift to take care of.

***

Getting my family to sit down and have a heart-to-heart talk wasn't exactly easy, but my God, it was completely worth it. Leading up to this meeting, weird stuff had been happening to me that made me keep a distance from my dad. For example, we would be in the same room and I'd go from perfectly normal Ana/daughter to all of a sudden having graphic images and thoughts of incest with him. Pretty much like this:

Ana's Thoughts:

Friends theme song stuck in head Hmmm…I'm going to watch Friends! And make myself a tuna sandwich, oh yes, yes.

Dad enters room

I look at him

Unwanted Incest Thought: I want to fuck you

….What!? No I don't….

Unwanted Incest Image: *graphic image begins to percolate in brain*

Oh, God, no, please! Stop. Why the hell am I imagining this!!?!?!?

Unwanted Incest Thoughts Continue Full Force: I want to fuck you

Ana forces herself to leave the room and face a very weird, creepy question

Ana's Consciousness: Well…I mean…do you want to?

(Every millimeter of my soul cringes in anticipation)

Ana's Reply: No. Of course not, I don't want to have sex with my father.

(Soul sighs in relief)

Normal Ana: Oh, okay, thank God. *goes off to watch the next season of Friends*

These are called intrusive thoughts and have nothing to do with who you are or your true intentions. They're actually the hallmark of covert OCD. I don't know if your brain is anything like mine, but if I repress something, anything, it blows up the size of Jupiter on steroids. I have a feeling my dad is the same way, because once the three of us sat down to talk, the amount of guilt and shame my dad had stored inside of him poured out like an oozing wound. Like the tumor had not only metastasized the tissue in his bladder, but also the tissues of his soul. Sitting there, I told him that even though I thought I was okay with him coming back, I still harbored resentment towards him, that I was afraid of him leaving again and leaving my mom in pieces.

He sat there, stunned, listening to me speak, every part of him that used to be "tree mode" left, and he cried for about ten minutes straight telling my mom and me how sorry he was, how guilty he felt, that we didn't deserve any of that pain, that he loved us both so, so, so much. I had never seen my dad cry so much and so hard in my entire life. I kept telling him that I forgave him, that it was okay, that I loved him, until words couldn't mean as much as action could. The three of us embraced tightly, I felt the love emanating from my mom and my dad engulf every cell in my body. I was so goddamn grateful for that moment, that writing this now, I realize this was the definition of Thanksgiving, not sitting next to each other passing around a piece of delicious dead bird on a specific day of every year.

CHAPTER 8
Room 4321

Your biggest fears do happen. Not all of them, but some of them.

They will arrive at your doorstep, and you'll think you might know how to face them, but you don't (not yet at least). And you can't ignore them, because they will pound the door like a freaking SWAT team. I was nine when the beloved Universe slammed a door in my face. It was a random day as an average third grader when I was selected to witness the precipice of pure tragedy. It took the shape of jalapeños. One moment, I was in my living room, cuddling with my Build-A-Bear, John, fixing his Air Force outfit as the television hummed the tune of the SpongeBob SquarePants theme song, and in the next moment, my father was bent over, clutching his stomach and gasping for air, wheezing the way someone does when they beg for a breath of air, of life. I didn't understand what was happening, but I hugged John closer to me.

"He's choking on the jalapeños," my mom cried. "Call 9-1-1, Adam!"

My brother immediately grabbed the house phone and began to dial. The tone of my mother's voice indicated panic in its purest form, and I was paralyzed watching the scene unfold itself.

"H-h-hang up," my dad said. He regained his composure and stood to his feet. He was drenched in sweat, as his breathing returned to normal. I let go of John and hugged my dad as he explained to me he'd had one too many of spicy peppers. An acute sense of relief flooded the room, as normalcy returned, but the fear never left me. Every single day at around 3 o'clock I would pick up the phone and dial his number while he was at work, and he never failed to answer.

"Hola, Papi," I would say.

"Hola, mi vida."

"Are you okay? Are you alive?" I obviously knew the answer, but still, you know.

"Yes, of course." He'd laugh then tell me he loved me, that he would see me when he got back from work. At the time, he was a television producer at Teleplanet and would return late at night, usually with a surprise like a toy or candy. I was the happiest little girl whenever he got home, screaming "PAPIIIIIIIII!" as soon as I heard the door open. I didn't mind staying up late, waiting. Love is patient.

Ten years later, I was walking with my mom on the way to his hospital room, and I could feel the same panicky energy coursing through her. "What room is it again?" she asked. Dusk settled in, and a cool breeze swept my bare legs.

"I…I don't remember." I sighed. Really, Ana? You were here, like, yesterday.

"Well, then call the hospital," she snapped. "First you lose your keys, and now you can't even remember your dad's room number? Why can't you pull yourself together, Anaregina? You can't live with your head in the clouds all the time."

I wanted to cry, but I sucked it up and ignored her bitching. I called the hospital and asked a sweet nurse the room number for Rogelio Frias. "Forty-three-twenty-one," she responded. I thanked her then hung up. Four. Three. Two. One. It couldn't be easier to remember. As soon as I walked through the doors, I realized I was becoming very familiar with the hospital's surroundings (except the room number, of course). Pass entrance. Go up elevator. Walk through hallway. Observe nature paintings leading me to his room. It had become a monotonous routine.

But routines are comforting to me, because I know what to expect. Emotions though, that's a whole other animal that was quickly catching up to me. Throughout the entire walk, my mom scolded me and bitched, and I tuned her out, because that was all I could do to keep from exploding and causing a public scene, or worse, a trip to the psychiatric ward. Finally, we arrived at Room 4321, and the look on my dad's face said detachment. I could practically read the words "I surrender" etched on every crevice of his emaciated face.

"Hola," he croaked. We both said hello and gave him a light hug, careful not to apply too much pressure to his debilitating body. Apparently, he'd been harboring a kidney infection in addition to the tumor (which wasn't getting any smaller, by the way). He asked us how we were doing, and my pissy mom transformed into happy pixie fairy Mom. "We're good, everything is well." She smiled.

WHAT? I wanted to say. Instead, I cradled my phone in my hands.

"And you? How are you, Anaregina?" he asked.

"I'm okay," I lied. I guess I wasn't too different from my mom. He accepted my lie and continued to make small talk with my mom who took a seat in a chair in front of him which held my dad's overnight bag. I chose to sit on the floor instead.

"Why are you sitting on the floor?" Dad asked. "It's dirty. Sit on the chair."

"I'm good." I stuck to my spot and glanced to catch the expression on his face. I could tell he wasn't pleased with my answer. My mom sighed.

"Okay, how are your friends?" He seemed to tire with every question, but he really wanted to know, and I thought about how much it must suck to be stuck in the hospital every day.

"My friends are okay. Well, except for She-Who-Must-Not-Be-Named. She is having relationship-issues-which-must-not-be-named," I explained.

"Poor She-Who-Must-Not-Be-Named," my mom added, "she's only nineteen. That can't be an easy decision to make."

The emotional animal stored up inside me rattled its cage in anger. I'm nineteen. And yet, you expect a full-grown fucking woman out of me? I crouched lower, so the bed frame could hide my face from my dad, and the chair could block my view from Mom. Tears couldn't contain themselves any longer. But I didn't make a noise. Instead, I stared at my phone and past text conversations I had with other people, feeling like an asshole for not paying attention to my dad.

Wonderful, now guilt was on my plate too. I am going crazy. I am going to implode. I can't take this. Every sense of rationality and patience escaped me, and then I remembered my fallout with Phoebe. I shed more tears, because I couldn't text her since we were no longer friends, but in my imagination, a different scenario took place. I vented to her about the comment my mom had just made, and how angry, guilty, and scared I felt. I imagined Phoebe replying to me, "It's okay you feel this way. You are not going crazy. Just let them know how you feel." I imagined myself thanking her, and before I knew it, I grew the strength and courage to unleash the vortex of emotion inside of me.

I stood and let myself speak the truth. "We are not okay," I said, finally looking my dad in the eye.

"Anaregin—" my mom interrupted.

"No, Mom! It's the truth. Why are we going to lie to him? We are not okay. At least I know that I am not okay." I crossed my arms and continued to stare at my dad. "Why are you letting this happen?" I demanded.

"Letting what happen?" he asked, raising his eyebrows.

"You are closing up on us. You are distancing yourself. I look at you, and it's like you're not even there, like how you used to be. Why are you doing that again?"

"I…I don't know," he stammered, scratching his head.

"Do you…do you want to live, Dad?"

"Yes," he said, his answer quick and almost inaudible.

"I don't believe you!" I snapped. "The way you're acting, the way you're talking…it…it feels like you are dying," I said. I couldn't believe the words that came out of my mouth. My mom's expression oozed discomfort.

Suddenly, his eyes lit up, like I'd just set a fire in him. "What is there to live for?"

"What?" I couldn't believe what I was hearing. "Dad, how could you possibly say that?"

"I don't have a family anymore, my son is in jail, there's nothing I can do about it, and I'm stuck here being a burden on you guys."

"You don't have a family? Really?" I blurted. "We are your family, Papá. You have us, we love—I love you so much. You are not a burden to me, and while, yes, it isn't easy to be going through this, I don't care. I know you would do the same thing for me. That's what family does. It doesn't matter what happened in the past, what matters is right now. Stop feeling so guilty about Adam—it's his life, he put himself there, that was because of his decision, his mistake. The lawyers are doing everything they can to get him out as soon as possible, and they will. Soon enough, they will. You were the one who taught me that guilt is a waste of an emotion!"

"Yes," he agreed.

"Do you love me?" My voice became so small and vulnerable, but I felt so strong.

"Of course I love you, and Mama, and Adam."

"Exactly, then there is still a lot to live for!" I exclaimed. "You have to push through this. You are going to overcome this, Papá. There's nothing stronger than love, and I know love can overcome it." Silently, he began to sob. I asked him, "What do you want?"

"What do you mean?"

"Forget me, Mama, Adam. What do you want with your life?"

He paused to think about his answer. He seemed to be wracking his brain for the answer to a quantum physics equation. I could feel a sea of despair quieting inside of me.

"Isn't there a fantasy, a dream that you had when you were little?" I asked, desperately, half-expecting him to tell me that he wanted to meet my grandchildren.

"Honestly, I just want to swim. I want to be swimming in the ocean." He smiled, lost in his fantasy, as his eyes teemed with hope. It wasn't the answer I was expecting, but it made sense. And honestly, I felt the same.

CHAPTER 9
Help Is Here

- The First Day I Visited Help Is Here, December 15th, 2014

It was another hot, summer day in Miami, and yes, it's still summer in December. Those black Miami grackle birds were squawking and shitting everywhere. My greasy face leaned against the window of the red Prius. It was easy to access this memory. It still laid awake in my brain. In fact, I can still feel the frustration burning in my cheeks, as I sat in a little waiting room after finally getting out of the car, a room with beige walls and faux plants.

I felt shock. I felt disbelief. I was finally seeing Adam. I would finally be able to hug my brother. The four of us would be together again, and there would not be a murky glass wall between us after all those months. All those months of obscurity revolving around Adam's sentence, where we all (including himself) believed he was innocent, but careless in our eyes and guilty in the eyes of the court. Justice is in the eye of the beholder. Nearby, the social worker lady in her professional pantsuit spoke to my parents, who resembled a perfect concoction of fear and relief.

"There's one thing," the lady with the permanent grin said. She glanced at me. "That's his sister?"

"Yes, his sister," my mom responded with a smile plastered on her face.

The social worker lady wore a countenance of polite, fake embarrassment then continued to speak about my situation as if I wasn't standing right next to her. Just like in the TV shows.

"Well…" She fucking smiled. "You see, because of problems in the past, where people have pretended to be other people's siblings and brought drugs into our place, we only allow siblings of age twelve or younger to visit." And she looked at me with that fucking "sympathetic" smile.

"Are you really his sister?" she asked with a slight hint of—I would call it sarcasm, but that wouldn't even do it justice.

ARE YOU FUCKING KIDDING ME RIGHT NOW!?

I wanted to yell in her face. I wanted my words to stretch her smile all around her head. I felt like I'd just had holes drilled through my brain and heart.

"So, I can't visit my brother on Sundays?" I said with perfect composure.

You mean to tell me that while both of my parents can come to this place every Sunday, I have to be at home? When I've also been waiting seven long months for this fucking opportunity?

"No, I'm sorry." She raised her hands up like it was all out of her control.

It took every ounce of my being not to jump up and strangle her. I wanted to crush something. I wanted to scream. I wanted to do something—anything—so drastic that they would force a change to the rules of this place. She continued to speak to my parents, her in her little petite frame, completely oblivious to the stir of emotions rising inside of me. I looked at them like they were just bodies, communicating, reacting, existing. And I was a ball of emotion, a volcano ready to erupt at any given opportunity. My parents were so concerned about seeing Adam they didn't even seem to have a reaction to my shitty situation.

But then…Adam walked into the room. I was completely taken aback by the length of his hair. It was so short that when he turned around, it didn't feel like I was seeing my brother but a completely different person. Still, it was him. He was so elated to see us, the entire energy in the room drastically shifted, like I'd swallowed a scorpion, its poison temporarily numbing me.

I couldn't believe it. There was Adam. In the flesh. Jail-free. There was a light in his eyes I hadn't seen in a while. He hugged my parents. They were so full of indescribable joy I cannot possibly put it into words, and apparently neither could they, as all they could do was talk about his hair. I handed him the Subway sandwich we'd brought him, and finally…he embraced me.

I felt so grateful, my arms full of my brother's love, but I also felt fucking uncomfortable knowing the social worker lady was watching. I felt her smile on me like a scorpion about to sting me in the throat. She probably thought I was his fucking girlfriend trying to sneak in drugs to him.

Well, I'm not! I mentally shouted at her. Adam let me go, and walked with us, as the lady took us on a tour of the facility. Carefully, I observed every detail, every corner of every room, as I imagined being in Adam's shoes, having this environment as my temporary home.

Well, it was a lot nicer than jail. That was my first thought. There was a large room with a small stage and rows of seats in front of it. Behind that room, crossing a hallway, there was a nice kitchen, sparkling with cleanliness.

"This is where the culinary guys cook," my brother said.

"It's nice." My mom nodded, and the SWL lady nodded and agreed that it was, in fact, nice.

Yep, a lot homier than jail… I thought. We were led to the basketball courts where I immediately felt the eyes of the other rehab guys on me like magnets. They all wore white shirts and basketball shorts. It made me feel confident and very self-conscious at the same time. We walked by the bunk beds which were empty and neat and had a smell I could only describe as the smell of a clean boy. Everyone was speaking, and I was just imagining Adam tucked in here at night, wondering where his thoughts took him.

The lady took us to the garden which was where Adam worked. It made me feel more connected to him because when I went to TERRA, I was in the Environmental Academy, so this place took me back to sweet memories of sunshine and soil and carefreeness. The way he spoke about the plants and tended to them reminded me of the same energy those memories brought me. He knew all their scientific names. He felt proud that they were finally bearing fruit. It was strawberries, I think.

"So…how've you been?" he asked me.

"It's been rough," I said with a sigh. "But I'm happy to be here right now and actually see you live."

"Yeah, I know what you mean." He chuckled and patted me on the shoulder.

I felt the SWL lady's eyes penetrate me again. I might have actually rolled my eyes 2,453 times at her. I waited until I could see her engaged in conversation with both my parents again before talking again. "So, I can't visit you on Sundays because of their rule about how siblings older than twelve aren't allowed to visit," I said in a low mocking voice.

"I know, it sucks, but don't worry. I'll be out of here in no time. And I'll be able to help out."

God, I hoped so. I missed having my brother around and seeing him go through all this was really bruising my heart. I hugged him again, kind of awkwardly, as we walked towards the music room.

"They told you about the point system here, right?" he asked.

"Yeah, I was hearing something about that."

"Well, I could speed up the time by trying to get as many points as I can to get out of here."

There was something so odd, yet so refreshing to have him here in front of me. I could visibly see all of the change and resilience he'd experienced in the last couple of months. His skin had lost its yellowish sun-deprived tone and invited a golden tan to highlight his new muscles gained from working out at the gym here. Yet all I could think about was SWL lady thinking I was his drug-smuggling girlfriend for sure. I felt like Jane from Breaking Bad, but shorter, and the complete opposite, actually.

We arrived in the music room, and I was instantly amazed. There was so much to look at, my eyes went into a frenzy. On the wall next to me was a collage of photos of different artists who apparently had been to this place, or some other similar rehab place. The one with Britney Spears stuck out to me. In front of me there was a small stage with fancy equipment and enough musical instruments littered around the room to get a boy band hard.

"Do you get to play guitar now?" I asked Adam.

"Yes." He smiled. We both knew how much this meant to him. SWL Lady was sneaking glances at us, I could feel it, and I caught her doing it. I imagined myself shoving my ID to her chest, as her smiling sheep face begot regret for even asking me if I was Adam's sister in the first place. I decided to take the optimistic approach. Yes, it was true…within just a little bit more time Adam would be back for good. I would just have to wait a little while longer. I could do it, I could stretch it out. Then, the scorpion lingering around my throat bit me harder than the first time.

When nobody was looking, Adam leaned to my ear and whispered, "Do you think you could get me a pack of cigarettes? The Menthol kind?"

Oh, fuck me.

CHAPTER 10
Meeting the Other Man

Time was going so slowly and so fast simultaneously. When it came to my brother, Adam (still being a jailbird after almost seven months), it felt slow. And when it came to my dad, it felt fast as hell. But whenever I hung out with Will, time managed to freeze in the moment as if we were both made of amber, crystallizing memories that made our connection stronger. In fact, there was this one night on December 13th when we became our own versions of Bonnie and Clyde.

"Let's go to my park," I said, as Will sped off into the night with me in the passenger seat. We tried escaping the insanity that was co-existing with his five-year-old little sister and his hyperactive ball of crazy three-year-old siblingness. I loved them, don't get me wrong, but every time I hung out with them at Will's house, I was reminded why I should always use a condom no matter what.

"Okay," he said, driving. I always found it sexy, like he became one with the car, as he swiftly navigated us the way a cheetah would in heavy traffic. He never doubted himself.

"Shit, my mom is calling," I said, staring at my phone like it was going to pick up the call for me.

"Answer her," Will instructed.

Tell her you're going to eat at Denny's, Ana. You want to avoid the Hispanic mom panic right?

Concerned Mother: "¿Hola, Anaregina, dónde estás?"

Me: "Hi, Mom, I'm with Will. We're leaving his house."

Mom: "Are you coming back home? It's already past midnight."

I was about to lie to her, when for once, the truth decided to speak up instead. After all, I was nineteen. There was no need to make excuses anymore.

Me: "No, we're going to go the park."

Mom: "Anaregina, are you serious? At this hour?"

Me: "Yes. Yes, I am."

By this time, we were already close to my house, so I whispered to Will to just take me home, as I rolled my eyes, but still, it felt good to tell her that.

Mom: "You have to be home by one o'clock, Anaregina! I don't understand why you don't just come here. Do you not want to come home or what?"

Wow, motherly guilt was in full-force tonight.

No, it's not that (except looking back, yes that's exactly what it was). I just really want to make out with Will, and for some reason this is making me want to make out with him even more. But of course, I just stayed quiet and let her repeat the same sentences in nineteen different versions before I finally told her that it still wasn't one o'clock yet, and I had time before having to go home.

Mom: "I don't understand why you are being so difficult. You know you should be coming home by now. And do you know that, at this time, the police go around checking parks to see if there are teenagers doing things they shouldn't be doing? Not that I am saying you are going to be doing that, but that is exactly what they are expecting."

Me: *quietly listening* My intuition was speaking to me—Ana, go back into the house right now. Your mom is completely right about the police and the park at this time.

Unbeknownst to her, we were parked right in front of my house. I could have kissed Will goodbye and been a good, docile daughter, calmed her worries with my presence. But a teenage rebel inside of me had awoken from a deep slumber, and she was not at all happy. She was pissed, and she was horny.

I weighed out my options:

Talk and make out with Will here, parked in front of my house, risking Jodie escaping the yard to see me as she always did (which would alert my parents to the fact that I was home). Or…go to the park, talk, and make out with him there, but totally risk the police thing.

I opted with telling my mom that I would be home at one. I was going to the park, but she shouldn't worry about any police encounter. But I swear to the Universe, at that moment, it was like fate was listening and saying, "Nuh, uh, uh…you will have a police encounter," while shaking a pudgy finger in my face.

Will left my driveway and drove the five minutes it took to get to my childhood paradise. He parked beneath a lamp post where a red truck was parked across from us with foggy, tinted windows. I felt exposed and remembered last summer when I hooked up with Ponyboy a couple of parking spaces in front of us. I shook off the memory, poisonous dust clouding my head. Sometimes I really hated myself for reminiscing about him while being with another guy.

Will had cut the engine and was turned to me in his seat. "You're so gorgeous, you know that?" He reeled me back to the present. I smiled and leaned into him for a kiss, but before long, we both made our ways to the back seat. As he sat on the left side of the seat, and I curled up into a ball on the right, I grew more and more curious about what Will Grayson's core was made of, even though my vagina was like, "Yo, it's been four months since I've had contact with a penis. I'm getting pretty curious too!" I ignored her. For now.

"Why did you keep telling me you thought you were crazier than me the night of the drum circle?" I looked directly into his dark eyes.

He looked right through me, then glanced away. I could sense his discomfort, so I touched his hand, reassuring him I wasn't going to judge him. I mean really, who was I to judge?

"You know, I've only told one other person this, which is Brian, who I've known since middle school..."

"You don't have to tell me now if you don't want to," I reminded him.

"No, I think it's time I tell you. I actually want to tell you. It's just not easy to talk about." He chuckled nervously.

"I understand," I said.

Then, I watched as layers of him peeled away like an old onion. He told me about his senior year, how it was unlike anything he'd ever heard of. I don't feel right revealing the details of what he told me that night, but I will say the gist of it. He contemplated the workings of reality and sort of lost himself in the process. As he continued to pour his inner demons out, I understood why he felt so afraid, so alone. Even putting myself in his shoes for five seconds made my stomach churn. I had no idea that questioning reality to such an intense point could make a person lose their minds, but at the same time, I was fascinated by how it all began with one thought in mind, and ended with one thought in mind.

"...and it wasn't until I accepted that this…" He gestured to the world around us, "is all a beautiful lie, that I came to terms with it" A weight seemed to lift off his shoulders and dissipate into the surrounding air.

"You know, Will, I have a feeling you're not the only one to ever feel this way," I said.

"Well. I'm the only one I've ever known," he replied.

Then, like the artists we were, we proceeded to show each other poetry that we'd written. I'd always thought my poems were shitty, but Will seemed to genuinely like them.

"What time is it?" he asked after reading my last poem.

"It's almost three in the morning," I laughed.

"I don't want you to get in trouble."

"I won't. I won't. Don't worry. She hasn't called."

Meanwhile, fate was laughing at us, as we peeled off our shirts and start making out so passionately I could no longer ignore Susy (the nickname I gave to my vagina as a joke years ago, and then it just stuck).

"Do you wanna…?" he asked, between heavy breathing.

I answered him with a moan, as his hands roamed my curves, and the fresh, sweet scent of his lips traveled to every nerve ending of my body. I nodded, and he unzipped his zipper, the sound putting me on the edge of the seat. And then I remembered we said we wouldn't do it in a car.

"But this isn't how we said..." I took a gulp of air between moans. "…we wanted it." Another shallow breath.

"I know, but I just want to so bad."

"I want to too," I said, as I cupped his face and kissed his lips with full force.

So, what if the first time we do it is in his car?

"Whatever you want," he whispered.

Like that's going to make it any easier.

After about four minutes of indecisive moans and kissing and teasing, Will pulled away, reaching over to where the shift stick was. I was confused until I heard quarters clinking together.

"Heads or tails?" he asked. "Heads we have sex now, tails we don't."

I giggled, fist at my lips. Of course, he would make this decision with a coin flip!

"Heads," I called. The anticipation was killing me, and then he flipped the coin. The moment it landed in his hand, my mother's prophecy came true.

"Ana, put your clothes back on." Will shuffled around the back seat, his energy turning nervous.

"What?" You have to be shitting me…

"There's a cop driving towards us." He retreated to the back seat, already getting his shirt on and zipper up. Meanwhile, I began cursing the decision to wear a jean crop top that had like ten buttons to button.

"Fuck, I knew it!" I said. My heart started to race faster than Usain Bolt from the Olympics.

I was still on the second button when a light flashed through our window, accompanied by a knock and a strong voice. "Open up!"

Will swung open the door on the other side, and I heard him shakily greet the officer who dubiously asked us what we were up to tonight. The moment I heard the officer's youthful voice, I sighed in relief and thanked the gods of chance, fate, and backseat sex. We're going to be okay, I thought, crouched down on the seat like the Hunchback of Notre Dame in a pale pink bra.

***

"Do you have a minute to talk about some gay stuff?" Leslie, my confident, adorable, quirky coworker would tell unsuspecting passersby while she was canvassing, in a voice so raspy, sultry, sexy, and deep, that yes! I totally had a crush on her! This was a surprise for me. Although all of us at GRC agreed that any human being, no matter what orientation they were, usually got a crush on Leslie when he or she met her. I never thought I would actually have a crush on a girl, but I also never thought that my dad would be gay, or that one day, I would meet The Other Man, or his "friend," as we called him.

When I was in elementary school, I remember watching TV and eating Fairly Odd Parents-shaped Cheez-Its, bored out of my mind, when suddenly, an interesting documentary came on. It was about a man who got married to a woman and had kids with her, and then came out of the closet TWENTY YEARS LATER! I knew what being gay meant by then, and naturally I thought of my parents and our family. That's so crazy! I thought back then. Thank God that's not the case with us, my naive, innocent mind conceptualized.

My dad had always done a fairly decent job of masking that part of his life from my brother and me. The only clue I ever picked up on didn't even register as 'gay.' I was in my early teens when I started to scroll through my dad's phone out of innocent curiosity when I encountered a photo message of another's man genitalia and immediately released his phone from my grasp. It was like accidently discovering a top-secret code I was not supposed to know about. Naturally, I felt confused and instinctively told my mom about it. She got angry and told me that was just a game that some men play when they're older. I thought it was weird, but accepted it, and dismissed it. I realized now that my mom was grappling for excuses to make for my dad.

I was sixteen and in one of my weekly therapy sessions when my chubby, gray-haired looks-like-Santa-Claus therapist explained to me that my dad was gay (my dad had him as a therapist before I started to see him and had okayed this). My reaction was exactly: "YOU'RE FUCKING WITH ME, TYRONNE!" Then, the memory of the penis picture message made complete and total sense.

Three years later, there we were in yet another hospital room in the cancer unit part of the building where the rooms are larger and have a light that shone over the bed as if we were part of a studio set, and the cancer patient was the main character. I was sitting in a cozy chair next to my dad with my phone in my hand, trying to think of something funny to say as my mom was talking to him, when suddenly, the door opened.

"Oh, hello," the tanned, bald man with a perky butt said.

"Hello," I said sweetly. He introduced himself as Rafael and firmly shook my mom's hand, trying to mask his surprise of seeing us. She smiled warmly at him and introduced herself as Xiomara. She also had no idea who he was.

I was flabbergasted.

Here I was, observing both of them, half-expecting the scene to escalate into a standoff between Russia and the US during the height of the Cold War, expecting my dad to start explaining the potentially awkward as heck situation we were unwillingly thrust into. I tried to examine him but deemed his facial expression as unreadable. His whole body and face grew three impenetrable layers to shield any form of human conflict. He did not utter one word, but then my mom and I evacuated the room a couple of tense minutes later. As soon as we were out of the hospital room my mom released her smile, and I watched her transform into a woman who has just seen the man her ex-husband had been with. She crossed her arms and scoffed, like a teenage girl riding the crimson wave.

Giddily, I texted Will and snapchatted Monica letting them know I had just accidently met my dad's "friend."

***

December 2014 felt like the longest month of my life. There were upcoming laboratory test results on my dad's cancer status which would reveal whether the cancer had spread to other parts of his body or whether the tumor was shrinking. The anxiety of waiting for those results was fucking agonizing. Paranoia festered in me, as I constantly imagined the scene in The Fault In Our Stars where Augustus Waters tells Hazel that his test results "lit up like a Christmas tree" and then I cursed myself for having watched that movie. I failed my first college algebra class and mourned over it until I had I-failed-my-math-class-but-fucked-my-boyfriend-for-the-first-time sex two hours later, and then tried out a CrossFit class with Rachel for the first time, which was fabulous.

Anxiety was making me feel crazy and trapped. Like a freak who overthought and overanalyzed every single moment about the past, present, and future. In my head, the results were going to light up like a fucking Christmas tree, and then it would fast forward to me wearing a black dress at my father's funeral while Ted and Barney hugged their inconsolable best friend. Even in the story I was writing, it just so happened that the dad of the main character was going to die somewhere near the middle. I was both relieved and slightly disappointed when my dad told me that the tumor had remained the same size and had spread to his groin. I couldn't stand not having control over this and hated myself for feeling like I couldn't even enjoy one moment with my dad without thinking about his death.

"That's the hardest part," I told Lily over Skype. "That as much as I tell myself 'just enjoy every moment with him, like you would with anyone else,' I always feel like I can't. The thought of him dying is always there."

***

Sometimes when I'd be having protected sex with Will, I would fantasize about him getting me pregnant, only so I would have the reassurance that my dad would get to meet my first child and be my baby's grandpa. I never told Will about this fantasy, because I didn't actually want to get pregnant. I just simultaneously liked and disliked entertaining the idea. My fantastic boss, Zoe, let me take a week off work after I told her about my dad being in the hospital nursing a stubborn tumor, which at first I thought would be great, but it only removed one of my distractions, magnifying my unwanted thoughts and worries to the point where I intentionally cultivated a new manageable distraction for myself—Ponyboy.

More specifically, being torn between Will and Ponyboy.

To make a long story short (ha, can I even do that?) I was this >.< close to breaking up with Will just to possibly crawl back into Ponyboy's arms based on the premise that Ponyboy may or may not have still been in love with me. See, we had talked on the phone for three hours the night Rafael took my dad back to Baptist hospital, yet I couldn't bring myself to ask him whether he did or did not, and then I ended up taking my first of many breaks with Will only to realize that I should've probably stayed with the guy who would "go on my hands and knees for you" (his words), as opposed to the ghost of my eighth grade lover who wasn't calling me back.

But hindsight is always 20/20, isn't it?

CHAPTER 11
The Game of the Ninjas and Car Keys Sword

The pounds were melting off my dad's body faster than an anorexic girl on cocaine. He no longer had a butt, and his clothes hung off his skin, when before his muscles used to intimidate my past boyfriends. I could feel these changes in my ribs, and change makes my ribs hurt.

"Anaregina, hurry up, or we're leaving you," Dad said. He was going with the simple jeans and his favorite blue jacket. I liked getting parented by him again, even though that was one of my mom's classic lines, but whatever.

"I'm going, I'm going!" I insisted, finishing applying my liquid eyeliner. The little lash wings must be perfectly even, even though that's impossible.

"Mama is ready. We're just waiting for you."

"Okay, ya voy," I whined. I glanced at myself in my mirror. I looked good. My high-low flowy dress always made me feel like an earthy goddess which was perfect for where we were headed for no special occasion. The Peacock Garden Café. I adjusted my handmade-in-Mexico-by-my-Mexican-best-friend-Alex flower crown, and ten minutes later we were in the family Prius on our way to Coconut Grove. Because I was behind the wheel, the Universe was on high alert for all our safety.

Breathe, Ana, I reminded myself. We entered the parking lot beneath the restaurant that reminded me of Batman's cave where I learned the definition of patience as we waited for the next available parking spot.

"Good job driving!" my dad reassured me, as we got out of the car and headed for the parking garage's stairs.

I hugged him hard. "Thank you, Papá. I love you."

"I love you, too."

"And I love you, Mama." I smiled at her in her pretty white dress. Just so she didn't think I wasn't feeling it for her too.

She smiled back and chuckled, telling me she loved me too. I could tell she was happy to see me happy. Or act happy, at least. We strolled into the enchanted garden of an entrance where a pretty hostess guided us to a table in the outside corner of the restaurant. My parents scanned the menus, while I eagerly waited for bread to arrive so I could restore my anxious energy.

"What are you going to have?" Dad asked.

"I'm probably going to just go with the angel hair pasta," I said, "And lemonade. You know, Papá, it's actually because of you that I always order the angel hair pasta. The last time we came here, that's what you ordered and I loved it."

"Really? I don't remember that." He scratched his head. I reminded him that it had cut up pieces of tomato and blocks of cheese. "Oh, I think I remember now. I was thinking of going with a salad this time."

"I could order the pasta and share some of it with you." I smiled.

He genuinely smiled back. Cancer can weaken your body, but it could NEVER weaken your smile. NEVER. A cheerful, bald waiter with an ear piercing arrived to get our orders, and I devoured the bread before anybody could start a conversation.

"We're just waiting on two more people," my mom told the waiter.

"That's okay, I'll be back." He smiled, as he collected our menus.

I observed the restaurant and took a picture of the view—both mental and on my phone. Trees decorated with lights, potted plants, and colorful orchids dominated the scene more than the people dining on the home-style wicker chairs. I felt at peace. Then, the thoughts came. Thoughts of death and what it would be like not to have my dad around. No, no, no! I was just started to enjoy myself! I screamed internally. The waiter returned with our drinks, and I found myself sipping my lemonade like I was furious at it. Just like that, I began slipping into a bubble of misery that made it seriously difficult to breathe and a full-time job to act "normal."

Still, I forced a smile, because we were trying to have a good time.

"¡Hola!" Lina, my mom's best friend, exclaimed, arriving at the table to join us, temporarily bursting the bubble.

"Hola," I said, as she bent to give me a kiss on the cheek.

Anezka, Lina's twenty-two-year-old daughter greeted us all and scooted to an empty seat. We exchanged hellos then gave our full, undivided attention to her one-year-old son, Jay, the happiest baby on Earth.

"Say hi, Jay," Anezka cooed.

The afternoon sun seemed to set in his brown eyes, as he burst into a fit of giggles before he could finally squeal, "Hiiiiiiii!"

That set everyone off laughing from sheer joy. Just watching him, I forgot all about my nagging thoughts and worry. Anezka sat Jay down in a high chair next to my dad who gave the baby his car keys to play with. Jay reacted as if he was given the greatest gift a human being could ever receive. Then, he threw the keys on the floor.

"Here, Jay." Dad pretended that the key was a sword and they were both ninjas. Jay could not contain his laughter and my dad fed off his youthful energy. The thick veins in his hands and arms seemed to glimmer with life, and the sound of his laughter was one of which I was all too familiar.

"Hyyywhee!" the baby gasped. Inside, I did too. Hey, I am actually enjoying the moment for once! Loving the way he made my dad bend down every two seconds, Jay threw the keys on the floor again, and my dad continued to enthusiastically pick them up and go along with the game of the Ninjas and Car Keys Sword. I didn't know it at the time, but eventually, I turned this memory into my dad being my baby's Grandpa, and even though it wasn't true, I allowed myself to believe it and to cherish it forever.

CHAPTER 12
Snapstory

Christmas came and went, and still no Adam. I hated celebrating any holiday and seeing any sort of decorations with my brother gone, reminded that he wasn't going to spend those times with us. My trust for the judicial system became a giant goose egg, but the fear of the four of us never being reunited was beginning to dissipate, because a deep part of me was sure that the whole thing was going to last ten months. So far, it had been seven.

"Look at how pretty the geisha is." I crouched down and took a snapchat.

"Oh, wow, she is very pretty," Mom said. The doll in the glass case posed with a fan splayed open in her hand, as we all admired her in the store of Asian knick knacks. We were on our way to get late night-frozen yogurt, but my mom, dad, and I stopped to window shop, as if we'd never been to these stores before. Like a family trip to Europe, instead of froyo.

"And the jewelry is beautiful too," my mom added. I loved the way her dark eyelashes curled to the top of her eyelids whenever she smiled.

We walked by a little Colombian restaurant, then entered beloved Yogurtland. I sampled every flavor, except the gross natural one, and finally went with vanilla and chocolate swirled together. This process usually took me at least eleven minutes.

"Are you going to get some, Papá?" I asked.

"No, I'm still full from dinner," he said, patting his ghost of a stomach.

"Okay." I shrugged and gingerly drenched my frozen treat in cookie dough blocks, strawberries, and brownies. Talk about comfort food. The guy working there weighed my dessert and smiled, as he handed me a pink plastic spoon. My dad paid, and I thanked him through a mouth full of yogurt before we could even exit the tiny store.

"I want to sit over there," I murmured, pointing to the Colombian restaurant's empty table. "Can we?"

"Just ask that guy." My dad pointed to the young employee standing outside.

I inhaled the cool air and walked over to the dude. "Hey, um, c-can we sit…is it okay if we sit here?" I asked, twirling the tips of my hair. He was so cute, I had suddenly lost my ability to speak correctly.

"Yeah, it's fine," he said coolly.

"Thank you." My tense shoulders drooped, as I sank into one of their outdoor seats.

He walked back into the restaurant, and the ambiance of soothing Spanish music filled the air as we all took seats as a family (our own kind of family) and began to talk. As my parents chatted, I tuned out and simply relished my froyo (now I'm craving froyo) and thought of the past. The past has always been my pillow for any future worries.

I remembered the times I came to this shopping plaza with my dad and my brother after seeing a movie at Regal Cinemas. I remembered the pain on my mother's face when my brother and I would leave to visit my dad while she stayed home reading a book, the guilt I felt when I would come back and could tell that she had been crying. I remembered the times I came here with my junior year boyfriend Augustus after experiencing sex for the first couple of times, brimming with excitement. I was starting to feel guilty for slipping into my own world in the middle of a family outing and forced myself out as if waking myself from a dream.

"How did the holiday party at GRC go?" my dad inquired.

"You mean the Gayla?" I corrected him and smirked. "It was good. Zoe's girlfriend decorated the office so nicely. Of all the superlatives, they gave me 'Most Changed.'"

"Why 'Most Changed?'"

"Apparently, I was super shy in the beginning when I first started working there, but then I opened up more." I picked at the puddle of my melted froyo, searching for cookie dough bits. "Then Zoe made me a sign that said 'warrior' on it, and she said, I was a warrior." I put my hand over my heart.

"Oh, I think I saw it," Dad said.

"Yeah, I hung it up in my room."

"Did Will have a good time?"

"Yes, he liked it," I said. I was also starting to feel guilty that I spent too much time with Will and not enough with my dad, even though since the very beginning of my dad's diagnosis, he made it clear to treat him as if he wasn't sick. But still.

"Ay, Anaregina, you only like him because he treats you like a queen," my mom said.

Um, was there any better reason? Before I could even roll my eyes or protest my mom's theory that I have a queen-complex, my dad clucked his tongue and said, "Xiomara, let her like whoever she likes."

I smiled warmly at my dad, always being able to diffuse the pendulum of potential, chaotic tension between my mom and me. Mom scowled, and then my dad brought up a memory from our visit to Mexico years ago. I savored the nostalgia of my childhood more than the bits and pieces of cookie dough that were stuck behind my molars. Around midnight, we started heading towards the car, when suddenly I said, "Wait, wait, wait!"

"What?" My mom suddenly turned around.

"I want to take a selfie of the three of us before we go."

"For your Snapchat thing, or whatever you call it?" Mom asked.

"Yes!" I smiled, extending my arm with my phone in hand. "The app I'm always using."

My dad, being quirky, dipped his head and made a funny expression with his eyes behind my squinty-eyed mom and me, and I posted it on my story after the geisha. No filter.

CHAPTER 13
Club Madonno

The first girl I ever kissed was Hermione Granger in the back of a bus on a school trip to Animal Kingdom. We both had boyfriends, but we didn't care. I was petrified to kiss her beautiful, exotic face, because I didn't know whether I would like it or not. And then I'd have to go through the daunting process of coming out of the closet, or being halfway out, I guess. After thirteen minutes of nervous laughter with both of our boyfriends watching, I finally did it and realized that girl lips were just like guy lips, and as wildly gorgeous as she was, I didn't like-like her. BUT it made me feel a lot more connected to my dad. Like, Hey, Dad, I understand you a little more now.

That was my senior year of high school. Now about a year later, my bi-curiosity took me to higher avenues, confusing paths, or simply a place I could finally cross off my ever-growing bucket list. I went to my very first strip club, Club Madonno.

Mom: "Where are you?"

Ana: "We're still at Flanigan's."

Detective Mom: "Where are you going after that?"

Disobedient Me: "Probably Barney's dorm. I'll let you know."

Overly Protective Mom who I love dearly: "Okay, que te cuidas, te quiero. Y no más tarde que la una, Anaregina!"

Nervous Me: *rolls eyes internally* "Okay, adiós. Te quiero también."

Nagging Mother: "¡En serio, no más tarde que la una! Una y media máximo."

Annoyed Anaregina: *presses lips together* "Okay, Mama. Adios."

I hung up the phone. I didn't like lying but lying to your parents doesn't really count sometimes. Will took my hand and squeezed it, as I delivered a fake smile. It was his nineteenth birthday, and the whole day long, I swallowed my pain and tears so that he could actually have a happy birthday. His present was the album photo of his band Quantum Waves. I painted it on New Year's Day which magnified my guilt for spending the holiday with my boyfriend instead of my dad. But there's still next year I thought.

"Shit, dude, I can't believe you're already nineteen," Saul said. He looked wistful behind his thick glasses.

"And you're going to a strip club!" I chimed in. The salty scent of Miami Beach made my nose smile, even though I could smell the oncoming crowd which reeked of booze and cigarettes.

"With the people I love the most," Will gushed. Just kidding, that's too corny for Will to say. He probably just acted uberly gay with Saul making him beyond uncomfortable, as I pretended to be amused and gave my feet mental emotional support for being warriors in four inch heels.

"BARNEY, ARE WE ALMOST THERE YET?" I whined, kicking the back of my heel against the floor for one second of relief.

"We just have five more miles to go!" he shouted, startling his girlfriend, Marie, locked onto his arm.

"What?" she cried.

"I'm kidding, I'm kidding. We have about one more block."

"Ugh," I muttered. Well, just suck it up, Ana. I distracted myself from foot discomfort by observing the people around me. Women wearing provocative outfits and eager gazes, the homeless man lying in front of the fancy tattoo shop, busy waiters attending glamorous couples, and the police at every other corner. I loved downtown.

"We're almost there, babe," Will said. He gave me "I love you" eyes.

"Uh-huh." I nodded. My lips formed a tightly-pressed smile.

We passed American Apparel, a couple of other clothing stores, and restaurants before finally reaching the neon pink sign boasting half-naked women underneath. Oh, boy. The pain in my toes turned to giddy excitement mixed with a rush of "I can't believe I am an adult, and I'm actually doing this!" feeling. Inside, I'd always felt like I was five.

Yet there I was, showing my ID and using Club Madonno's ATM to access twenty dollars all so I could see naked women dance on poles. The truth was, I did not see strippers. I saw human beings with imperfect bodies and vacant expressions in their disconnected eyes, breasts and butts saying hello in a hundred different ways, while their thongs seemed to make their butts appear smaller than mine (I would say mine is average size). It felt so strange and surreal.

"Would you like a dance?" A blonde stripper in a white, lacy two-piece asked me.

I giggled and said, "No, thank you," politely while quivering. This is my first time here. I'm still trying to grasp everything! I wanted to say. She smirked at me and at Ted who was tagging along next to me. I always felt safe next to him. We sat in what looked like a doughnut couch with rows, and where the doughnut hole would be was the actual platform where the girls danced. I sat next to Will, who genuinely seemed more interested in me than in them.

"I still think you're the most gorgeous girl in the room," he said with a smile.

"I don't know, that one over there has massive boobs," I inconspicuously pointed out.

"Yours are nicer." He kissed my cheek. You're just saying that, I wanted to say, but he really couldn't tear his gaze away from me. Where were his raging nineteen-year-old hormones?

We lingered on the couch for a while, politely rejecting another woman who approached us for lap dances. The most entertaining part of the night was watching Ted talk to them and be tense in general. He looked so out of place in his plaid button-down shirt, sneakers, and glasses that gave off the impression that he'd never even seen porn. Then, there was Barney telling Saul about his last math final that he aced, saying "I fucked her right in the pussy!" in reference to the test metaphorically being a woman. Don't ask.

We're so nerdy, I thought. I love it. It would have made more sense to have a huddle of penguins from Antarctica here than us. The juxtaposition fascinated me. Until, it no longer did. And then, eventually, watching the lifeless girls swing their bodies around the poles became normal and boring, and I was quickly growing disappointed.

But then, Rosie appeared.

Rosie, a curvy-bodied brunette, emanated life, charm, and sensuality all at once from the moment she confidently walked onto the lit stage. I watched in awe, as she gracefully moved to the beat of the music and climbed to the top of the pole only to let herself fall almost to the very bottom while straddling her legs wide open and clapping her heels before her entire body and face practically kissed the floor. All with a charming, cheerleader-bad-ass-like smile on her pretty face. Finally, one performer who seemed to enjoy herself.

"Oh, my God, she's so athletic!" I gushed into Will's ear.

"Sounds like someone is having a girl crush."

"No, but seriously how the hell is she doing that? That's insane!"

"Yeah, that does not look easy," Will agreed.

"Let's go sit up close," I tugged on his sleeve.

"Do you have any dollar bills we could give her?"

I fished around in my wallet for Washingtons. "Yes," I murmured, "I do."

I felt like the entire room was watching us, as Will, Saul, and I approached the first doughnut couch row to see Rosie's talent up close. The crowd was vibing off her energy, as the people littered her stage with ones, a couple of tens, and maybe a few twenties. Beads of sweat dripped from her hairline, and then, she noticed me. "Look at you! You're adorable! Come 'ere," she cooed. Her brown eyes, gleaming white teeth, and short hair shone like the sound of her voice.

I smiled and laughed, not knowing what to do with myself, as we took a seat. I felt like a kid at a candy shop, and Rosie was one of those giant swirly lollipops. I took out a couple of bills, thinking I was just going to place them on the floor and retreat to my doughnut row when she shook her head at me and winked. She also stuck her tongue out in a sexual way that I can't really describe.

"No, no, no, cutie, it's like this." She took the bill from my hand, rolled it up, stuck it in my mouth, and then pointed to her cleavage which suddenly registered in my mind as a coin slot machine. I was both mesmerized and disgusted (money germs were now on my lips…ew!) Then, she did the same to Will, who let her know that I was his girlfriend, but she just laughed and said, "Who cares, baby?"

I care. I care very much. But I cared more about the fact that we were sharing our first stripper encounter and relishing the sight of watching my boyfriend stick bills in Rosie's boobs. I can't explain it. We continued to watch her charm everyone and then I found myself wanting my very first lap dance from her.

"Do you want a lap dance?" I whispered to Will.

He put his arm around me, "No, not really, but I think you do."

I laughed like I'd been caught in the middle of a lie. "You can have a lap dance if you want. It's your birthday, I really don't mind."

"You want a lap dance from her, don't you?" He chuckled.

"Yes, yes I do," I admitted.

I watched Saul go up the stairs to the lap dance floor with a beautiful blonde chick who was a natural flirt, and Saul could barely contain his excitement. I wanted to feel that same rush. And I wanted it with Rosie. Barney and Marie had already left to go have sex, of course. And that left me, Will, Ted, and two of Will's friends who were getting lap dances from other women.

"Okay, just wait 'til she comes up to us," Will said.

"Okaaaaay," I giggled like as if I was tipsy on vodka, except I hadn't had anything to drink. Now, I was the tense one of the group.

"But, Ana," Will said, "you can't kiss her. You guys can feel each other up, whatever, don't tell me about it. But nothing on the lips." He pointed from his neck up. His expression was solemn. Was my boyfriend actually jealous of a girl?

"I'm not going to kiss her, Will."

"I'm serious, like the whole night would be ruined."

I held out my pinky to him, and our pinkies interlocked, as I kissed my hand and said very seriously, "I won't." He kissed his hand too.

As I waited, a civil war unraveled inside me, as I judged the older men who were gawking at the strippers like they were sex toys, and I could tell by their gestures—one swine pet her ass like she belonged to him—the little respect they had for them. Or the strippers respect for themselves? Or me? Wasn't I the same for paying my entrance to watch this? What separated the "old, disgusting pigs" from me? I decided to let the "dehumanizing argument" go, as Rosie finally approached us. I morphed into the most, awkward, shy version of myself I thought I had left behind in middle school. It was actually Ted who initiated the conversation.

"Hello, what is your name?" He extended his hand like the proper man he was.

She shook it and said, "I'm Rosie, and you?"

"Ted," he said and then pointed to me. "And this is Ana, and this is Will." Will waved at her, and of course, I giggled nervously while playing with my hands. Closer up, I could see she was in her late twenties.

"Have you guys gotten a dance yet?" she asked.

"It's actually our first time here, and no we haven't," Ted said, looking more comfortable.

"How old are you guys?" Rosie asked.

"We're all nineteen," Ted replied.

"Oh, my God, you guys are babies!" she exclaimed with a laugh.

Ted asked where she was from, and she confidently told us that she was from Detroit but ended up finding herself here the way an interesting character from a movie would reveal a layer of herself.

"How are you able to do all of that? Like, like…was it hard to, you know, learn?" I asked, in awe of this woman. I peeked at Will for a moment.

"I just took a class, and it all went from there." She flipped her pretty brown hair.

So, can I get a lap dance from you and finally find out whether I'm bisexual or not?

"Wow, you're really good," I said, feeling like I was lavishing her with compliments, but it was true. She was the best of the performers.

"So, it's your first time here, and you also haven't gotten a dance?" She was talking to me. Rosie, the stripper, was talking to me. Her eyes were akin to chocolate almonds.

"Yes, it is, and nope," I said quietly.

Rosie threw her head back and laughed. "She's so innocent and adorable. Oh, my God!" She gushed, bringing a hand to her lips, and I was suddenly really comfortable with the vibe she was giving off. Natural, down-to-earth.

"Can I just take her home?" she pleaded to Ted. Ted smiled, and Will laughed nervously.

"Do you do a couples' lap dance?" Will asked suddenly. A couples' dance? What, he didn't trust me enough for me to have my own?

"No, we don't, but I'll give you one for free if you give me twenty minutes." She looked right at me, hands on her perfect hips. I know I must've turned every shade of beet red, because my cheeks burned. Oh, my God, my stripper has a crush on me! Rosie started telling Ted how my "innocence" was so appealing to her, and I could totally relate. That was how I felt about Sodapop and Emmett. Even though I didn't take Emmett's virginity, the prospect of it was so terribly fun.

Rosie would occasionally shake her boobs, as if it was the most casual thing to do and naturally flip her hair while talking to Ted. Standing there listening to them, I wrapped my head around the situation I was putting myself in. Rosie glanced at me again. "Can I just take her home?"

All I could do was look at Will's surprised expression and suppress my laughter.

"So, what's the strangest thing that's happened here?" Will, being his direct self, asked.

"There's so many stories, man. One time, this guy came in with his girlfriend, and he asked me for a lap dance, and the girlfriend got so pissed that she was actually this close…" Rosie put a foot of distance to her cheek with her hand, "to hitting me, and I was like, 'Hell, no! I'll kick your ass!' It was over there." She pointed to the dark corner by the bar. "They had to escort her out, because she wouldn't stop yelling. The jealous girlfriends go crazy. Which is like, what the fuck man, I'm not here to fuck your boyfriend, I'm just here for your boyfriend's money. Why they would bring their jealous girlfriends is beyond me!"

"Yeah, I can imagine," Will said, nodding.

An hour later, it was finally my turn to get my share of Rosie. That sounds so weird to write, but whatever, it's true. Heading up the stairs ready to lose my lap dance virginity, I mentally took photographs of the moment, as Rosie led me to a theatre box seat and told me to wait a little while longer.

As I sank into the plushy seat, I had no idea what to expect. Was she going to kiss me? Wait, no, Will didn't want that. Was she going to rub her butt against my thighs? Would I get turned on? I didn't know. My knees shook with anticipation. And then, suddenly, she arrived in a red bra and tiny black booty shorts, asking me if I wanted her bra to stay on, so I simply nodded. She continued to tell me how cute I was, and I couldn't have been any more awkward as she faced away from me and sensually shook her butt to my face in a cat-like motion. My gaze fell on all her tattoos, especially one of a shooting star on her shoulder blade. She glanced over her shoulder at me, smiling, reminding me that she respected whatever I'd want, and it didn't have to be awkward.

"And don't worry, I'm clean! We always wash up before." She added with a smile. I smiled back at her, and then I got a face full of clean-smelling boobs. Yes, I got motor-boated.

Am I turned on? I honestly asked myself. Because I honestly wanted to know.

No, I'm not. I honestly replied.

Well, Rosie's really hot, so I guess that means I'm not bi. I must've just had a girl crush. You know, attracted to her confidence.

She must've sensed that I wasn't really all that into it, even though she continued to dance half-naked on me, so she took the opportunity to tell me more strange, funny experiences she'd had with other men. It was ordinary sleepover chit-chat, except she was half-naked and dancing on me. I tried to memorize her moves, so maybe one day, I could, you know, pull some tricks out of my sleeve in the bedroom (that shit takes real practice). Before I knew it, it was over, and I thanked her very politely, and once she was gone, I proceeded to tell Will every detail.

"I didn't get turned on though!" I said, crossing my arms.

"That's funny. You're disappointed, because you wanted to fit in with the rest of your coworkers by at least being bi." I pouted my lips at him. I was always totally see-through to Will.

"But, hey, at least now you know."

"Yeah, that's a relief," I sighed, confused, as the wind flirted with my hair.

***

"How is your book coming along?" Dad asked from his hospital bed. We were in another big room where the lights shone down on him.

I sighed. Disappointed in myself. "I stopped writing it." I stared at my chipped nails. I could feel my tension make a home in the back of my head, my neck, and my back. I should really go for a run or a swim… Or better yet, have a mind-shattering orgasm.

"Why?" he asked in a concerned tone. I stared at the IV drip connected to his arm. "You were getting so far along."

"I stopped writing it, because Will told me he loved me."

"What does that have to do with it?"

"Papá, I can't write a book about a girl trying to get over a guy for the past seven years while someone else is loving me. It makes me feel wrong. I don't want to feel those emotions as I write and have him love me at the same time. It feels like I am lying to him in a way." I stared at the tiles of the pristine floor.

"Anaregina, it's okay to write all that and be with him at the same time. It's like that author from Lolita…what was his name?" He paused to think. "I don't remember, but the man wrote an excellent novel about a man who falls in love with an underaged girl, which had nothing to do with who he was. He had a wife and kids."

"Yeah, I've heard of that book, but I haven't read it. And you know what? You're absolutely right, Dad. It doesn't matter if I write about my past love life while being with Will," I said, grateful that he understood me. I felt guilty for forgetting to bring playing cards like he requested and made a mental note to bring them next time.

I don't know or understand why random memories hit you at the most unpredictable times, but sitting there with my dad, I remembered a time I was in fifth grade, getting ready to go to the fifth grade soirée, and I was crying as if my dog had died, because I didn't look the way I imagined myself to look. I wanted hairless legs, perfectly curled hair—my fifth-grade crush was going—and I was embarrassed that both my parents were coming with me and my grandma. On top of that, my fifth-grade teacher picked my friend, Poussey, and me to read some sort of graduation speech that I didn't feel ready for. Nothing was going the way I had imagined, so I threw a mini tantrum, making my mom, grandma, and dad furious, because I was hell bent on not going. I ended up arriving late with patchy hairy legs, natural wavy hair, and I still had a blast.

The very next day, my dad took me to eat breakfast at IHOP and taught me a lesson over buttermilk pancakes which I will never forget. "In this life, Anaregina, you need to learn to be more flexible."

CHAPTER 14
Cirque du Soleil

"What are you getting your family for Christmas?" Lucas, my relatively new coworker, asked me one day out of the blue.

The cure to cancer.

"You know, I keep thinking about it, and I still don't know. What about you?" I asked politely.

"Well, my sister loves Taylor Swift, so I'm buying her tickets for her next concert," he said, flipping his young Justin Bieber styled hair out of his face. PERFECT! I KNOW EXACTLY WHAT TO GET MY PARENTS FOR CHRISTMAS NOW! I thought. No, not Taylor Swift tickets, although I wouldn't mind seeing her perform live. TICKETS TO GO SEE CIRQUE DU SOLEIL FOR THE FIRST TIME EVER.

After nights of praying, sobbing, and listening to the song "Fix You" by Coldplay, January 7th arrived, and my dad was in fact healthy enough to go. As I've probably said before, the Universe and I are on pretty good terms.

"Bye!" I waved cheerfully to my CrossFit companions and exquisitely hot coaches. My dad parked in front of the gym, the one place I could ooze out all of my anger and stress instead of waking up and wanting to kill an innocent bunny for no reason. The guy at the front desk told me to have a good time.

"Hola, Anaregina," Dad said, as I opened the car door.

I stepped in and lightly closed the door behind me. "Hola, Papi."

"Hurry up, so we're not late," he said, all moody. His hands clutched the leather steering wheel.

"Dad, we just finished, and I'm already in the car," I laughed. We had gotten in an argument earlier before dropping me off about how I should ask my dad if he could drop me off at the gym hours prior to the gym time instead of last minute. He was right about this.

"When we get home, hurry up and get ready. I don't want to be late."

"Okay, Dad, I get it." I took a sip from my water bottle. Despite the cool down, I was still panting like a dog in a desert. I examined my dad's expression, which seemed so stressed.

"I just hate being late to things," he said bitterly, as if I didn't know.

"I know, I do, too, but we have enough time. It's not even six yet." I smiled meekly. And besides, rarely do the Frias get to places on time.

His eyebrows bunched together, all the wrinkles in his face having an argument with one another. "And I don't want Mama to be stressed, because you know how she gets."

"I know."

"So, I really want you to hurry up, don't take your time please."

"Dad! Okay! I get it!" I barked. Guilt kicked me in the pit of my stomach soon after my outburst. "I'm sorry," I quickly added. He took his eyes off the road for a moment and looked at me like I'd grown two extra heads. I played with the lid of my empty water bottle.

"I'm so sorry, Anaregina," he said solemnly.

"For what?" I asked, confused. The black grackles were back, creating a beautiful picture of their togetherness on the cables connecting the street poles along Kendall Drive. One bird would leave a cable, and then a good twenty would follow it into the sunset.

"For how I was acting when I dropped you off." He let out a heavy sigh. "I was just stressed and worried about being able to make it to the show or not. The medications make me feel so tired, they affect my emotions. I'll be feeling numb, but then I get so moody, it's just out of my control," he said, exasperated. "So, I'm sorry."

So, taking cancer medication was like PMS times one thousand, I decided.

"And I know how much going to this means to you." His voice cracked. Wow, he was really getting emotional. Two lumps congregated in the back of my throat. He was right—going to Cirque du Soleil had been on my bucket list for years.

"That's why I'm so happy that you're going, Dad. So, don't be sorry. It's okay, I understand."

"You're the best daughter I could have possibly asked for, Anaregina. You really are. You're so special. I am so happy that you got these tickets for us. Such a thoughtful gift, and it shouldn't come as a surprise, since it's coming from you. I'm just so glad I c-could g-go," he began to sob violently while driving. I worried about whether he should pull over or not, but then I immediately did the same.

"I'm s-so glad you could come too, Papá. I was also afraid you wouldn't be able to, so thank you. You've been so strong, and I'm sure Adam will be able to come with us next year."

"Yeah, hopefully…" He started to laugh at how emotional he'd gotten.

Then, I started to laugh too. For a moment, I wondered if anybody driving their little cars could see us crying and laughing through the silent windows and felt self-conscious. What would the guy in the Honda next to us think about a father and daughter crying their eyes out and simultaneously laughing? Then, I smiled to myself. It didn't matter. I had everything I wanted right by my side. My dad would be well enough to make it to the show.

My heart couldn't have felt fuller if I'd tried.

If only the drivers next to us knew our whole story.

CHAPTER 15
The Girl with the "Rotten" Heart

I'm a list girl. I love making lists, and when I was little, it was making contracts. I remember making a contract with my grandma stating that when I grew up, I was not going to marry a man. I was going to have a lot of dogs instead. She laughed and told me that when I was older, I would change my mind. No. No way. I stayed firm in my belief, took out a pen, and wrote my contract on a napkin. Then, I signed it. There—it was done.

I don't know where this passion came from, but I recently made a list of the top ten feelings I've ever experienced, and number two was rage. The kind that comes with shattering a plate. It was so cathartic and metaphorical, of course I wrote a shitty poem about it. I clung onto the white ceramic plate, pacing around the kitchen like the crazy person I am. I clung to all my fears and emotions, like it was my life, like it was my soul, and after a couple spouts of resistance, I flung it to the floor with full force. White shards of glass littered the floor, glittering like fresh-fallen snow. Immediately, my angry heart slowed down followed by a sense of lightness and freedom. And as I started sweeping up all the pieces, I swear the song, "Firework," by Katy Perry, started to play. Now, I felt empowered. Baby, you're a fiiiiiirework! C'mon, let your cooolors burst! I sang to myself like I was powerhouse Adele herself.

And to my dogs, of course.

Jodie knew. Jodie understood. She listened to the same songs I listened to while crying myself to sleep at night. My only anesthesia to insanity. The only way to drown my thoughts so I could actually sleep at night. There will be bad days, the song insisted. Be calm. Loosen your grip, opening each palm slowly now. Let go. Be confident. Know that now is only a moment, and that if today is as bad as it gets, understand that by tomorrow, today will have ended. Be gracious. Jodie heard the way I held my breath until the last lyric of the song, Be calm. Loosen your grip, opening each palm, slowly now – let go.

The truth was, I unwittingly started to treat my dad as though he were already dead. I wasn't seeing my therapist at the time, so there was nobody I could tell this to. How could I tell those close to me that I was treating my dad as if the cancer had already consumed every particle of his body? I couldn't. There would be judgment for sure, and that would be admitting defeat to his battle.

Then, I met Eve. It's funny how the Universe brings you the exact people you need to meet at exactly the precise moment you need them. It was another weekday of going to work, transitioning from the tired, sleep-deprived, broken girl to the happy-go-lucky gay rights activist ready to tread on all the "no's" and "they can go to hell" strangers told me.

Ana's Thoughts while driving to GRC (Mom in the driver seat):

I really need therapy

...but I have Will, and he's basically a therapist

Yeah, but he's also your boyfriend who you love

I love my therapist!

Okay, but it's a different kind of love

Do you even love Will?

Yeah, I do. But I'm not—in love—with him.

I don't care, I can't tell him about this. I can't tell anyone about this. I'm miserable. I think I am depressed. This isn't fair. Why the fuck is this happening to me? I didn't want to wake up this morning.

"Hello!" Enzo greeted me when I walked through the door. Enzo, my older, wiser, gay guru with brown eyes that seemed to emanate an all-knowing glow, like harboring all the secrets to the world. Or at least my universe. I forced a smile at him, feeling the desire to continue living. We were both Virgos. We understood the struggle of being us.

"How are you, boo?" he asked cheerfully, his vaporizer in his hand. He always wore bright-colored socks that popped out of his All Star Converse.

"I'm...well, you know…" I shrugged my shoulders. And he really did know. He would give me rides after work and the kind of golden life advice that made actual gold seem like something you'd find on the bottom of your shoe.

"I know, honey." He patted me on the shoulder, and a boulder of tension eased instantly. "But we're going to have a good day today!"

I pulled up a chair and sat next to one of the tables where we did "cash out," which was counting all of the money we made and recording statistics like whether people paid by check, credit card, or cash? How many yeses did we get? Divide the average amount of money our group made. I was disappointed to learn that every math teacher I'd ever had was right—we do actually use math in the "real world."

Enzo #2 hugged me from behind, and I instantly felt 9,201,995 times better. You wouldn't expect it by looking at him, but he's gay too, and he gives the sort of hugs that make you love life again.

"Hi, Ana," he said sweetly.

"Hello." I gave him a tired smile.

The rest of my coworkers greeted me with their own kind of warmth and love that made me feel safe and secure. We played the announcements song, which was probably "Boss Ass Bitch" or something. The worries of my emotional state melted away. We separated into groups to do our morning training to be better canvassers, and as usual I was in charge of persistence training. There were three main necessary trainings—mindset training, unflappability training, and persistence training. I think I never lost perspective over my situation, because I applied these trainings to my life.

Positive Mindset: No matter what, you keep that mindset positive the entire day, baby. Focus on the task at hand.

Unflappability: The world gives you shit, but you remain resilient. You don't give up on your goal.

Persistence Training: You keep going, keep persisting, until you realize it is time to stop, accept the situation for what it is, and let it go. On to the next task.

Smile. Wave. Positivity. Say, "Have a good day!" Even though you're really telling yourself to have a good day (but them too, of course!).

"Time for announcements!" Leslie shouted. We all gathered in a circle, and Charlie, my good friend with a brunette afro passed out little white pieces of paper with what we were going to announce today. I always had the role of being the weather girl. "…which is really great for the Congress," Charlie wrapped up the main memo. It was so early, sometimes announcements on the LGBT community wouldn't register in my brain. I always listened to the goals of "togay" though. I always took them seriously. Talk to at least twenty-five people and sign up as many partners as you can. We called our members who contributed monthly "partners."

"And what's the weather gonna be like togay?" Leslie asked, staring at me expectantly. The rest of my coworkers focused their eyeballs on me. I could feel my heartbeat quickening and smell the teeny spritz of nervous sweat from my armpits.

"DO MEANGIRLS!" Johanna stage-whispered.

"Okay," I muttered, rolling my eyes, pretending to be bashful. I got into character as dumb, blonde Karen. No offense to blondes, by the way.

"So, like…" I trailed off, twirling a strand of my hair. "The weather togay will range from…like…the…high seventies." I lightly cupped my left breast and then my right one making everyone laugh. "With like...a fifty percent chance of rain." I glanced at the map behind me, acting totally clueless. "You know what that means?"

"PERFECT CANVASSING WEATHER!" Everyone shouted in unison.

My mood lightened, as we completed the rest of the morning ritual. We said our names, our preferred gender pronouns—to this day, I am still her-she—and then said a random question to get to know each other better. Today's question was: "Who is your favorite superhero?"

Oh, that's easy. Spider-Man, of course. He's a superhero AND a nerd. It doesn't get any more perfect than that, I thought. I revealed my superhero crush and turned to my new coworker, giving her a high-five to "high-five it off" to the next person. She wore a light blue hat with sparkles that said, "Let it go," with matching pants covered in silver sequins. Around her waist was a fanny pack, which I thought was a little odd.

She waved to everyone. "Hi. My name is Eve, and my preferred gender pronouns are her and she, and I would say my favorite superhero is…can I just say Taylor Swift? I love her. She's like a superhero to me." She put her hands to her heart.

She's so nice and sweet. I want to canvass with her!

"Sure," Charlie chuckled. "Now we're going to announce the canvassing crews of the day."

"What's a canvassing crew?" we asked in unison with the same tone kindergartners use in class. This was for the new co-workers, we obviously knew what it meant.

"Thank you for asking, guys!" His eyebrows reached the top of his tan forehead. "A canvassing crew is your team for the day led by your mighty field manager." He smiled sarcastically. I loved him. As everyone read who was in their crew off the paper, where they were going, how much money they were going to make, Leslie slipped me my paper with my crew members on it. I adored the anticipation of not knowing who I was going to work with and where I was going to canvass that day.

I looked down at my sheet and smiled. "Alright, guys, I have a crew. Denny, Eve, and I are going to Miami-Dade College Wolfson Campus, and we're going to raise eight-hundred dollars!"

I glanced at Eve, her smile raging with glee and then at Denny who seemed excited as well. Then, we huddled up in a tight group like my swim team used to do before a competition, as Leslie ordered, "Touch hands or we don't win championships!"

We layered our hands together. I put mine on the very top.

"Alright, guys, put your left hand in, and why the left? Because the right is misguided. Your right hand on your head because we need to give them some education. Your right hand on your heart to show them some love and your right hand on your butt cause they're a pain in the ass."

Leslie directed our cheer to the best part, "Okay, let's give it up to bisexuals…and on three…we're all going to shout out our favorite Mean Girls quote!" We giggled, as she gave us a moment to think. "One...two...three!"

"You go, Glen Coco!" I shouted at the top of my lungs, amongst, "You can't sit with us!" "Boo, you whore!" "On Wednesdays, we wear pink!" "That's so fetch!" "She doesn't even go here!" And I'm pretty sure someone said, "I can't help that I have a heavy flow and a wide set vagina!"

Oh, the perks of working at a liberal non-profit organization. I gathered my binder, lunch bag, crew members, and oh, our equality sign stickers. "You guys ready to go?" I asked.

"Yeah," Denny said coolly.

"Yes, and I will be doing the honor of driving." Eve grinned.

"Yay! I'm really glad I finally get to work with you," I told her. "Everyone here talks about how nice you are, and I'm just here like, 'Who is this new Eve girl? And why haven't I met her yet?'"

"I know. I'm glad I get to work with you too!"

Denny trailed behind us, as we walked towards her mustard yellow car parked next to a fancy house. We crossed the street, and I admired the familiar early birds who were living in the area walking their groomed poodles so early in the bright morning light. Mind you, 10:30 AM was early for me.

"Is it your first time going to Wolfson Campus?" Denny asked.

"It is, actually," Eve replied.

"Mine too."

"Don't worry, guys, it's a great site, lots of young, liberal people," I reassured them. We got in the car, and I took the passenger seat, eager to discover the essence of Eve, what made her so special.

"Okay, good, and you guys, don't worry, I am an excellent driver. I just have no idea where we're going." She put the keys in the ignition and stretched her hands on the steering wheel, revealing several tattoos on her arms and a plastic cord that rested on her forearm.

Hmm…

"Don't worry, I got you. I know how to get there." Denny pulled out his phone and opened up his GPS. I felt a little nervous about Eve driving at first, but as soon as she got comfortable with Denny telling her where to go, I did too. Now, for the probing questions to begin…

"Are you guys good with the A/C? Let me know if you want me to change it. And the music too," Eve said. Okay, so she is caring…

"I'm good," Denny said from the backseat.

"Me, too. I like Taylor Swift," I added.

"Oh, my God, I love her! Like you don't understand, she is my girl! All of my tattoos are the names of her album." She pointed to her forearm tattoo that read: "1989."

"Wow," I said, genuinely impressed. "That's real passion."

"Yeah, if I could meet her, that would make my life."

"Take the next turn at the light," Denny directed, pointing between the two front seats.

"I feel you," I said. "So where did you go to high school?"

"I went to Killian, and you?"

"Oh, do you know Monica from Killian?"

"No, she graduated after me. I'm twenty-two, what about you?"

The song "Twenty-Two' popped into my head. "I went to TERRA. I'm nineteen, and now I am going to Miami-Dade," I paused, "Kendall Campus. Where do you go to college?"

"I am actually not going to college right now," she said slowly.

But why? Don't you want to pursue an education and eventually get a career? You're already twenty-two!

God, Ana, don't judge her, I told my brain.

Okay, I won't, but like why not?

"Why not?" My voice came out a little high-pitched.

"Well, in high school, all I did was sit there in class and listen to boring teachers teach me subjects I wasn't really interested in."

But you could discover what you really like in college!

Ana, stop.

It's true, though!

She continued to speak in the sort of tone a person uses when they are about to let you in on the inner layer of themselves. "I've been sick my whole life, pretty much, and over time I realized, you know what, life is really short, and I don't want to spend it stuck in a classroom all day, so I decided to work odd jobs like this, like I actually really enjoy this. I love all of you guys. Coming here, I felt like I was joining a family."

"I know, me too," I agreed, smiling. "So, you don't think you'll ever go to college?"

"I have a heart condition called Idiopathic Endocardial Fibroelastosis which basically means I have a malfunctioning, rotten heart…"

I clutched my stomach. That explained the IV coming out of her fanny pack.

"People with this condition are given ten to twelve years to live, and the ones who live extra take extremely good care of themselves 'til the point where it becomes obsessive. They don't even go out of their homes, because they're so afraid of getting sicker." She turned her gaze to me while I was in mid-gasp. "And I thought, you know what? I don't want to live that way. That is not the sort of life I want to live, if it means less time, so be it. At least I'll be happy doing the things I actually want to do."

"Oh, my God…" I felt both guilty and empowered hearing this. How could I complain about my life? Here was this young woman so cheerful about life, knowing she wouldn't be around for very long, just making this conscious decision to be happy, and I was screaming into my pillow every other day.

"I know, but there is still hope in finding a heart transplant for me. I've been on the waiting list for seven years. You would think I would have one by now, but those things take forever to come, and sometimes they don't come at all."

My heart sank to my curled toes.

"And if you happen to get that transplant, then…" I trailed off, trying to delicately choose the right words. I felt like I was swimming in Jell-O, as I thought of my dad and him dying.

She finished my thought for me. "Then I would go through with the surgery that same day. I actually have a beeper that will go off the instant I find out there's a heart ready for me." She smiled her bright warm smile. "And I'll be able to live a long, healthy life after that."

"Wow," I said, her story resonating inside of me. "Thank you for sharing that with me. Hearing this has really given me perspective on my life." My voice came out tiny and feeble.

Eve shrugged, her eyes focused straight ahead. "It hasn't been easy. There are days when I don't even want to get out of bed, days I have locked myself up in my room and stayed there in the dark all day, but you really have no other choice other than to keep going!" She lifted her arms off the wheel for a moment, exasperated. The sun rays hit her glittery hat and sparkling pants, casting little beads of light throughout her car.

"I can only imagine," I said in my most compassionate voice.

"My ex-girlfriend left me, because she loved me so much, she couldn't imagine losing me so quickly, and it got to the point where she literally treated me like I was already dead. Like in her mind…" Her eyebrows knotted together. "I was already a done deal."

Guilt gnawed at me suddenly.

"Like I'd already died," she went on. "She mourned my death and felt like she had no choice other than to break up with me, because it hurt her too much." Her eyes narrowed on the road ahead of us.

"And we were engaged to be married," she added. I could see that it was still an open wound by the sound of her voice. Out of genuine instant trust and as a way of showing her she wasn't alone, like, "Hey, you're not the only one who gets fucking boulders thrown at them," or in her case a meteorite, I told her about my dad and his Stage 4 cancer.

"I also have days where I just don't feel like getting up, like it takes me so much energy." My voice cracked a teeny bit. "And I'm not even the one suffering like my dad is."

"I'm sorry you're going through that, Ana," she said, "But whatever you do, do not treat your dad like he is already dead, okay?" I suddenly realized that Denny was still in the car with us. It was like he had silently retreated into the backseat. "You can't do that to him," she went on. "Your brain might be preparing for the inevitable, but he's still here. He's still alive and needs you."

I nodded, flabbergasted.

I hadn't mentioned a word of my secret feeling to anyone, but then again, there was no one I felt could understand. Until Eve. She saw right through me like water. The girl with the "rotten" heart spoke to every fiber of mine with a strength so real, so gentle, I couldn't believe it was happening.

She got her heart transplant a couple of months after that.

CHAPTER 16
Those Three Words

My parents never told me how many months to live my dad had. I don't know if that would have helped or if it just would've made it worse. All I knew was that there was no cure, that "this is a disease that isn't going to get any better, something that he is going to have to live with," the doctor had told my mom. My greatest nightmare was coming true, so it was no surprise I kept a distance from his cancer. I never met his doctor, and to this day, I can barely conceptualize how this ruthless disease crept into our family, cell by cell. I kept wondering why I wasn't processing it right, why wasn't I behaving like a character from the sad cancer movies?

When I was fifteen years old, I went through a manic episode when I truly believed that my dad was on the verge of death, and not just that, but amidst suffering delusions of grandeur, I believed—no, I knew—that the cure to cancer was at the bottom of the ocean, somewhere deep in the coral reef. I remember telling this to one of the nurses with the utmost confidence, as I passed by a large painting of a coral reef. With a glimmer in her eyes, she told me that if I truly did know the cure, to please discover it quickly, so I could help millions of people. Was she crazy to trust a young girl in a psychiatric ward? I was obsessed with death, cancer, and helping people as I was again now on this cool January night. But I wasn't underneath a spell of mania, and there was no shield to protect my reality of the situation. Just the constant, nagging feeling of helplessness like a crying little girl tugging at the bottom of my shirt.

"I want to scream, but I can't," I confessed to Will over the phone.

"Just get a shirt and scream in the shower to drown out the sounds," he suggested.

"No, I don't want to do that," I paused with thought. "Wait, I think my mom is coming. I'll call you back. Bye, babe, love you."

"I love you too, Ana."

I snatched an old shirt that hadn't seen the light of day since middle school and tucked it beneath my arm for the crying little girl inside of me who needed to scream like her life depended on it. I entered my dad's car in my backyard and curled up in fetal position, as I balled the shirt into my mouth and let out the demonic screams held prisoner inside of me.

Scream. Stop. Cry.

Scream. Stop. Cry. The pattern repeated itself until I deemed my cries to be too loud. What if the neighbors would hear? What if I would wake up my parents?

I wish I was alone…

Moments later, I heard the car door open and immediately, I stuffed my tear-saliva-snot shirt in the corner of the car, as I wiped tears away. I expected to see my mom, given that she is the lightest sleeper of the house. But…

It was my dad emerging from the patio.

We were about to have a conversation that would rearrange every paranoid bone in my body. The stars edged themselves a little closer to listen to his words, their magnitude so strong, I think the constellations might have been rearranged as well. The universe revealed a secret to me through my father's mouth that night.

I admitted to him my deepest fear, the one I'd had since I was a little girl, about watching him choke on those damn jalapenos. His death. I could feel warm comfort emanating from his concerned expression and loving arms. I can't remember the exact words we exchanged, but more the comfort and security of his presence. My inner child finally satisfied, terribly spoiled by the unconditional love only her father could quench. Then, three words crawled out of his mouth from a place few human beings truly come to terms with—cancer or no cancer—they marched their way into my ears planting a seed in my soul that would sing its way to my brain like a popular song that dominates every radio station.

"Time is limited," he said.

How am I supposed to just accept that? How am I supposed to come to terms with our time being limited? I am only nineteen. I'm not even twenty yet. I still need you. I still need you Dad. You can't go. You can't leave. I have so much to learn. I have so much growing for you to witness and nurture, for you to be a part of. But no, time is limited. So, I would have to make the best of it.

CHAPTER 17
The One Where I Meet James

Don't doubt yourself, don't doubt yourself, the Hazel in my head told me. Hazel and I went to the beach last night, and I confessed my fears of the upcoming semester. Would I be able to pass my classes? Would I be able to handle work, school, boyfriend, and just LIFE, really?

It was the first day of my first ever spring semester. Gorgeous flowers were blooming at every corner—I'm kidding, it's Miami, so there were thunderstorms every goddamn evening in January. Naturally, I was wearing a flower-print sundress with my brown combat boots, as usual, hair and light makeup done. Don't doubt yourself, don't doubt yourself, Hazel's voice echoed in the walls of my anxious brain.

"Okay, where the heck is Building 9?" I whispered to myself, checking my schedule for the 2,015th time, half-expecting all of the room numbers, and hell, maybe even classes to morph into Sanskrit, because I couldn't believe my World History Class was at 9:50 AM, Room 9209 with Professor Whisper. I know where I'm going, I know where I'm going. Okay, fine, no, I don't. Somebody help me, please. I'm just a freshman.

"Excuse me, do you know where Building 9 is?" I asked a short, confident-looking guy.

"Yeah, it's riiight over there." He pointed and flashed me a toothy smile.

"Oh...oh wow, right in front of me!" I laughed. "Thanks, the 9 was blocked by the palm trees," I said, trying to save face. I'm not stupid, okay? Do not think I'm stupid. I marched over to the stairs, content that I was at the right building and still on time. Okay, now where is the damn room itself? I was at a crossroads. I reached the second floor of the cement building where I could either go left or right. Hmm, something tells me to go right. Yes, I'll listen to my gut. I strolled over and thought about my AP

World History teacher from ninth grade, remembering how incredibly handsome he was.

Oh, my God, I REALLY hope I have another hot history teacher. That would be perfect. Please, Universe, let me have a hot history professor. I will be able to pay attention for sure! And you bet your ass the Universe was listening, because I walked into that plain classroom witnessing a young, blue-eyed Prince Charming meets Game of Throne's Gendry. I couldn't believe my eyes. Then words flowed from his mouth in the glorious accent that is ENGLISH.

Oh…my…goodness, just writing this right now, I'm remembering the sound of his luscious English accent making music in my ears. He would speak about his Brazilian wife, and all I could think was, wow, they must be so beautiful in bed together…she is so lucky. I wonder if he teaches her history lessons on the go…

And somewhere in the middle of that internal dialogue, I learned about the Haitian Revolution. This might sound pretty boring, but I've concluded with my current romantic interest whose identity will remain anonymous that the majority of life is actually pretty boring, stereotypical, and cliché…but then, of course, it has its moments that makes you feel like you're not just another cluster of dust cruising by, but instead a floating star. And sitting in that very classroom was a boy who would later make me feel like one.

"Hey, you're in my history class, right?" Beard Boy asked (he totally knew we both were in the same history class).

"Yeah, yeah, I am," I said with a meek smile.

"Your name's Ana, right? You sit towards the middle, always asking questions," he said (he totally knew my first and last name).

"Yup. That's me, Hermione Granger." I tucked a strand of hair behind my ear.

To be honest, I don't remember if I said that because my stomach was busy growling at me to feed it or I was trying to grapple with the fact that I was mingling with a stranger instead of walking myself to Subway.

"I'm James. Nice to meet you," he said

"You too," I said. ANA, GO EAT, LEAVE HIM NOW.

"Hey, uh, you want to go grab something to eat maybe?" His thick black eyebrows perked up with hope. He was trying so hard and being so nice about it, I felt bad telling him no.

Ana's Thoughts:

But, Ana, you have a boyfriend…not just that, but he is a total stranger!

Yes, but he is in my history class.

Okay, but your mom warned you about guys in community college! They're not like high school boys. He could be a rapist.

I scanned him over. He wore Converse, jeans, a long-sleeved black shirt, and a purely innocent expression on his face. Not that rapists couldn't wear Converse, jeans, a long-sleeved black shirt, and an innocent expression, but I just didn't peg him as someone who would hurt me.

He seems harmless, Ana.

Will wouldn't like this.

So, tell Beard Boy you have a boyfriend.

"Are you even hungry?" He popped my mental civil war bubble. There was something warm about the sound of his voice, like he might've rescued abandoned cats in his spare time.

"Starving. Let's go to Subway," I said, surprised by how readily I agreed. "It's right across the street from here." Perfect. I didn't want to cross the street by myself.

One messy meatball sub and a surprise broccoli cheddar soup from him later, I subtly dropped the I-have-a-boyfriend bomb on him, which sent a rippled effect of disappointment across half his face. I say half, because the lower half was being brutally consumed by a pitch-black beard that would make any Viking jealous just looking at it. He spoke about his passion for Airsoft, and I found myself staring at the beast of his facial hair. A family of mice could live and hide in there. I could never kiss that. It must feel like kissing a goat.

Yeah, then why are you here sitting in front of him like it's a first date, Ana? Imaginary Will merged. He eyed me suspiciously, intensifying the guilt I already had from savoring the soup James bought me, which is exactly what made it feel like a date to begin with.

Will you relax, Will? I already told him I'm with you. You should be proud of me. Besides, look at that beard. I don't find him attractive. I'm allowed to have male friends.

Whatever. Just tell me in real life later.

I will, and you'll be glad you're dating someone as loyal as I am.

"It's been a while since I've gone airsofting. What about you, what's your passion?" He pointed his sub in my direction.

"Me? Writing. I want to be a national bestselling author," I said with a confident smirk, as my imaginary fight dissipated.

A smile spread across his face, even underneath that beard, making me squirm a little in my seat. "That's amazing. Really amazing, Ana."

***

"So, you left this Will kid for that guy?" Jacob probed, thrusting me back to the present and our Staples surroundings. The employee who was putting away boxes hadn't left yet. In fact, he was closer to us, and I was ninety-nine percent sure he was also listening to my story.

"No, not exactly, but goddammit, exactly what I didn't want to happen happened!"

"Explain."

"Well, we would have lunch together every Tuesday and Thursday after history class, and we just got pretty close, like I would vent to him about everything, and I liked how no matter what was happening, I knew I'd be seeing him at 11:05 AM. A nice constant, you know?"

"Yeah." Jacob nodded.

"I don't know. He just kind of became my counselor. Except he had a really big freaking crush on me. It got to a point where I felt like I had Will as my actual boyfriend and James as my school boyfriend. Even though we obviously never did anything, and I almost always paid for my own food."

"Uh-huh, so then…"

"Then that freaking Lizzie McGuire cliché started happening to me which I was livid about!" I slammed my hand on the arm rest.

"Which cliché?"

"The one where you have a boyfriend and a sweet best friend who likes you and always listens to your problems, and then you and your boyfriend start having problems, so you go to vent about it to your caring best friend who has an even bigger crush on you now that he knows you so well, and eventually you wind up with him!"

"So, you did fuck him." Jacob, who'd been on the edge of his seat, sat back.

"No! No, Jacob. No, I did not. I am not that kind of girl. Actually, when I felt like we were getting way too close, I came up with the excuse that I was going to start using Dade's gym during that time, so we would be parting ways, and he was all, "Well, Ana, you have definitely been the highlight of my life lately," making me feel even more guilty. Still, I was glad to separate from him, because James would always happen to text me when I would be with Will, and then Will would say, "Oh, my God, you're going to leave a diamond for a rock just like my ex-girlfriend did."

Now, Will might have very well been the diamond in this situation, but his rollercoaster-like depression no longer seemed worth the glittering moments we had. Yeah, wonderful, you're a deep-ass artist, but if we go more than two days without seeing each other it's like our relationship has struck an iceberg, and I don't really care about the value of the diamond, because it isn't going to save me from drowning…it's actually going to drag me down. But a rock would save me, a sturdy enough rock that I could take a rest on, set me straight during my Titanic hell state of being. A rock with light brown eyes and mile-long eyelashes, and now a beard that had been shaved off, revealing an attractive face to vent to after all.

CHAPTER 18
Suicidal Thought Territory

I could no longer take this anymore—this stress, anxiety, and constant tension in my entire body, the ache in my ribs, the pressure on my chest. I felt like I didn't know my mom anymore. We couldn't relate. And Adam? Adam was no longer in jail, but still in rehab.

God, I was so angry every Sunday, waking up knowing I had to do chores while my parents got to see Adam. I refused to do them. I would cry most of the day instead. I needed the opportunity to release my emotional tension, then mend the pieces back together. But I hadn't been getting enough sleep lately because of having to wake up every day early as hell for a fucking mini term I was required to take on how to be a better student. Making quota at work was becoming difficult. Some days I woke up determined to break up with Will for good, and other days, I felt like I could not endure another moment without him.

I want to kill myself.

The thought slithered into the landscape that is my mind, like a garden snake emerging from a rose bush. I want to kill myself. It became a siren wailing in the back of my head, but the lights were off. I glanced at myself in the mirror of my bathroom. I could not see myself. The strong Ana I knew was nowhere to be found. I saw bags of blue sorrow under my tired eyes, untamed tendrils of impending doom, each split end of my curls a metaphor for my inner state of being.

I want to kill myself.

The strong voice that kept me going had faded like the end of a good pop song. I was just too tired, drained in every way possible.

"Anaregina!" My stressed-out mom called me.

"Sííí…" I meekly replied, staring at the mirror.

"Come over here," she called from the living room.

We were going to have a family meeting. Concerning me. Even though this shouldn't have been about me. It was about my dad's well-being, I was not the one with cancer. Me, I could just kill myself.

Jesus, no, how could you think that, Ana?

How could you be so selfish?

"I'm coming, Mom," I croaked. I brought my face closer to the mirror as if I was making sure it was really me staring back. I trudged to my living room and plopped myself on the couch facing both of my parents.

I felt like the exhaustion was pulling the skin off of my face. Like at any moment my skull was going to collapse in on itself. I was exhausted from the anticipation of my brother's return. I was depressed that my father wasn't getting any better. Despite all this, life wanted me to go on.

I arrived at the dining table and sat at a chair.

"How are you?" My mom asked. She looked impatient, as she crossed her legs together and started to play with her hands. I hated the fact that that was probably exactly how she was as a therapist for other families. Minus the impatience.

"I'm fine," I lied.

"Really, how are you?" My dad asked. He looked undeservingly worried about me.

I just want to die.

I gulped back the truth. "I'm okay, Dad," I said. Maybe I could believe my own lie if I said it enough times.

"Anaregina, I understand that this hasn't been easy for you," he said.

"That is true," I agreed. I focused on Jodie, sitting beneath my feet, wagging her tail periodically. I petted her softly.

"It hasn't been easy for us either," he said. I couldn't help but detect a little anger in his voice. My head shot up to look at him. "Mama has been going through a lot of stress at work, now that people have left certain positions, and she's been doing everything she can for Adam, for me, and for you."

"I understand," I said. That still didn't change the fact that I was depressed.

"But you don't seem to be okay…" Dad's eyebrows raised.

"I mean, there's nothing in my life that is happening to me exactly. I am healthy, and I am here, still employed and enrolled in school," I said, crossing my arms. What more did they want from me?

"Exactly, and she still isn't happy." My mom sounded a little exasperated, looking to my dad for support. I remember a friend of my mom once told me that having a therapist for a mother is one of the most difficult things to endure.

"And you are?" I hissed.

"Yes, I am," she said.

"Really?" I said. Shut-up, Ana, you're just going to make things worse. "Okay, Mom." I laughed. A cloud of silence lingered over our heads for a moment.

"I know I am okay. I know that right now, exactly everything is supposed to be happening exactly as it should. I've been taking your father to Mike, his reiki. He saw Suzanne who helped me him a lot, he's been able to talk a lot more to Adam, and Adam is the best he's ever been. I really feel his inner change, like this experience is turning him into the man he has been meant to be all along…" she rambled.

All I could think was yeah, but I don't get to see him. And yeah, fucking right, Mom, you're not okay. The other day you told me you felt like we were all fictional characters in your life, and that a part of you is dying, a part of you is in jail, and that you control what happens to everyone. I don't remember what she said about me. I debated whether my mom needed to see a psychiatrist, and then I realized that this was just her way of getting through the pain. It reminded me of the times we fought so much to the point where she claimed, "This isn't real, this is all a dream," making me more upset. Talk about denial. At this point I was thinking about Will, wavering between feeling angry at him for still being depressed and wanting to give him a blowjob. Not because I was horny, but because at this precise moment, I would rather give a blowjob over this. I called it "The Blowjob Mood."

"Are you listening to your mother, Anaregina?" Dad asked, underlying anger hissing in between syllables.

"Yes," I muttered.

"I just don't feel like you're okay," Dad said. "Don't you understand this isn't easy for me, Anaregina?"

"I'm sorry, Dad," I mumbled. Hello, guilt in my gut.

"I wish I didn't have this cancer. I hate that I can't help around the house anymore, that I am tired all the time, that I am causing more stress on your mom's shoulders and seeing you this way hurts me more. I feel like there's nothing I can do about it. Like I am a burden. It's exhausting…really exhausting," he said, anger dying down a bit with his words.

Me on the other hand…

"And I feel so bad about that, Papá, but I know if it was any of us, you would be taking care of us just the same. While technically, yes, it is a burden, it doesn't matter, it's for love. So, you're not a burden. Don't say that. I'm…" I took a deep breath to suppress a wave of tears. "I'm exhausted too."

"But you have everything you need," my mom reasoned.

Was she crazy? Did she think that all I needed in this life was food and air and shelter? I was losing my father! I never got to see Adam!

I glared at her. "Dad is sick, and I can't see my own fucking brother during all of this, because of some stupid fucking rule that place doesn't bother to fix. Do you think that's having everything I need?" I snapped, then felt bad for it. I felt impotent—a whiny little girl not getting her way in life.

"That's going to be over soon," my dad said. "And you know why they have that rule. It's not against you personally."

"I know, Papá, but it still isn't fair. You guys leave every Sunday, and I'm left alone at home to clean, and I don't even have energy to do that. Then Mama gets mad at me and just expects more of me, and sometimes I feel like I can't. And I don't think she's really okay," I paused to glance at her. "I'm not saying that in an accusing way, Mom. I'm just telling you what I see and what I feel," I said, breathlessly.

"That's your anxiety speaking," she said. She crossed her arms. "Am I really not okay?" she asked my dad. "Because I think I am. I read my passages, I meditate, I still make time for myself, but now she's making me question whether I am actually okay or not."

"How… How can you…" I said. How can you be okay? Don't you see what's going on? I wanted to yell. Tears boiled in my temples, the engine for their heat churning in my stomach. None of this felt real to me now. Maybe I was a character in her fucking book after all.

"Xiomara, let's put ourselves in her shoes. I know it's really difficult for you on Sundays when you go see him, but you have to understand that it's out of your control. Just like my cancer. This is the hardest thing I've ever had to experience, but I am fighting it the best I can, Anaregina."

"It's still not fair," I cried. My inner child stepped up to the stage. None of this was fair! My mom visibly tensed up. I was messing up her "okay-ness." I wanted to be a crab and live at the bottom of the ocean, have my one little breathing hole. I wanted that so bad right now.

"I know, mi vida, I know." Dad reached his hand out to me. I felt a tiny bit better.

"Have you been taking your anxiety pills?" Mom asked, sitting there in her classic therapist Mom pose.

"Just a crumb every now and then," I sighed. I hated taking them. I never liked a pill governing my state of being. Not if I could help it.

"Well, it's there for whenever you need it," my dad said.

"I know," I sighed again. I wanted to feel better, I really did, but… "I'm going to go now." I excused myself and got up to walk to the bathroom. My dad looked like he had something more to say, while my mom just sat there looking indifferent. Jodie shadowed my footsteps, worried about me. I locked myself up in the bathroom and let out a huge rush of air.

It was one in the morning, and I had to get up in the next four hours, so I started straightening my hair. It took about two hours to straighten, then I painted my nails crimson red, distracting my suicidal thoughts temporarily. I glanced at myself in the mirror. Still didn't see my reflection staring back. The girl staring at me was pretty, sure, but unfixable. Applying an oil to my hair to make it glossier, I was simultaneously me and not me. Not-Me walked herself to the kitchen, unafraid of the cockroaches that never ceased to cruise the cupboards at night and stood in front of the knife block.

I wasn't even thinking about it. Mechanically, I grabbed the carving knife I had only ever used to cut chicken or a steak. I want to kill myself, the siren blared in my head. I sat down, criss-cross applesauce on my couch, holding the knife in my hand. It was both heavy and light, and I felt so strange looking at this from this perspective. Where my skin was the potential meat. My cat, Gin, left the room without making a sound. Uncaring beast.

This isn't me, I thought.

Lightly, I traced the outline of my foot with the edge of the knife, and then I let it glide across my ankle to the top of my calf, and back in a circular motion, like it was a figure skater and my skin was the frozen ice. This isn't me…

I slowly applied more and more pressure a couple of inches away from my ankle, making my skin tingle like the famous 5 Gum commercial even as the edge of the knife left that spot. The moment I felt an eighth of an ounce of pain, I would drag the knife back into another circle motion on my leg. I inspected the knife like it might grow a pair of eyes or something. Not me... not me…

The sound of light footsteps disrupted the silence, and instinctively, I hid the kitchen utensil behind the couch cushion.

"Anaregina?" my dad mumbled. "What are you doing awake right now? Son las tres de la mañana."

"I…I couldn't sleep," I stammered. He was in his usual PJs—a white shirt and plaid blue PJ pants.

"Why not?" He leaned against the wall, looking concerned.

"Dad, I think I'm…I think I'm depressed," I said. Suddenly, a load lifted off of my ribs. He sat next to me and laced an arm around my shoulder. Looking at me without saying one word, I knew he understood me completely. My dad knew depression all too well. "I feel like I'm not enough, like I'm useless, like…like I should just go," I said. I didn't have the energy to cry anymore.

He embraced me in his arms and stroked my hair. I squeezed him as tight as I could without hurting him. I inhaled the scent of my father's skin, soft soap, and aftershave. Like light rain after a storm.

"You are enough. Love yourself," he said, squeezing my shoulders.

When I exhaled, a familiar voice returned to my mind. You…just need…to...breathe, Ana.

And so I did.

CHAPTER 19
My Chickens! My Chickens!

6/1/14

Dear Adam
Life is happening to you
Like it happened to me.

So, grow, learn, grow strong
Mold your fibers of your being
Into sympathetic strength.

And free your mind on your own
Because when you do
Then you'll truly be free.

~ Your sister who loves you very much – Anaregina

Spoken like a true soul who was once trapped, not in a jail cell, but a psychiatric ward. It seemed fitting in a way, that one sibling would get institutionalized in a hospital for misdirected teens (I believed, truly believed, I was an angel that descended from Heaven to protect my best friend, Rachel, and I could morph into a demon—a clear metaphor of my repressed, tumultuous feelings towards my fifteen-year-old life at the time) while the other sibling would become a jailbird for seven months, humming the melody of injustice at its finest. Yeah, my parents had a handful, I know. But that's what happens when two artists (both my parents are writers, and my mom is talented with painting and drawing as well) marry—you get emotional, creative creatures bending the strings of normalcy one word, or in Adam's case, tune at a time.

***

2/4/2015

Dear Ana,

Yeah, I remember that summer in Mexico, and I'm still glad you listened. Ha, ha! I think what I was trying to do was get you to play an instrument in the future, but I'm happy you broadened your horizons. You'll always have great taste in music if you listen to artists with soul no matter what the genre or style. It's great that you found someone who is also interested in talented bands. I have several "Tool" albums and I even saw them live once at the Bank Atlantic Center. "Nine Inch Nails" is also good. That style of industrial music was very original when it first came out, and to this day, it's still popular. If you check the CD case that says "Metallica" you'll find "Undertow," "Aenema," and "Lateralus" by Tool. I've always thought of them as the "Pink Floyd" of our era, and another band that started around the same time that's also very cool is the "Smashing Pumpkins." Check them out when you can. I miss you so very much too but don't worry, because my lawyers are doing all they can, so I can be allowed to leave and visit you at home for the weekend. I'm already up to 68 points as of this Sunday the 5th and at 90, I'm allowed to spend Saturday and Sunday at home, but first we must be patient while the wheels of bureaucracy get everything turned out.

I know how you feel in regards to the emptiness in your heart. I also have realized just how much you and I are bound by love and understanding of life. Let me assure you that when I return, all the time we have spent apart will be erased and we can begin to build an even better relationship. Going through hell and back has made me realize that there is no one but you who knows me and comes closest to understanding me. You've seen and been there for me through all the best of times and the tough times. I will always be your brother and forever protect and love you from anyone or anything.

I know how difficult things have been for you, especially caring for Papá and helping Mama, but don't worry. I'll be there soon to complete the family and do all I can. I'm already halfway done with this program and I think I'll be coming home sometime in March. I'm doing all I can to speed up the time. I do think I'm doing well, and yes, I've definitely changed for the better. The only thing on my mind is making up for all the things that have happened and paying off my debts.

I hope you're doing great in college and still enjoying your job. I haven't heard much about your boyfriend Will, but if he listens to bands like Tool and NIN, he must be a good guy and I look forward to meeting him. I especially can't wait to be home again and see you, Papá, Mama, and all of our pets. I wonder if they'll recognize me. I'm pretty sure they will but still. Hopefully my presence will help Papá's recovery and lighten everyone's mood. I have ideas on how to fight against his enemy, like eating organic foods and getting him to do things which will brighten his demeanor. I've been practicing how to sing and play guitar at the same time very well like Jimi Hendrix so that's something I plan to do for him on days he feels like the pain is too much and on days where he needs some soul. I'll continue to write to you while I'm in here. Just send a letter by mail and I'll do the same.

I love you so very much,

Your brother,

Adam Frias

I decided to wear my red dress with a hipster pattern strewn across it and black eyeliner top and bottom! I felt like a gorgeous minx, and of course I absolutely had to document this on my Snapchat story, because otherwise the look would go to waste. I posed for my selfie in my parents' bathroom, then applied the filter that made your skin glow a sort of orangey hue, a character from The Simpsons, basically. That has always been my favorite one. Just smooths out allll your imperfections!

I opened Will's snap.

You look great.

In his selfie, he had a closed lip smile, which I loved.

Today, my family would finally, finally, FINALLY be coming together in our own home. With our own kitchen utensils, our own cups to drink from, our own chairs to sit on as we loved each other outside the confinements of jail and the hospital. No cancer, no rehab, no courtroom date thing shit, no jail, no hospital, no problem! JUST A NORMAL FAMILY. You could only imagine my elation! And my parents! Oh, my parents had sparklers lit in their eyes. Adam would be back! His first day home, and guess what, motherfucker (sorry, I don't even know why I'm cursing at you, beloved reader)? WE WERE THROWING A PARTY!

Yes, that's right, somehow someone managed to detach me from my unhealthy relationship to celebratory selfies on my Snap story, and now I was sitting at the dining room table observing my live, physical brother sitting right across from me (he was beginning to look like a hologram behind the dirty glass at jail), as the delicious scents of Domino's pizza wafted into my nose.

"This feels so surreal that you are actually here," I told Adam.

"I know, I feel pretty surreal being here," he said, smiling.

"I can see that," I said. Everything about Adam was different. Everything. The main thing being that he went from having his wild, clavicle length hair shaved right off to a buzz cut.

"It's good to finally meet you, man," Will said with a genuine smile. He placed his hand on my knee, feeding off of my glee.

Mama emerged from the kitchen brandishing a stack of red Solo cups for all of us, which were basically Adam, Will, Mama, Papá, and Adam's best friends, John, Larry, and Sam. Oh, and me. Mama was glowing.

Just as I felt eager for the pizza to make its way into my mouth, I felt eager for my dad to return from the bathroom, because while cognitively, I knew we were all in the same house, I needed to actually witness the four of us together (plus company) with my own eyes, all of us physically together. I needed to relish the moment for at least three eternities. You'll never value family time so much as when you're torn apart the way my family was.

Finally, my dad strolled into the dining room while I served myself my second slice of pepperoni pizza. It seemed as though he'd left his cancer in some room next door to us, because he too glowed with happiness.

"Don't eat all the pizza without me!" He laughed a joyful, heartily laugh. "I'm well enough to have some."

"Of course, Papá," Adam said, reaching for a plate. "What do you want?"

"The one with everything." Papá smiled like a young boy at a children's party.

Adam served him two slices, and I just sat there taking in the totally normal scene, the beauty of its simplicity.

"Just one," Papá said, taking a seat next to him.

"Oh, yeah, my bad." Adam took the second slice and placed it on his plate. It was insane how much had drastically changed in the last few months, but in this moment, everything was exactly the same as it was before. This was my family. All here. Free. Eating pizza together. I squeezed Will's hand, and he smiled at me. I don't think I could've been any happier than at this moment.

"We wanted to throw you a big party," Mama told Adam.

As soon as she had mentioned having one, I imagined a big "Welcome Home Adam" banner, balloons engulfing the scene, and all, but my brother shook his head slowly. "I don't think I would've liked that. Sorry, Mama."

"I know." She smiled and stroked his head.

"Man, this pizza is great!" Johnny exclaimed, sliding the slice right into his large mouth. Despite his famed gluttony, this boy looked like four extremely long toothpicks attached to a thin trunk.

"I know, right?" I gushed, as though I'd baked the pizza myself. Larry nodded his head in agreement, and Sam was so quiet that I literally forgot his presence at times.

"I still think Mike's is better," Adam said. His voice sounded as if he'd aged ten years, and the way he looked at everything reminded me of the way a pet behaves when it's in a new place for the very first time. He was definitely adjusting.

"Hey, for real Adam. It's so nice to have you back," my dad said, sounding like he'd lost ten years of age. He placed his hand on Adam's shoulder, and I held back fresh tears.

"It's so nice to be back here," Adam said. "I mean, it feels a little weird still to be honest, but everything is so much better."

"If you knew how badly we wanted this," Mama said.

"UH-HUH," I added.

Adam's eyes glazed for a split second, then his smile infected everyone at the table. I was too exultant to have thoughts, until I reminded myself to take a moment and be grateful. For their presence and for our inhuman resilience and luck it took to get here. But the pizza was too good, and Adam had rehab stories to deliver. We reminisced over memories of Mexico when somehow, the topic of chickens came up.

"Oh, man, at Help Is Here, we keep these chickens in their coops, and one time this possum came and terrorized the chickens, which was a problem, because my group was in charge of keeping them in check, since their eggs are used for the kitchen. So, my friend was getting really pissed off about it, because he really likes taking care of the chickens, and every time we'd catch the possum terrorizing the chickens, we always arrived too late to do anything about it. The possum would either leave or play dead where we couldn't see it, and this was like seriously aggravating the shit out of my friend, because he just really, really liked the chickens and wanted them to be in peace. So, every time the possum came, he would just lose his shit and start blowing up, yelling like, 'WHAT THE FUCK, MAN! WHERE THE FUCK IS THIS POSSUM GOING? I SWEAR TO GOD…LEAVE OUR MOTHERFUCKING CHICKENS ALONE!' And I would try not to laugh and just be like, 'Hey man, calm down, they're alright,' but the dude would just have this insane look in his eyes and defend the chickens like they were his life. Until one day, I don't know what happened exactly, but somehow, he managed to get ahold of the possum, and he literally beat it to death, just yelling at it in defense of his precious chickens."

We laughed, even though I felt sorry for the possum, but the amazing thing was, I could feel the underlying tension of the story behind my brother's charming way of telling it.

"That kid obviously had a lot of anger in his life, but the possum paid the price."

My mom, being the epitome of psychotherapy, commented, "I take it he went to see a psychologist after that?"

"Oh, of course." Adam threw his hands in the air. "I just remember him crying, 'My chickens! My chickens!'"

***

Will and Adam's friends left soon after the pizza. My dad went to sleep, because I guess the excitement had taken a toll on him. I was sitting on the beige couch in the living room. Adam was in the kitchen with my mom. So, what happened to him? my mind repeated over and over again. What was the truth of the entire situation that had landed my brother in jail for seven months? I sat there pondering until something prompted me to get off my ass and go find out.

Adam and my mom had migrated to the dining room, and I joined them, sitting in the head honcho seat at the end where an enormous painting of a tanned woman holding flowers watched over me. I interrupted their conversation like a typical Miami driver cuts off another driver in the street without remorse. Sorry, but I'd been waiting way too long for this.

"So, Adam…" I prepped him. "Now that we aren't talking through a telephone that's being monitored… Can we know what really happened the day you got arrested?" I asked.

His whole vibe changed. He wasn't comfortable talking about it, but I needed to know, and his body language said he was going to anyway. "Uh, yeah, sure," he mumbled.

My mom crossed her arms. I know she wanted to know this piece of information just as much as I did, but at the same time she would've rather had her forehead pinned to a wall than to relive that day.

"Well...uh...what do you want to know exactly?" Adam asked.

"Like everything," I said cautiously.

"Okay, well…I was trying to help Skyler out, and this guy decided to lie about what really happened, and then I got arrested," he said. His arms were crossed. "That's basically it."

"Okay. But like…" I paused. "What are the details?"

He let out a heavy sigh. We were such opposites of each other. Whereas I splurge on details, so much that my last boyfriend even told me I talked too much, at which point I developed an insecurity I never had before (but screw him, right?). Adam was as ambiguous as a leaf frog camouflaged in leaves.

"Well, that day, I went to the dog park with her. We went with her dog, and then when I took her back to her house, I spoke with her boyfriend who was pissed at me and trying to start a fight, so I just told him to calm down, then the both of us left the house…" His gaze met the table, then the ground.

And she was obviously cheating on him with you, I mentally told him. "And then?"

"Nothing," he grumbled. "I went to band practice with her and we drank a little."

My mom shook her head and sighed.

"And then?"

"And then, he texted her two hours later saying he called the police and told them someone broke into the house."

"Which wasn't true?" I interrupted.

"Exactly, that was a lie. He was just trying to get me back."

"But what about the tire iron?" I asked. I remembered the charge was specifically for breaking in and entering with a weapon.

"I had that in the back seat of my car to protect myself in case of anything. I always do. Most guys have something like that in their trunk."

Fair enough. I knew that Will happened to have a bat in his trunk. "Alright, so the police were there when you got there…"

"Yes, and that's when they arrested me," he said, annoyed. His countenance was a mix of regret and torment. I knew I should've stopped peppering him with questions but given the nosy sister I am, I couldn't resist.

"How did that go?"

"What do you mean? The officer was this white guy who kept yelling at me while he put me in handcuffs then drove away. I knew there was nothing to say to make the situation better. I knew the best thing to do was just to remain silent."

"And what did Skyler say? Why didn't she talk to them and explain the situation?"

"She did, she just didn't say enough."

"How did you feel while it was happening?"

"I felt scared," he said, staring at the table as though he was transported to that very moment, that very day.

I dropped the Spanish Inquisition towards him, now that I could see the pain reflected beneath his eyes, behind his corneas, right through the lens. He'd had enough of the past, and honestly, so had I.

3/4/15

Dear Adam,

I just got out of therapy with Tyronne right now, which was somewhat helpful, but I don't know. I still feel emotionally clogged, or emotionally exhausted, I should say. You know I love Papá and want to be as supportive as I can, but after a while, it just takes a toll on you. Just seeing him sick and noticing the pounds melt off of him breaks my fucking heart, but this past weekend, despite how surreal it all was, it felt amazing, because I was afraid that the four of us would never be together again. *You don't understand how grateful and happy I felt you were back. I can't wait until you are back permanently. I'm getting really sick of the waiting game as I'm sure you are too but it's FINALLY coming to a close.

**This is really, really sucky timing, but for a while I've been desperate to get away from everything even if it's for two days, and I'm finally getting that chance this weekend from Friday to Monday. Barney and a couple of his best friends invited me to go to Lafayette State Park, which is between Gainesville and Tallahassee (7 hours away), and I made the decision to go. I feel really bad that I won't be able to see you, but I hope you understand and hope you can forgive me. I will see you next weekend, and we will spend time together and talk and just have a good time. I'm thankful that you can come every weekend now. I feel like it will make the transition from there to here much easier, and besides once you come back, we will make up for all of the lost time! We really, really missed you and need you, so just having you back for a little while turned Mama and Papá into different people. There was light in their eyes I hadn't seen in a while, and they looked five years younger. You mean a lot to them and me. I love you very much and I know you'll understand.

Love, your favorite sister, Anaregina Frias :) <3

*I feel like I didn't show it as much, but I was

**Excuse my grammar errors

CHAPTER 20
The Trip

Acid is not for everyone, let me tell you.

Just kidding, I didn't go on that kind of trip! As aforementioned in my letter to Adam, I got my wish of getting away with my friends. I suppose my suicidal soul was communicating with Barney's intuitive soul, and they came upon mutual understanding to go to the quietest place on Earth: Lafayette State Park.

"Guys, we need to get kitchen utensils," I said, mostly to Barney, since he was the pack leader of the friend group. Although sometimes it was Ted. But I'm also kind of the alpha, because we always do what I want to do. Anyway, we were wandering the aisles of BJ's, hunting and gathering food for the trip. Barney, Saul, and Will were so excited, they were behaving like baby monkeys on Adderall, not that I have a clue how baby monkeys on Adderall would act, but I can only imagine.

"Shit! You're right!" Barney examined our massive shopping cart of mostly junk food. I felt like the mother of the group, coming up with the sensible ideas. Slowly, it dawned on me that I was the one who'd be in charge of cleanliness, making sure everyone was well-fed and tucked in at night with a classic Ana bedtime story. What I wasn't expecting, however, was the giant SHIT that Will's growing depression took on me.

It actually began to escalate while we were at BJ's. I don't even remember what the hell we were arguing about, probably something stupid, but then he started getting all dark for no fucking reason, and I had to just sit there and take it like Han Solo convincing my son to join the freaking Light Side (if you've seen the movie, you get what I'm saying, and if you haven't, well then you're welcome for not spoiling it for you).

"So, you're just going to stay like this?" I said with a gentle, caring but also what-the-fuck-really? tone.

"Ana, look I'm trying, okay?" he said in the most depressing, dejected tone ever.

We huddled near the Weight Watchers treats display stand, so completely enveloped in our fight, we didn't notice the woman standing right behind us tentatively reaching in for the chocolate muffins. She wore such an awkward expression, I almost wanted to burst out laughing mid-fight. I love the juxtaposition of funny moments occurring in the middle of steamy, tense fights. Oh, yeah, my fights were steamy. This little BJ's fight with Will was just a drop to the storm that was going to shatter all hell later.

"Okay, Will," I said, dropping it.

He'd been distant and dark with me since the moment I saw him today. On an intuitive level I felt as though he was growing jealous of Barney, but even more so with his best friend, Saul. More on that later. Let's fast forward to the next day, when I was suffering hard core anxiety from the moment I woke up. My brain was a mash-up of thoughts between cancer...death…depression...anxiety…hello, do you have a minute for gay rights? No? Alright, you have a great fucking day! and rewwwinndd. The entire time at work I could feel my pulse quicken on the side of my temple, as though I'd somehow grown a heart with an irregular heartbeat there. And then I faced the thing I loathed more than cockroaches…

ALIENNA HEALTH INSURANCE.

OH. MY. GOD.

I can't even type this from how HEATED I am remembering this horrible, horrible health insurance. Let me give you some context to the story before divulging into a full-page rant on these motherfuckers!

I needed health insurance. I got it. With my dad, actually. It cost a whopping two-hundred bucks a month. One month into my insurance, they lost my freaking account or whatever the fuck it's called! Okay. Fine. Whatever, everyone makes mistakes. I was sure it would be fixed in no time. Optimistic me cheered on. Meanwhile in reality, I was paying hundred-dollar therapy sessions while having to pay the damn two-hundred-dollar bullshit insurance. I spent a total of SIX hours on the phone with these people and got NOTHING solved. AT ALL.

Just take this as an advisory warning…insurance companies are a metaphor for adult life fucking with you to test your newly acquired status. I thought I would enjoy venting about this, but I detest it so much I don't. Fuck Humanna. Fuck it so hard. Fuck it so hard, it bleeds. You call. You repeat all your personal info at least four times, and they send you to like six different departments which all make you wait at least ten minutes before anyone answers. Then…the annoyed, clueless person you speak with does not give ONE FLYING FUCK about your problem. Just when I got the people who might be able to help me with finding my own goddamned insurance, the call…fucking…dropped. After ONE hour of being transferred, being put on hold, accumulating to the other FIVE hours prior to this last sacred attempt. I think I actually felt steam come out of every orifice in my body. The worst part was that by that point I was beginning to give attitude to the people, because I just couldn't contain it anymore, so I really felt like they might've "accidentally hung up" on me. I imagined terrible things happening to this manipulative, money-sucking company, my first hope being that someday I would publish my true feelings about them somewhere, somehow. And goddamn it, I am finally doing it! I'd never been so angry in my life to the point where a really weird, eerie calm just swept over me, and I felt strangely at peace. But not in a good way. I couldn't explain it.

"Oh, yeah, insurance companies are awful like that. That's why people go postal," my therapist told me sessions later. Yes, that was it—I had been feeling pre-postal.

"I don't know how you deal with that," Will said. We were in his car parked outside of his house.

"I tried. I tried, that's all I can fucking say. I tried, I'm just going to let it go and enjoy this well-deserved trip," I smiled. I probably looked like the chick from Gone Girl at this point.

Inhale. Exhale. Inhale. Exhale.

Next day, Barney and Saul were outside my door at 6:30 AM while I was still packing my things, heart racing like I was in the middle of a swimming race. Is this even real right now? Am I really going on a trip?

Barney drove like a maniac without a head and missing appendages. To make things worse, his car was falling apart, growls emanating from the car making me fear for my life and pray to the Universe, but I enjoyed the thrill ride nonetheless. I think we all had that dual emotion in ourselves, as Barney drove the monster on wheels. We arrived at his girlfriend's house in one piece, then had to wait for her to finish getting ready. Ten minutes, she promised.

An hour later, we were back on the road headed towards Lafayette. Morning greeted us in the friendliest way: the birds were chirping and the sun streamed through the clouds, making the green in the trees glitter.

"Ana, I really think you have high blood pressure," Will told me as we were leaving Marie's house.

"Well, that's great of you to tell me."

Why tell your girlfriend she has high blood pressure and make her worry, causing a higher blood pressure? Why not just tell her reassuring, calming words like, "Hey, beautiful, there's nothing to be anxious about. We are going on vacation!"

But no, some guys could be true idiots. Albeit, us girls can be complicated too but still damn it. I retreated from the conversation Barney,

Marie, Saul, and Will were having until we got to the drive-thru of Starbucks.

"I have to pee," I announced. I left the car and dashed to the bathroom, feeling self-conscious about showing half my stomach in the cropped shirt I was wearing, and even more self-conscious that I was holding in my stress tears. I had to pull myself together.

"Listen to me, Ana," I whispered to myself while staring intently into the mirror.

"You are okay, okay? I know you're angry, and you're scared, and the high blood pressure comment ticked you off but, Will didn't mean it in a bad way. Just relax. You're going to be fine! Let it go. You're okay. You're okay. You're okay. I promise. It's going to be fine. Just have fun!" The anger left my expression, but I could still see fear embedded in my little brown irises.

"Just enjoy the time with your friends!" I got myself to smile and breathe again. Okay, I had this. I strolled out of that bathroom like Starbucks became my runway, and I was its supermodel selling self-confidence. I got back in the car and felt the joy that came with being in college and going on a road trip with only your friends, no parents. Marie was driving, so I felt safe, safe enough to nap, and let my demons rest.

When I woke up, we'd arrived in Lafayette, and I was stunned by the silence that embraced me. We parked in front of a cute, safe-looking motel with a small pool across from it. It was two stories tall, and our room had two queen-sized beds. The warm yellow walls gave it a homey feel, and the beds were so comfy, Will and I had sex in front of our friends three times! Just kidding, we wanted to, but it felt too awkward to actually follow through even though we were beneath the covers.

"Guys, let's go explore this place!" Barney suggested.

"Alright, yeah dude, let's go walking in the forest," Saul replied.

We left the motel, armed with enough granola bars to feed a small elementary school. The silence in the forest was precious. I could hear every leaf fall to the ground, the fluttering of a bird's wings from a far distance, and Will found a deer footprint! The majesty of the tall forest trees swallowed us whole, and I finally felt at peace while gazing at a still pond in front of us. Sunsets were celebrated by nature here. Every creature had a part in making it known. I stood on a handstand to view it upside down as well.

"You better not let me fall!" I told Will, as he grabbed my legs.

"I won't." I heard the smile in his voice.

"This is so nice," I mumbled, all my blood rushing to my head.

Marie did the same with Barney, and I noticed how incredibly loud we sounded in this place, like whispers were shouts, and light steps were giant stomps. Night eventually collected the beautiful pieces of the day, and we returned from our expedition, tired and hungry. I made Nutella and peanut butter sandwiches for everyone, excited to sleep in the comfortable bed. Yet a gnawing sensation in my stomach grew as my friends quieted their voices, and it was just Will and me.

"Ana, I have to tell you something."

"What is it Will?" I asked. I knew it wasn't good from the sound of his voice.

He went on to tell me how horribly depressed he was, how he could barely contain himself, and now like me, he was also feeling physical symptoms of depression. I realized suddenly, that together, Will and I were like the blind leading the blind.

"You need help, Will. I know you think you don't need anyone's help, but I really think you should see a therapist."

He sighed. "I think you're right." I could see him feeling better after our talk, but me? I felt worse. A full on stomachache ensued.

"What's wrong?" He probed.

How do I nicely say, damn-it-Will-I-was-finally-starting-to-feel-better-but-then-you-dumped-your-shit-on-me-which-feels-so-unfair-because-my shit is so muchfuckingworsethanyourshit, AND I feel like your mom right now, or your wife of fifty years?

Instead, I made an analogy about my plate being full, that I could barely, barely handle it, and that right now my plate got even more full than before when all I wanted was to have fun, relax, and let go. He apologized for not putting himself in my shoes at this moment and ended up feeling worse. Making me feel worse! Ugh, it was like a never-ever-ending cycle. I gave up any attempt to lighten the situation and just let out what I was truly feeling. It was a mix of pain, awe, and beauty from earlier that night when we were on our way back to the motel, and we stopped the car in the middle of the road just to gaze up at the stars. I had never ever seen so many stars in my life. It took me back to the time when I went camping in Fish Eating Creek with my dad, and my brother and I were able to see all the shy stars emerge with the others.

"It was so fucking beautiful," I said, as tears streamed down my cheeks. The air conditioner hummed softly, as I went back there with my mind. It was like witnessing a whole other galaxy, a place so mysterious and holy, nothing on this Earth could compare with that sort of raw beauty.

"I think…" I said, closing my eyes. "I think when my dad's time comes—you know, whenever that is—that this place is exactly where he is going to go. And this is where I'll come to see him."

CHAPTER 21
The Ana-tific Method

1. How much stress does it take for the subject, Anaregina Frias, to ingest one Alprazolam (Xanax)?

2. Drawing from extensive recorded data consisting of the following stressors: her boyfriend felt like committing suicide the night after she established where she would like to see her father in the afterlife, she accidentally swam in a pond with septic water (to say I was now swimming in shit was both figurative and literal), and during the five-hour ride back to Miami, she endured the tension leading up to her suicidal boyfriend proclaiming, "I think it's the best thing for me to leave you." All this was followed by a plea to stay together and an uncertain promise that he would try and get help. We also found evidence of her anger regarding her brother's absence from home, but hey, at least she got to pet a cow named Darcy and cross that off her bucket list!

3. If these stressors are combined in one weekend, then Anaregina will take a crumb of her expired anxiety pill, which will have no effect whatsoever, leading her to ingest a quarter of her father's Alprazolam.

4. By placing Anaregina Frias in the shower alone with her thoughts and scrubbing off any septic shit germs that may still cling to her skin, she will experience the worst anxiety she has ever experienced in her lifespan. Including, but not limited to heart palpitations, sweating profusely (yes, even in the shower), trembling like a frightened Chihuahua, chest pain, nausea, numbness and tingling in all her appendages, and dizziness. In the experiment, her confused, startled brother asked what was wrong as she let out a short scream into a towel and found herself planted on the couch admitting all of her concerns to her parents. "I'm afraid that if I break up with him, he'll kill himself!" In the best interest of their daughter, they tried

to soothe her with calming words but even this was not enough, as words cannot penetrate the unbalanced brain chemistry as a pill can. The father chops up one-fourth of Alprazolam and gives it to her daughter. The subject ingests it without a hesitation, not even water.

5. It was concluded that after the pill was administered, the subject slipped into a coma-like sleep in a matter of minutes and did not wake up until the very next day.

6. "It was the best sleep of my life," the refreshed subject said then promptly went back to sleep.

CHAPTER 22
Remedy to Anxiety

Even the birds were elated to awaken on such a beautiful morning, because they would not shut up about it, as they flitted from tree to tree. James and I had just gotten out of Professor Whisper's class and were enjoying our hour-and-a-half break at the running track behind Miami-Dade College. I wouldn't call Dade "pretty," but it definitely has its vivacious personality accompanied by a glorious sky and tree-filled horizon. I was babbling about my life to James, while he just walked alongside me, patiently listening on a breezy, March day.

"It's pretty strange," I said. "I feel like I can compartmentalize (my favorite word at the time) all the aspects of my life right now. Despite how hectic they've become, I cannot let it get to me if I really try, but the one thing I just cannot swallow is when I have freaking relationship issues."

"Ah, yeah, I get you. They suck. What are you going to about that?" He scratched his head.

"I'm going to…I'm going to…not stress about it, first of all, and second of all…I guess I'll just talk to Will." I sighed. "That's all I really can do."

"Yeah, you're right about that."

"And everything else, well, everything else," I laughed a little desperately, "I don't know. You know how I feel. With obsessing over my dad's death and everything. I mean, my therapist told me to look up the survival statistics of people with Stage 4 bladder cancer, and it said five years. Meaning that I will be twenty-four. I could get a lot done in five years." My imagination quickly took me to my graduation, followed by my marriage with my future husband, and a dog, then my newborn baby. Yeah, it could all happen. My dad could get to experience all those things with me. ESPECIALLY the publication of my first bestselling novel! I smiled at the fantasy of that becoming a reality, considering I was halfway through writing my first novel.

"Five years?" he asked.

"Yup." I blinked. It felt better to think about all that could occur in five years, as opposed to death, death, death.

"Wow, I fucking hate cancer," he blurted.

"Oh, fucking tell me about it," I laughed. I felt so much better talking to him. Although it was starting to feel like I had a boyfriend at school, but without the dates or kissing or sex. We were standing in front of the cement bleachers, staring into some rose bushes, while it occurred to me that maybe I should study or eat to get my mind off of everything.

"Do you want to sit down?" he asked.

"Yes, and eat, and stop being stressed for at least five minutes of my day. I would absolutely love that," I laughed sarcastically. On the outside, in front of James, I always pretended like I had it all together. But he knew, deep down, that I was hurting. As it turned out, Beard Boy (even though his beard was gone) was the kind of guy who would nurse a kitten back to health, then love him like a son.

"Ana…" His voice took on a sympathetic tone.

"Yes?" I smiled, taking a seat on the bleachers.

"I'm just putting myself in your shoes and really trying to feel out your situation. I mean, I know that I can't really, obviously…" He rolled his eyes. "Because I haven't gone through that, but I am trying. I remember when I was with my ex, Miley, and her dad's Alzheimer's was getting worse, I felt so helpless, even though I really wanted to help her. Instead I just got depressed." He shook his head wistfully. "And then you know, she broke up with me."

As his words registered with me, I dropped the everything-is-okay act, the smile fading from my face. He had told me a lot about Miley and how much he loved her but was an "idiot at nineteen." I felt like James was nineteen-year-old Will now, and I was Miley. I leaned my ear closer to him. James always talked so quietly.

"Ana, I think you're handling this the best way possible. I think you really are. There's no other better way of handling it that I could imagine."

"Thank you, James." I smiled a real, genuine smile. "That means a lot to me, that you're telling me that."

"It's the truth. And look, the best advice I can give you (correction—this was actually the best advice I'd ever received) is to just look at it like this: you have your way of looking at the whole situation, your mom has her own way of looking at it (she chose to believe that his cancer was not real which ignited the series of arguments between us), and I'm sure your brother and your dad have their own way of looking at it too.

"Just accept this, and try not let other viewpoints bother you. I know this is hard, trust me, I know, but just try. And as far as the cancer itself, well it's being dealt with the best it can. He's getting treated, you guys are well-informed, you know the doctors are doing everything they can, and you're all being there for him the best you can. Now, as far as what happens, that is beyond your control. You have to accept that. Whatever happens will happen, but that isn't for you to worry about,"

CLICK. CLICK. CLICK. CLICK!

A series of light bulbs went off in my soul. The birds in the huge cypress trees morphed into angels singing Ave Maria, and all of a sudden, everything just made sense. About life.

"You. Are. Absolutely. Right," I said, feeling my eyes widen and my chest expand with the holy breath of the secrets of the Universe. "God, you're so right. I feel like you just organized my mind. Like you just organized everything, and I could see it clearly."

"You're welcome, Banana." His bright brown eyes smiled.

CHAPTER 23
Knock, Knock. Who's There?

I was home alone on my laptop in my PJs. My dad was getting acupuncture, and the last time he did that, he wasn't back home for another four hours. I called Will. Will who finally told his mom about his depression, got a therapist to talk to. Will who was focusing on his band, and CrossFit, and finally getting employed at a shoe store called Vans.

"Hey, gorgeous," I said, as soon as he answered. Reversing gender roles and gender stereotypes was our thing.

"Hello, handsome."

"So, I'm feeling pretty lazy to get ready right now, and you know…take a shower, get dressed, and all that..."

"You want to shower together at your house, then head over mine?"

"You know me so well." I smiled.

He chuckled. "Alright, babe, I'm on my way."

He clicked off. I sighed of delight. Oh, the feeling of having a boyfriend and being home alone! Such a magnificent feeling. It was like even the house could feel it. If the walls could speak, they would be saying, so where are you going to do it this time? The living room? Family room? The dinner table? Now, the walls were gossiping with each other like old ladies at the booth of a Denny's diner. They should do it on the dining room table. They giggled like the naughty old lady walls they were. I glanced at myself in the mirror. Messy hair, no makeup. But I didn't really care. Will found me beautiful regardless. Even if I didn't shave any part of my body. Those were top quality boyfriends, if you ask me. I impatiently surfed the web while waiting for him to arrive. I checked the time. 2 PM.

C'mon, Will, hurry up. I don't want to be overconfident about this.

Nah, you have plenty of time, I reassured myself. I sang to my dogs for a little bit, and Jodie just wagged her tail, as we eagerly awaited Will's arrival. Okay, maybe not her, but me yes.

It was almost 3 PM, and he still wasn't there.

I called him. "Hey, are you on your way?"

"Yeah, there's just a shit ton of traffic," he replied.

"Oh, okay, gotchu…" I paused, thinking it was weird that he was taking so long, traffic or no traffic. "Yeah, I was just checking, 'cause you know, normally, you're here a lot sooner."

"I'll be there in ten minutes, no more."

"M'kay…"

"I love you…"

"Love you, too." I hung up, admittedly starting to get annoyed.

I killed the ten minutes with Snapchat, Instagram, and Pandora, all the apps I used the most, excluding Spotify. Now, I was starting to feel antsy. The walls were saying to me, hey, maybe you should just get ready and leave with him. There was a knock on my door, and my heart syncopated with his steady knocking. It was the knock of athirst love. I opened the door and Will came bouncing in with his gorgeous smile and camo book bag on. We pop-kissed hello and went straight to my bedroom, not wasting one second of our precious alone time.

We started kissing, his hands running all over my body, and before long, we were shedding each other's clothes. "To the shower?" he murmured breathlessly.

"Yes," I said, my hands wrapped around his neck. Jodie watched us as she always did whenever I got intimate with him. She shot us this look that said, "I know what you two are up to," and I imagined her having an English accent, as she nodded her head disapprovingly, clicking her tongue at us. I laughed, interrupting our moist, steamy kiss.

Suddenly, I felt the walls closing in on us, as dread replaced my…thirst.

"What is it?" He pulled back and looked at me.

"Nothing, it's just… It's just… Yeah, like, I think we should just shower and leave."

"So, no sex?"

"No sex. Well, I mean…" I chuckled. "Not in my shower—here right now, at least."

"Oh, c'mon, baby," Will cooed. Rational Will completely left the building. And frankly so had Rational Ana. We continued our making out session all the way to the bathroom where I turned on the shower, and then, the gut feeling returned, stronger than ever.

"We really should just shower, trust me. I'm getting a gut feeling about this."

"Well, I mean, if anything, your dad won't be able to see us."

That wasn't exactly reassuring. I mean, my dad would see Will's car in the driveway and hear us moaning in the shower, but whatever, I took it. The water streamed down our naked bodies, and I felt both sexy and self-conscious at the same time. Like, yeah I'm wet and naked! But also like…okay, so please turn around, as I awkwardly wash my vagina, please, and thank you.

I'd always had some sort of reverse psychological phenomenon inside of me where I actually felt more turned on if I told myself that I couldn't have sex. "No…no…we really shouldn't…" I giggled. Will began planting kisses all over my legs, as he sat down beside me. I hadn't even used my loofah yet.

"Why, baby?" he asked in my ear, as I crouched down behind him. Intuition utterly replaced with unquenchable thirst.

"Um…um…you know…" I muttered. Now, little baby moans followed my words, as he slid his fingers into…how do I put this in a way where I still sound classy and elegant? Into my Garden of Eden. There we go. Pleasuring the blooming bud that is my…lotus flower. Yeah, that's it. The steam was making me a little dizzy, but not enough to stop. Get a condom! a tiny voice screamed in my head and faded away, as Will's joystick started to flirt with my meadow, making my "petals" moist with anticipation…

"Arch your back for me, baby," he whispered so, so sexily. I listened to the smoldering sound of his voice, a sultry smile breaking on my face, as we got rained on, the sound of rushing water drowning out the outside world, when all of a sudden…

KNOCK. KNOCK.

GUESS WHO'S THERE?

YEAH, THAT'S RIGHT. IT'S MY…

FATHER.

"Anaregina, are you in there?" His voice came out choppy, awkward.

I instantly felt Will tense and back away from me, becoming completely paralyzed.

Yes, yes, I am here. Just me. Only I am inhabiting my bathroom. It is just regular good old daughter me taking a shower.

"Yeah, Dad, I'm just showering. I'll be out soon." I sounded so convincing that I practically believed myself. Except that…

WE COULDN'T HAVE MADE IT ANYMORE OBVIOUS BEING THAT WILL'S BOOK BAG WAS ON FULL DISPLAY IN MY ROOM LIKE AN EXHIBIT AT A MUSEUM ALONG WITH A TRAIL OF OUR CLOTHES LEADING TO THE BATHROOM LIKE HANSEL AND GRETEL OF COMPLETE AND UTTER SHAME.

"I know you guys are in there," my dad accused, his tone infused with one of those if-I-had-a-middle-name-he'd-use-it-right-now kind of tones.

"Well, you were a sex addict! And I'm your daughter, so it only makes sense!"

Just kidding, I didn't really say that to my outraged father. I actually laughed a little bit out of sheer nervousness. I think it was a mix of disbelief and just, ahhhh, I fucking knew this would happen.

"We're going to get out now," I said, defeated. I mean what else are you supposed to say in this situation? Don't worry, Dad, we weren't having steamy shower sex. We were just about to, but the act itself was not happening, as you knocked on the door interrupting my innocence. No worries.

"I am going to be in the kitchen," he muttered through the door.

"Okay," I said, shutting off the shower faucet handles. "He's probably going to act like nothing happened," I reassured Will, as my dad's footsteps trailed down the hallway.

Will didn't say a word. He slowly unfroze and mechanically stepped out of my bathtub. I wanted nothing more than for him to disappear into a particle of steam that clung to the green walls, and by the way that he looked at me, I knew he would have preferred that too.

"Just put on your pants." I handed him his khakis and boxers. "And then change in my room," I asked of him. As Will used my towel, I used what would be my brother's towel to dry myself off. It felt so fucking dirty and wrong. "But first, I'm going to get my clothes really quickly, so that I could change in here."

"Okay," he said. My boyfriend was starting to look like he'd rather be shot in the balls twice than face the situation he was in.

"Hey, be grateful it isn't my mom. She would be going crazy right now," I said, wanting to put a reassuring hand on his shoulder. But I felt like I couldn't even touch Will without feeling disgust in myself. He nodded, zipped up his pants, and I slid into my room and snatched Margo's borrowed overalls and a black crop top. I might as well go to my creative supplies closet and cut myself a red letter A and pin it to my forehead.

I changed, brushed my hair, and went back into my room, feeling partially confident that my dad would just act like none of this had happened, and it would all disappear. Will was fully clothed, and he'd picked up his book bag from the floor as he sat down on my bed. A prisoner of his guilt, I was sure. We slipped into our world of thoughts for a while, my mind venturing to a memory of talking to my friend, Adela, in our high school algebra class.

I was about to open my mouth to speak when I heard my dad's voice from behind the door, and then it opened. "Are you guys done?" And he was not happy.

I turned around and instinctively told him, "I am so sorry, Papá."

He nodded, then I realized I would rather be shot in the crotch twice right now than look into my dad's eyes. No, three times. No, no, four. Yes, four times, for sure. I could take the sting.

"I need you to leave right now," he ordered Will in a stern voice.

Will nodded and mumbled something that sounded like, "Yes, sir."

"I need to speak to my daughter for a couple of hours."

"I understand, I am sorry." Will strapped his book bag on. I actually don't remember if he apologized at this exact moment, but my mind is saying that he did. Both their faces were masked of any sort of emotion. No, no, no, this isn't what I wanted! I cringed. I wanted to leave with Will, study at his house, and surgically tie my hymen back together.

Will left without saying goodbye to me, which I still don't hold him accountable for to this day. Then, I committed mental suicide. I went outside to the yard to the corner of our fence, so I could cry alone in my own shame. The tears streamed down effortlessly. Most guilt tears do.

You knewww it, Annnaaaa. You had a gut fucking feeling and you ignored it for Will! I berated myself. I buried my face in my hands, as Jodie came to the emotional rescue, wagging her tail as if to say, "I still love you, though." The sky was burning into twilight, my favorite time of day.

I petted her, calming myself down. It's been scientifically proven that petting an animal lowers your blood pressure. Well, I could use a zoo at that moment.

"Let's go for a walk," I said, smiling at Jodie. Her light brown eyes lit up like there were little fireworks in them. I dragged my dignity together, went inside the house to get her collar, and just as I was about to grab her leash before escaping, my dad said, "Sit down, I need to talk you."

Why can't we just act like that didn't happen? I internally screamed. Sighing, I walked toward the living room. "Okay, Papá," I surrendered, plopping down on the couch where the plasma screen he bought us for Christmas dominated the scene.

"Look, what you did isn't wrong. You are an adult, and you can choose whatever you want to do with your body…"

Instantly, guilt tears shot through my eyelids. His words didn't make any sense to me. If I wasn't doing anything wrong, then why was he making such a big deal out of this? "I'm sorry, Papá, I'm so sorry," I cried. Then, I dared myself to look at him in the eyes and pleaded, "Please do not tell Mama. Papá, please don't tell her." There's a no-sex-in-the-house rule because "it is disrespectful" and that's how most, if not all Hispanic girls grow up. Including Adam.

He sighed heavily. "Anaregina, I've lived my whole life with secrets. I am no longer doing that. I am going to tell her. You didn't do anything wrong—"

"She's not going to think that!" I interrupted him. Now I was whining. Now, I felt sixteen again. I put my hands to my forehead. "Papá, I need to leave the house. I need to take a walk, I'll be back," I said, heading to get Jodie's leash. She started prancing around like a Mexican jumping bean.

Images of my mother screaming at Will and me filled my head. How could her daughter be nineteen and not a virgin?

If there was something that I held sacred to, it was having my sex life be a galaxy away from the universe my parents lived in. Besides, in my head, I was planning to tell her when I turned twenty, because she lost hers to my dad at twenty. Or so she confessed to me once. I stepped outside and drank in the sun and soothing wind, as peaceful clouds melted together in shades of pink and marmalade orange.

I called Rachel and left her a voicemail detailing my current position. Instantly, I knew she would find it funny, and by the time I strolled to the lake by my house, the weight of the situation had left my tense shoulders. My chow-chow mutt baby couldn't have been more ecstatic that she was getting a walk out of this.

"I love you, too," I said, petting both of her soft ears. "Let's go back now."

I took a deep breath and walked back towards my house.

As soon as I was inside, I heard, "Hola, Anaregina, please sit down with me." My dad's voice, calm and reassured, but still…WHY ISN'T THIS OVER YET? I internally screamed. "Okay," I surrendered.

Again, he reiterated what he told me earlier about how I hadn't done anything wrong, how I was an adult now, and how it was my body, so I could do whatever I wanted with it, that I had nothing to feel guilty about, blah, blah, but this time he added, "So, now that you are doing adult things, now I don't know if you're having intercourse or not, that's your private life, and you don't have to tell me…"

Good thing, I was never planning on telling you that, Dad.

"I think it means you need to behave more like an adult here at home now."

What? Well, I was not expecting to hear this…

"You know, the three of us are adults, and we live in the same house, so if you're going to be acting like a teenager by doing things like that, which again, it's normal…well, I want you to help Mama around the house more by cleaning when she asks you to, and even when she doesn't. You could also maybe help with cooking."

I sat there stunned, internalizing his words.

Part of me thought, yes, of course, Dad. But another part of me felt like reaching sexual maturity shouldn't mean some sort of tradeoff when your parents found out. I was fighting outrage but was still too ashamed to express it. In hindsight, I think it was really my dad who was stunned and outraged in trying to grasp the concept, that yes, ever since he left the house when I was sixteen, I did some growing up and rebelled in my own way.

I accepted the fact that he was going to tell my mom. I could tell he wasn't going to change his mind about that. But still, a part of me hoped he wouldn't, hoped to rid myself of the anxiety of waiting until my mom got home from work.

When she finally did, two surprising thing happened. First, she accepted it right away and didn't even flip out or get angry at me. Second, what began as a family meeting discussing my teenage ways evolved into…well, one of the most profound, loving, and pure moments we ever had as a family. Picture my dad sitting next to me on the sofa trying to comfort me, as I was dressed in my own anger, then somehow it all dissipated the moment I realized what was happening. My dad got to be a real father to me in the earlier event, somehow making up for the years he missed out on in my life at home. I was grateful. We spoke about how hard it was not having Adam home, but how strong we were to be going through hell together. The three of us embraced like it was the last hug we might ever have.

At least that's how it felt.

CHAPTER 24
Meet Kit-Kat, Your 305 Psychic

I need to go. I need to go. I need to leave. I need to get out of here.

My stomach felt clenched. Or maybe it was from not eating much while canvassing during the day. I needed to be alone so I could cry, at least lock myself up in my room, in the dark, and feel the warmth of my covers rub against my skin. It was one of those days where I could see myself from outside my body talking to people, smiling at them, wishing them a great day, giving them an equality sticker despite their shitty refusal to help.

I was in the office, surrounded by my coworkers who wanted to get to their lovers, their Netflix, their food and their pets. Their voices were serene waves above me, but I was in a dream underwater, and I needed something tended to. My eyes begged me to bleed tears the way a neglected bladder begs to have a relieving date with the toilet. Please, debrief me already so I can get the fuck out.

"Who's next to be debriefed?" Charlotte called through the closed door. It had a poster on it outlining all the rules we had to abide by while driving to sites. Never text and drive. Always wear your seat belt. No alcohol or drugs before or after arriving on site.

"Me!" I sounded like I was cracked out.

"We're on it!" Charlotte answered. I inhaled and exhaled slowly.

"Is Kit-Kat back from site?" I glanced in the direction of Monica and Enzo. They shook their heads. I couldn't believe of all days, I was going to ride with her. I'd only met her once before, and now I needed to endure this while holding back all my stress.

Enzo, Monica, and Charlie conversed while our other coworkers completed the tedious cash-out process. I forced myself to laugh at the appropriate times. I needed to release tension somehow. Kit-Kat arrived while I was debriefing with either Charlotte or Leslie. It could have been a dolphin debriefing me, and I probably would not have noticed.

"You'll do better next time! I love you!" Charlotte said, as I got up to face the door. Quota had become an unattainable clown that laughed and hid from me whenever I needed it most.

"I love you too," I answered. Get me out of here already.

It bothered the fuck out of me that most of my fellow gay rights activists had done so well, whereas I had barely made half of that green bitch of a clown. Monica stepped inside the office for her turn, and I felt joy upon seeing Kit-Kat's face. She reminded me of when I was little and going through my tomboy phase, when having my hair down was a sin, and flowery dresses were downright disgusting. I waited for her, organizing the office to keep myself from thinking about Will and how shitty things were going with him.

"You ready to go, cowgirl?" Kit-Kat asked, as soon as she got out.

"Oh, yes." I felt a fake smile crease my greasy face.

"Let's head out!" She marched out of the office. Something seemed different about her since the first time we'd met. She had been my first ever OBS (which is a person trying to make staff) on the day I had to pack for the trip, the day my pulse seemed to be knocking through the vein wall to my temple every five minutes. I continued to feel like I was underwater, concentrating on not speaking or crying for the next fifty-eight seconds. But I kept wondering what about her had changed, something about her vibe kept persisting.

"Dude, today was a good one. I met a lot of interesting people. Not like last time I worked, I met the biggest assholes, man! I got so heated. I had to be like, 'Kit-Kat, control your anger, don't unleash it on them.' But today was actually pretty nice." She smiled, exuding maturity. "How was your day?" she asked, genuinely interested.

I met her gaze and opened my mouth expecting the usual, "It was okay" followed by an indifferent shrug to come out, but instead, an emotional unleashing began.

"It sucked. I didn't make quota. And the rest of my crew did. Honestly, Kit-Kat, when you first met me, and I was training you, I tried my best. Believe me, I am beyond glad that you made staff. I was really, really stressed, and just suppressing a lot of emotion."

"Yeah, I took one look at you today, and I could feel your energy was off." Yes! Confidence! That's what was different about her! "What's bugging you?"

I looked both ways, as we crossed the street from Virginia Road to CocoWalk with the sun beating down on us relentlessly. "My boyfriend!" I screamed. Obviously not loud enough for the pedestrians around me to hear, but loud enough.

"Ah, boys. They can be very immature at your age. What are you? Eighteen? Nineteen?"

I made some sort of grunting noise in response. "I'm nineteen. And because of all the shit that I've been going through, I feel like I'm already halfway to practically being a woman. But my boyfriend…" I laughed humorlessly. "Oh, my boyfriend, who's also nineteen, by the way…" I searched for the right words. "It's like I am dating a freaking boy when I want to be with a man!"

Wow, I couldn't believe those words had come out of my mouth. What did this mean for me and Will?

"Ah, yeah, he's got a lot of growing to do. Women do typically mature faster than boys. I mean, I don't feel exactly qualified to be giving you advice given that I'm a lesbian, and I've never had a boyfriend, nor do I hope to ever have one in the future…" She raised her hands up and made a funny, disgusted face. "But I can safely say that part is true."

"It's really annoying," I complained. "I don't understand why he can't just get his shit together," I sighed, feeling a teeny bit better.

"With time, my friend, with time." Kit-Kat guided me to her red car, and my head exploded, as though I was underwater again. I climbed into the passenger seat and observed the way her hands confidently embraced the steering wheel, as the calming music filled the car. Up, from the water I surfaced, amazed by the advice Kit-Kat was giving me.

"Don't take work so personally, stay humble from work high days, and don't let the low days define your normal days. At the end of the day, bitch about it for ten minutes and then just let it go. Tomorrow is a new day."

"That's exactly what I needed to hear!" I exclaimed, turning my body towards her. I was finally starting to feel a little better, but the tension in my chest and back persisted. I wondered if she always kept her natural brown hair in a bun. She looked so mature. A bun!

"Yeah, homegirl, you've got to spit out your issues!" She glanced at me. My stomach rumbled. It had been hours since I'd eaten, but instead of being "hangry," like I usually got, unshed tears ferociously knocked behind my eyeballs. Just focus on what Kit-Kat is saying, Ana, you could cry and eat your heart out at home.

"You know, sometimes you have one thing as your outlet, and you rely on that your whole life, but then it gets to the point where that thing just isn't enough anymore…" She paused to think about it. "Like I have a friend who would play music as a release, but it wasn't 'til he found jiu-jitsu that it all sort of came together for him."

"Like me with writing." I laughed sarcastically. "Which I haven't even been doing!" I felt so disappointed in myself. Why was I letting life get in the way of my dream?

"Oh, you write? That's awesome. What do you write about?"

"Fiction, but I want to write sci-fi, too." I felt like a repressed woman from the Victorian era. "What's your release? I also love to work out a lot."

"That's cool. You're an artist. And I like to write too every now, and then. I do jiu-jitsu, which I feel has taught me a lot about myself, my temper, and just life in general."

"Ha, life!" I laughed.

"Then there's always music to soothe me. I am a big music fan," she said. I was beginning to feel extremely comfortable with her, like I could open up, and she would just listen judgment free. Maybe it had something to do with her big boobs? I re-read her tattoo on her forearm. Something about life with a little red ladybug on the side.

"Yeah, I honestly don't know what I would do without music. I can't go to sleep with just my thoughts. I need music there to drown them out." I clenched my hands. The late afternoon sunlight streamed through the windshield, penetrating my eyes. "I'm a really emotional person," I added with a laugh.

"Wow, you really are an artist," Kit-Kat slowly said, glancing over at me every so often. "And, oh, trust me, so am I. There have been times when I have cried to the point where I am hyperventilating."

I thought of her tattoo. When we first met, I asked her about it. She told me her favorite aunt died of a drug overdose, that if she were to come back to this life she would come back as a ladybug. I would come back a red rose, or maybe a golden retriever.

"Does it get easier as you get older?" I asked. "Because you know PMS is still a real freaking bitch to me."

"You learn how to handle yourself better, but your hormones are still wild during that time."

I sighed. I'm probably getting my period like tomorrow.

My eyeballs grew tired of taking punches from the unwelcome tears, and finally, they made their appearance on land. The sun warmed my face. I took a deep breath and silently cried. I waited until Kit-Kat noticed. As soon as I felt her looking at me, I said, "Yeah, I'm going through really rough shit right now, and for some reason, I just can't hold it anymore. Which is weird, because normally I can. There's been lots of times where I get rides from other coworkers like Johanna or Enzo, and I feel like this now but I'm able to hold it in. I don't know why with you, it feels different. Like I've known you for a long time or something."

It has to be the maternal big boobs!

"It is one hundred percent completely okay to cry. Not only is it okay, it's necessary, and don't worry, I have that effect on a lot of people." She smiled like a wizard from a place where people can predict your future and take you to other galaxies. Happily, I let myself cry my sad tears, as I told her about my father's cancer and my intuition that he was going to go back to the hospital soon, and that Will's depression wasn't really helping the situation at all.

Enter movie moment with movie-like lines, as the sun cast the spotlight on psychic Kit-Kat and desperate Ana on Killian Road, a street down from Miami-Dade Community College.

Psychic Kit-Kat: "That really bites, man. I am really sorry to hear that, and I do hope your dad gets better with all my spirit. But as far as your boyfriend goes, that will pass, I promise. All of it will pass really. I can promise you that one year from now, you will be laughing without a care in the world. I promise you."

Crying, but now genuinely smiling Ana: "Thank you, I really hope that you're right."

I fantasized about my future self, laughing until my stomach hurt on March, 18th 2016. It made me so happy.

305 Fortune Teller: "You will see I am right. You're okay right now! You're letting it out, and the rest will all come into place with time. It's like what I was telling you earlier about finding another release. You are releasing now which is okay, Ana."

Sentimental Me: "Thank you, really, thank you."

Wise, soulful Kit-Kat: "Your problems are Mentos inside you, and there's liters of diet Coke in you, you need to spit them out, or you'll explode." I laughed at the metaphor, but it worked. Good one, Wise Kit-Kat!

She proceeded to tell me that her mom was a psychiatrist; that all her life she'd grown up learning the psychology of human emotions, and how just like me, she was very keen on feeling people's energies. When she told me to write down my negative thoughts, then watch them burn, Kit-Kat became a witch before my eyes, a good witch of course, with soft brown eyes, and translucent silk skin. I thanked her again for all her advice, and she gave me a bear hug when she dropped me off at home. Yes, the maternal boobs, for sure.

The whirlpool inside of me finally evaporated, and with it a shitty poem was recorded on my hot pink iTouch:

You think
Her tears are drops of rain that drip down little hills making small
Explosions as they hit the ground
No
My tears are hurricanes that flood
The Himalayas 'til the top as they bubble up inside
You think
She's down, she's blue
No

I can't be alone with my thoughts at night
Because it gets so overbearing I need music to drown them, to soothe me
You think
It's just another boy in her life
No, he's a human being
With emotions capable of reaching the depths of the Mariana Trench
You think
She's nineteen, she's hormonal
No. Yes. Wait, no…I don't know
All my emotions are eating at my stomach clenching my insides
They're the Mentos in my Diet Coke body
But they're also my drive, my inspiration, the reason I can survive
The reason why I KNOW on this planet, I, Anaregina Frias, will thrive.
A writer, a human being
Trying
Striving
Achieving.
All that I can be, and all that I will be.

CHAPTER 25
That's Life

I was right about my intuition telling me my dad was going back to the hospital. However, I had no idea it was going to be the last time he would be at home, still able to stand and talk to me like a regular father.

I was also right about getting my period that week too. Things with Will were getting a little better. He went to his first therapy session and made his mom happy by working at Vans, the shoe store (okay, fine, that made me happy too). I wasn't writing a novel like I wanted to be, but I was enrolled in a beginner's writing workshop for people like me who wanted to publish their first book! This became the rock I could rest on whenever I felt myself drowning underwater again. I felt like a real writer, which was important, because I had no idea that a couple of months from now, I would muster the courage to show my Creative Writing 2 teacher a personal poem of mine I thought was at the very least decent, and he would then crush my self-esteem as an artist with his assessment, "This is so cliché" and "Just start over."

Well, Professor, this may not have made it to Miambiance Magazine, but—oh, would you look at that? My cliché poem is published right here in my very first book along with "No Air," which you deemed "unremarkable work on such tired theme."

This poem was me retelling real life, okay? I am sorry if dad-gets-cancer is such a "tired theme," but nonetheless, I grew from that, so thank you, Professor Killdreams, and thank you, Snotty Girl who gave me a 2 on "Room 4321." I, too, agree with you that the ending was way too abrupt. As my mom says, C'est la vie.

Broken

By: 2015 Anaregina Frias

It began the moment she stared into the mirror
She saw a beautiful girl
Porcelain skin, bright eyes, shiny hair
Pearly white teeth inside a plump lip mouth
Suddenly tears began to form inside the eyes
They turned black
She stared at her lips as they became chapped and began to bleed
She could see every wrinkle in every pore
She was depleted of her beauty
She was entering the Twilight Zone
Livid, she broke the mirror
Shattered it to pieces with the hairdryer in her frail hand
She stared at the fragments of the once whole mirror
She saw her pearly whites shine even whiter now
For now, she could truly see herself

Broken, but alive.

CHAPTER 26
I Probably Still Have Daddy Issues

There are conversations you are going to have with your parents that you will never, ever, in a trillion past and future lives ever expect to have. Take right now, my mom walked into my room while I was putting away my clothes, and she handed me a black, lacy lingerie thing called a negligée that she probably used the night she conceived me! I literally turned the other way and laughed while my cheeks burned (a week ago, we were talking about how it hurt her when she found out that I'd had sex with more than one guy). Well, there'd always been an unspoken conversation with my dad about my daddy issues, which we never got around to discussing until now in late March.

In the span of re-reading that paragraph, things with Will got shitty again. Why. Why. Why was I still with him? I kept asking myself. Why did I still think so much about Ponyboy?

If Will knew how much I thought about Ponyboy, he would leave me for sure. Hands down. I bet all the chocolate chip cookies sitting in Publix right now. I started to think about all the issues I'd had with guys in the past, and I kept coming back to Ponyboy. Then, the conversations with my therapist, Tyronne, started. I remembered when I was around sixteen when he told me with a look of awe in his eyes that I still loved Ponyboy. Then, I remembered sitting down on his leather couch in his small, cozy office, as he looked me in the eye and said, "Sweetie, the reason you have such a strong attachment to Ponyboy is because when your father wasn't all there, that's when Ponyboy came into the picture. Ponyboy would tell you how special you were, make you feel as amazing as you are, and encouraged you. That's why it's so hard for you to let go."

It made sense in my sixteen-year-old mind.

Now, I was nineteen. Now, I entertained myself by imagining all the guys I'd dated (four, not including Jacob, the white daisy, and Andrew, the weed on my Wall of Flowers, because he dumped me after a month) gathered at a long table, like the Last Supper all talking about me and what it was like to date me. I can confidently conclude that they'd all agree I moved at the pace of a tortoise (I would say turtle, but haven't you noticed those fuckers run pretty fast?) and that I wake up annoyingly late.

As the meeting proceeded, someone would bring up Ponyboy, and I'd feel like he would be the purple tulip and then they'd all throw their hands in the air like the way hardcore football fans whine when their team loses a point. The red rose would probably start blushing and show apologetic gestures for having unconsciously intervened in all my following relationships. Then someone would be like, "Just, just go home, man." And he would stand up and leave with his tail tucked between his legs, a sad puppy face.

I don't know why I imagine these sort of things and get perverse emotions from them, but I do. I also don't know why when I am pissed at someone, like genuinely pissed, I completely downplay my true feelings towards them once I confront them about it. Inside, I'll be screaming my head off to that person, but the moment I have the chance to show one ounce of irritation, I reduce my rage to humor. And I hate having this done to me! For example, if you're angry at me, just tell me, don't act all passive aggressive about it, or try to hide it. This wasn't meant to become a tangent, just like this conversation with my dad wasn't meant to get serious and heart to heart.

"Papá!" I walked into the kitchen with my arms crossed, my lips pursed (but remember I am not really mad, I'm just joking mad).

"Qué pasó, Anaregina?" He turned to look at me. All of his muscle was completely gone.

"I think...I think you gave me daddy issues," I said.

He leaned his hip on the counter to look me in the eye, as he told me in one of the most serious, genuine, sincere tones he has ever used with me. "Oh, yes. I definitely have. And lots of them too. I think I still am, actually." He smiled at me apologetically.

Wham! I was completely taken aback by his honest response. So much so that I had to really take a step back before I could cultivate my answer. To my surprise, my words flowed effortlessly. "Yeah, Papi, I'm not mad at you or anything, but it's just true. You've given them to me. I remember one time I was with Tyronne, and we were talking about how difficult it is for me to let go of Ponyboy, and then he told me how I had become so attached to him around the time that you became depressed, and you weren't really emotionally there for me anymore."

I felt bad telling him this, but it was truth. And to my surprise he agreed wholeheartedly.

He nodded. "That's true. I see it in your relationship with Will. You are transferring the relationship I have with Mama to him."

"What do you mean? How?"

"Right now, my relationship with Mama has come down to her taking care of me, and from what you've told me about your relationship with Will, it sounds like you're taking care of him."

An eco-friendly light bulb flickered on in my brain.

"You mean like with his depression?"

"Yes," he said, as he diced slices of cheese for himself.

"Wow, that does make sense."

"You may not see it right now, but you have been trying to change him, and he isn't going to do that for you. You cannot change someone. They aren't going to change unless they themselves are ready to make that change for themselves."

Here was my dad, standing on his two feet, in his PJs, spewing words of wisdom and human psychology to me. I was stunned. And grateful. And I was getting every ounce of my dad's attention. His presence, his breath, his love.

"And I agree with Tyronne about Ponyboy," he added. "He's, ay…what's the word?" His thinking eyes gazed away for a moment, then he said, "Emotionally conflictive. Like me."

"Wow, Papi, I never thought we would be having this conversation," I said, standing next to him. Unaware, so utterly unaware that if I knew this would be the last conversation with him, healthy enough to be on two feet, I would have hugged him. I would have said, "I love you" a thousand times over.

But I didn't. C'est la vie.

CHAPTER 27
Pain Starts with Pee

"I just want to break a plate," I told Will while slouched like a pissed-off teenager in the passenger seat of his car.

"We could go buy those plastic ones that break. You want to go do that?"

I laughed but it wasn't a real laugh. "Yes. No. I don't know."

"What's wrong?" he asked, truly worried about me.

I remained quiet, trying to formulate my answer coherently. There were no words in my head that could accurately describe why I was feeling the way I felt. No logic to back up the tears that ran down my cheeks that met the tip of my chin all too frequently.

"I don't know," I scoffed. The sky was acting shy from the way it hid behind one enormous gray cloud. I wore all black today.

Emotions like these, so deeply rooted inside of you, emerge at the most random times, and usually at the most inopportune moments. It can only be explained as pain from the very core of your soul. And there's no logical explanation to describe what your soul feels. I don't know why of all the souls that could have arrived to this planet Earth on September 20th, 1995, mine came into being.

My simplest answer was well, to be a writer, of course!

But my soul's soul's soul's soul's soul knew that it was something deeper. Perhaps simply a coincidence—a spontaneous reaction. But either way, every single moment that my mother and father lived in order to finally have the moment where I was the fastest little sperm to meet with my ticket into existence happened exactly as it should. As it has for the rest of humanity. We're just a bunch of cells that never stopped replicating.

It just so happened that my father's cells were at war. The war of all wars. And all I could do was pretend to be this warrior who could only watch the chaos unfolding in the battlefield. Every day. Every day, I asked my dad, "How are you feeling?" and he said "okay," or "fine," until one day I realized that he was just acting like there were no gunshots. He was trying to protect me from getting any of his blood on me. Every day, I heard the screams of agony that escaped my father's soul enter my ears and shatter my being into crumbs of who I was, swinging on a pendulum of powerless and powerful. Every day, his shrill cries seemed to grow weaker, sharper, but less powerful. The enemy grew full force laughing at chemotherapy's pathetic attempts to destroy it, as it sharpened its claws on our backs.

"Radiation is the last resort," I told Hazel one day at school.

"And if that doesn't work?" she asked.

"Well, then…" My silence hung in the air.

"That's it," she finished my dreaded sentence.

Now, whenever I asked Papá, "How are you feeling?" he could not lie any longer. I was no longer blinded by his falsifications of love. His shrieks of pain made nails scratching a chalkboard sound like angels singing a church hymn.

Every day, he had to pee.

Every day, the pain would come.

Every day, he went to war with a fucking toilet, for crying out loud.

And I listened to the battle cries, the gunshots, the blood filling up the hospital walls.

Pain. Pain. Pain. Pain. Pain. Every day. Pain. I couldn't just see his pain before my eyes, I could practically taste it as if it were my own, as if it transferred through osmosis to my brain. My cells may have multiplied on their own volition, but my dad's blood was my blood too. He just couldn't see it yet.

CHAPTER 28
Chicken Soup for the Departing Souls

If there really is a hell, it's here on Earth. Inside hospital rooms.

Satan isn't one to take you there. No, this demon's name was Radiation. Radiation was so hellish, he could make Satan piss his pants then drink his own pee if Radiation ordered him to do so. He was ruthless. Pure poison taking delight in clogging every cell with even more unbearable, excruciating agony. I know this with my whole heart and soul, because on days when I was working, fighting for the gays out in some Starbucks or wherever, I would receive a text that would choke my heart and nearly asphyxiate my entire being every single time.

It was from my dad asking me, my mom, my brother and Rafael to pray for him because he was about to go into radiation treatment. He sent his love and appreciation in a couple of characters.

"Are you okay, Anaregina?" My coworkers would ask me. They all knew what was happening.

I always gave them a cookie cutter reply. "Yeah, it's my dad asking me to pray for him, because he's about to get Radiation." The master of Satan, the one Satan bowed down to every day.

"I'll pray then," some of them would be kind enough to say.

And I would sigh so low and full of sorrow, it would reach the depths of Satan's soul.

I continued on. Wake up. Eat. Brush teeth. Work, eat, work, work, eat. Cry. Sleep. Next day: wake up, eat, brush teeth, go to school, vent to James, see Will, think of Ponyboy, try and sleep. I eventually accepted that sleep was an elusive fox I was lucky enough to catch for a couple of hours at a time. Going to the hospital every week no longer gave me anxiety. I became Miami's most confident driver. I could drive in the dark, drowning in my own tears on my way home. I would sing "Beautiful Pain" by Eminem at the top of my lungs.

I'm standing in the flames
It's a beautiful kind of pain
Setting fire to yesterday
Find the light, find the light, find the light…

I hope no one sees me crying, I would think, furtively glancing at the drivers next to me. They never saw me, they were always caught up in their own destinations, their own kinds of problems, their own personal hells.

"Yes, I'm crazy," I would angrily mutter as if anyone who did happen to see me could hear me. The lights turned green, one after the other.

"But I'm also insanely brave. It takes courage. Real courage to willingly drive yourself to face this kind of pain every day. This is the pain that comes from loving someone so much, so much, that their pain becomes your own, because love transcends. It pains you to see someone you love suffer to that degree, someone you love so much, but you do it in anyway because that's how much you love. And that is real love."

I turned into the main entrance of Baptist Hospital and found a decent parking spot. As I walked to the elevators that would take me to the cancer unit, I thought of the lives of the nurses, I thought of the other patients I'd see, and I thought of their families, and how they must be feeling. This hospital resembled a beehive. Everyone buzzed around, nurses wheeling away patients to new rooms, doctors chatting with other doctors, clusters of families holding back so much emotion in their fearful faces. I glanced at the pictures of birds, the beaches that littered the walls. I'll be there again one day, I thought to myself. For sure. I will.

For now, I had to slip into my costume of a warrior-daughter-cheerleader to cheer for my dad on the sidelines. Or I could be myself, a nervous, depressed basket case. Surprisingly, accepting my sadness felt a lot better than faking my happiness. It had become second-nature to me.

I opened the door to his room and was immediately hit with the smell of urine, uneaten food, and clean, medicine hospital scents, all hitting me in the face. I gulped it down. "Hola, Papi!" I said, happy to sound so genuinely cheerful. Did someone send me a good vibe out of nowhere? Where could I get more of it?

"Hola, Anaregina," he croaked. I focused on making eye contact with him, zeroing on his smile to not see how frail he had rapidly become.

"¿Como te sientes?" I asked as always.

"Eghhh…" He scrunched his face and made that "so-so" hand gesture.

"Have you eaten?" I opened the light brown, plastic lid off his dinner. It revealed pasta, a small steak, and slices of carrots with broccoli. There was also soup on the side, soda crackers, and an open, pint-sized carton of vanilla milk with protein in it (I am guilty of drinking half the containers myself sometimes). The scent of the food actually flooded my senses with joy.

"I don't really feel that hungry," he sighed.

"I know, Papi, but you will feel a lot better if you eat," I said. I felt like a broken record saying this. Mostly because I was always hearing my mom say it and the nurses say it. I wasn't liking the nurses lately. Some of them would talk to my dad the way an impatient mother tries to bribe her kids into eating their vegetables. And like a little kid, my dad would stubbornly refuse. He took one long sip of his milk.

"I actually feel too…I lack the energy to cut up the food, actually chew it and eat it," he admitted. I liked that we were being so honest with our emotions lately. It was so strange that just a couple of months ago, some flower on my wall was telling me my dad was so buff that he intimidated him.

I focused on the food, the soft, white sheets grazing my skin, the way my dad was looking at me, every ring in his eye revealing a spectrum of who he was and what I meant to him. Strength. Charisma. Hope. Pure and Unconditional Love. An unconscious maternal instinct kicked in me. I gingerly grabbed the fork and stabbed some pasta noodles, as I examined my dad's parted lips. We agreed without words that we were doing this. I instantly thought of Hazel that autumn day after math class when she told me that the pain became so much for her mom that Hazel had to spoon feed her.

It looks like now our feet were the same shoe size.

I stuck the food in my dad's mouth, careful not to stab him. As he chewed, I curled up closer to him, the way penguins huddle for warmth. If Hazel could do it, so could I. If Hazel could do it, so could I. If Hazel could do it, so could I… The mantra came to a stop when my dad shook his mouth. He was not enjoying the pasta anymore.

"It's starting to taste like nothing," he said.

"Do you want the soup?" I suggested. My tone was brimming with hope.

"Eh, yeah," he nodded. I felt like he only said yes to please me. Which was fine by me. The way a docile child wants to please their mom. It hit me then that I had never spoon-fed anyone in my life, not even a baby cousin or anything.

"Papi, I'm not really good at this," I complained, as a drop of soup dripped down his stubbly chin. He wiped it away with his hand and smiled his cancer-defying smile.

"Anaregina, just get a little bit of the soup in the spoon, slowly bring it to my mouth, and then wait to take it out," he said. He looked at me like he just explained to me 2+2, and I felt flooded with gratitude, following exactly what he said.

Yes, this is how it should be! Father teaching daughter! Not daughter feeding relatively young father. I repeated the task with as much patience and precision of a neurosurgeon performing brain surgery on the President of the United States. Occasionally, drops of soup dribbled down his cheek, and I would feel disappointed in myself.

"You're doing great," he reassured me with a smile.

"I'm trying my best!" I blurted with dramatized frustration. We both chuckled. Somehow this had become funny to us. We felt content. I would sneak in forkfuls of pasta for myself in between waiting for him to swallow the soup.

"I'm going to be a bad mother!" I cried, taking the spoon out before he had finished slurping the nutritious liquid.

He wiped his chin for the fourth time or so, and a calm, loving energy escaped his soul and infused his words, as they carried out into the air, warping space and time. "You are going to be a wonderful mother, Anaregina." I sat there, silent, stunned, completely unaware, yet intuitively aware of the future waiting to unravel.

CHAPTER 29
A Diploma for Sobriety

"Fuck, we're going to be late." I glanced at the time. Well Ana, you can't control time. I sighed with acceptance.

Naturally, Will sped up. "I'm not sure if we passed Opa Locka or not."

I gazed at the street, the small shops, the road signs. A blur of gray and peachy concrete colored walls. It looked the same for miles. We were lost, but I knew Will would find the way eventually.

"I can't believe the day is finally here," I said. The anticipation had me as giddy as a little girl going to Disney for the first time. Adam was finally coming back home for good.

"I know, me neither," Will said. He clasped my left hand with his right. I admired his long fingers and well-kept short nails. I loved how masculine they looked.

"I just wish my dad could be coming too," I said. My words hung in the air, each one an entity standing on its own, claiming energy too large to inhabit a human body. My annoying ring tone went off. Will gave me an empathetic expression, as he squeezed my hand.

"Hola, Mama," I answered. She said hello and asked where we were. I put the phone on speaker and let Will answer her the technicalities of our location.

"We should be getting there around the same time as her, babe," Will informed me. I nodded at him. He parked the car swiftly and with expert precision. I wondered if I was the only human aware that it was possible to feel more than two polar opposite emotions at once. Sadness, and happiness. Pain and pleasure. Anticipation of something good, dread for something bad.

I could feel myself slipping into a dark hole… But we will all be together again soon, I reminded myself. I felt saved from my own fall.

"You ready, baby?" Will smiled at me. I leisurely stepped out of the car. He planted a peck on my forehead. "Let's go."

I sighed. "I really hope they haven't called Adam's name yet." I felt dumb for crossing my fingers, but I did it anyway. Couldn't hurt.

We slipped in through the main entrance where a tall man greeted us, asking us where we headed. "The graduation ceremony?" Will said. Quick and to the point, always a Will characteristic. The man directed us to the media center where the small stage was. I wondered if Will was thinking about his dad too. Since we're in a drug rehab and he's always known his dad with the scent of booze stalking every word that had ever come out of him.

We entered the room filled with young men seated in rows of green chairs. I spotted my mom in the last row, and we sat next to her. Her face beamed with the same anticipatory energy that coursed between the cream-colored walls.

"Did Adam already go up?" I asked. Please say no.

"Yeah, he already did," she said. Her expression contorted with the same remorse I felt earlier. My mom and I forever connected through our emotions. I spotted Adam sitting somewhere towards the front. We waved at each other. Happiness seemed to be dripping off of his whole face and body. Some man on stage was announcing some dude to go up, and we all gave him our ears and eyes. The man with the mic was the director of the place. Apparently, only that guy and my brother were graduating from the rehab today. I loved seeing all the boys' faces brimming with hope, love, and excitement that they were going to be up on that stage too. I tried attaching stories to each face, because every single guy in this room no doubt had their own unique story just like my brother's and unfortunately, I could only imagine what it took for them to get to here.

There's the troublemaker…

The joker…

The one who always talks a lot.

The way they communicated with each other, the way they laughed together reminded me of a camp for all boys, a sacred brotherhood, a group of young men eager to get back into the world, all tied together for more or less the same reasons. Of course, I scoured the room for the cute ones. One with eternally long eyelashes and a bright white smile stuck out to me. I looked at Will from my peripheral vision to see if he noticed. His gaze was glued to the front of the stage. Adam's name was being announced again. The group of guys cheered like he was Troy from High School Musical who'd just won the basketball game.

"Would any of Adam's family members like to say anything?" the director man asked. Yes! No! Yes! My insides screamed. I sank in my chair a tiny bit, shy all of a sudden, and decided my wave of nerves wouldn't control me. I sat up straight and nodded.

"Go ahead," he egged me on. The entire crowd of guys turned to face me and "whoo'd" like they were monkeys in heat. My cheeks were enflamed, and my ears began a roasting party of their own.

"It's okay, Ana," Will whispered. I could feel his temporary vibe of "stop woo-ing at my girl like she's the last woman on Earth" by the way he tensed up, or at least that's how I interpreted it.

"Hi…" I waved awkwardly, clearing my throat. "Uh, hi, yeah, Adam, as your sister, I just want you to know I am so proud of you graduating from here." I paused to think of what to say next and listened to the sound of my voice as if a little critic popped out of my ear with its arms crossed and judgment boards with numbers in its hands. "It's been so long. So many days of just waiting…so the fact that this day is finally here, I am just so grateful. I am so proud that that day has finally come. I love you, and we are so happy to have you back." A cloud of applause thundered through the room, as if I had just given a speech for being the first woman to win a Nobel Peace Prize. Director Man had to shush the repressed monkeys in heat twice.

I cringed back into my seat and let out a small sigh of relief. Will squeezed my hand, as his plump lips formed a smile. My mom said a version of the same thing I said, but much more eloquent and Mom-like, of course. A couple of other directors spoke words from their souls and the bottoms of their hearts, as people always do at graduation ceremonies. One said, "It's sad to be seeing you guys go, but I never want to see you in here again."

We all laughed. Humor even in the darkest of times. I felt grateful.

Once the ceremony was over, we reunited with my brother and embraced each other. I was surprised he was friends with everyone, and everyone seemed genuinely sad to see him go. They said things like, "Take it easy, man," and "I'm going to miss you, man," followed with pats on his shoulder. We stepped outside into the humid night and took pictures with Director Man, and I made sure to thank him and his team for all of his work and obvious dedication to their jobs.

"Ay, Adam, Papá really wanted to be here," my mom said after we finished photographing the memories.

"I know," Adam said. He was too delighted to be sad about that fact.

"He wants to speak to you when we get out of here. He's really proud of you," my mom reassured him. Fuck cancer and its uncanny timing, I thought. It would lead him to the hospital just in time for Adam's graduation.

CHAPTER 30
Adam's Shitty Birthday

"You need to take Papá to get his medication." Those words broke my sleepy dream state.

"Uh-huh," I murmured to my mom. She left for work in an anxious tizzy. I didn't know it then, but I'd awoken to one of the most stressful days of my life, the day I saw my dad as a child and myself as the adult in charge. I got ready in usual monotonous way I'd been doing lately without really caring how I looked.

"Okay, let's go, Papá," I called to him.

"Give me a minute. I'm going to the bathroom first," he said. I cringed at his potential pain. I waited. I scanned Instagram like a programmed drone who does the same thing every day for ten minutes.

"I'm ready," he said, walking out of the hallway.

I gave him a meek smile, though it felt good to be independent enough to be helping out my dad. And to be driving!

"What hospital is your medication at?" I asked, my hands firmly on the wheel.

I immediately felt anxiety oozing off my dad. "It…it isn't the one on…uh…no, I don't think it's Baptist, Baptist." He was muttering and confused.

"Well, according to the lady on the phone, Baptist has a pharmacy that may have it or should have it," I said, but I wasn't sure myself. That lady sounded confused as hell too. The roads became a jungle of traffic, and my dad and I were lone survivors. We navigated ourselves to help, to safety. We just didn't know where the fuck we were.

"It's Kendall Regional Hospital we have to go to!" My dad burst out suddenly, relieved that he'd remembered this critical fact. His eyes were wide, innocent, and child-like. My grip on the wheel tightened.

"Are you sure, Papá?" I asked tersely. What was wrong with me? I didn't like the tone of my voice. It reminded me of those patronizing nurses.

"Yes, yes, I'm, yeah, I am pretty sure I am," he said, perched in the passenger seat like a child eager to visit his favorite candy shop but nervous to face the deadly dentist first.

"O-okayyy," I said, shrugging. It was his medication, so surely, he must know. He guided me to the correct hospital, but we ended up taking the wrong turn in the tangled jungle of Miami streets and ended up in a house driveway. I grew impatient. How could he not know how to get there?

He apologized for the fiasco, and I quickly forgave him, even as guilt bit me in the ass. Finally, we pulled into the hospital. It was the same one he'd brought me to four years ago when I had a series of sinus infections. The contradiction between today and four years ago startled me, but I couldn't afford to be Anxious and Afraid Ana right now. I parked the white Volkswagen, feeling like I was in an episode of The Twilight Zone, where now I was the caregiver and Papá was the sick.

"Where are we going?" My dad asked all of a sudden, panic-stricken. "Where are we going?"

"To the hospital, Papá, to get your medication." I looked at him, as worry filled the pit of my stomach. What was going on? I didn't like this new version of my father. Please, please, get it together, Papi. Please.

"Oh, yes, yes, that's right, I'm so sorry." Shame seemed to coat all of his facial features.

"It's okay, Papá," I said, an element of maternal care exuding from within, as I patted his back, soothing him down. As I helped him go downstairs, I thought of people with Alzheimer's and their families, instantly feeling sorry for them.

"Are you hungry?" he asked me. "Do you want to get something to eat?"

"Yes, I do," I answered. At the moment, food sounded like the best thing in the world. We could always get the medicine afterwards. We exited the gray parking lot and entered the warmth of a yellow, scent-filled cafe. The atmosphere and familiarity immediately put me at ease. I asked my dad if he wanted anything to eat, but he said no, so I indulged in a Caesar salad and a giant macadamia nut cookie.

"I'm feeling very weak," my dad admitted after my first couple of bites.

"It's because you haven't eaten," I said confidently.

"No, it's not that. I ate earlier," he assured me. My anxiety level started to go up.

"Okay, well, let's just get the medication and go home then," I said. Maybe that will help.

"Yes," my dad agreed. "I'm sorry, you haven't finished your food."

"Papi, it's okay. I'll just get a doggie bag and take it to go," I reassured him.

He sighed, and I sighed internally. I could feel him getting weaker and weaker even as we spoke. Draping his pencil thin arm over me, he leaned most of his body weight on me, as I helped him exit the cafe. I could feel the cash register guy staring at us. I could feel other customers staring at us too, feeling sorry. Outside, the security guard stared at us as well. I ignored the boa constrictor of anxiety slithering up my throat, as it clenched around my chest.

"Sir, let me get you a wheelchair," the security guard politely offered.

"Yes, thank you." My dad smiled at him. I smiled at the man in the uniform too, and for one moment I felt like I'd been rescued from the never-ending stress eating me inside. It felt good to have someone helping me help my dad.

But then… "I have to go to the bathroom," my dad announced. At this point, his bladder was a demon that demanded all his strength not to collapse on the floor. I helped him walk to the restroom, a challenge that would take another few minutes.

"Okay, Papi, I'll wait for you right here," I said at the door to the men's room. I had to use the restroom too, so I quickly dashed away into the women's restroom to use it as fast as I could.

Once I was back outside, the tall security guard returned with the wheelchair, and we both patiently waited for my dad to come out. When he did, he looked so relieved to see the wheelchair, but the tone of discomfort at the end of all his sentences wouldn't leave him.

"Oh, thank you so much," he said to the security guard, as he took a seat.

"You're welcome." He helped my dad to sit. "You folks have a nice day."

"Thank you." I smiled at the guard and began pushing my father in a wheelchair, something I never thought I'd do until he was much, much older.

"Do you know where you are going?" he asked.

No. No, I do not. I hadn't been more lost in my entire life. My dad was acting like a child, and somehow nineteen-year-old me had become the adult. Please help me. "More or less, well…actually, where is the pharmacy?" I asked, scanning around for signs.

He pointed the way, and once we arrived, the pharmacist let us know that there were no medications in his name waiting to be picked up. My dad tried asking her again. "It's under Rogelio. Frias."

She looked at him the way someone looks at someone when they are dying, full of sadness and hopelessness, an image I had only seen in movies. I felt like we were part of a circus and we were the circus freaks. Other customers waiting in line gave us the same sympathetic looks, so we left. No medicine in hand.

We were directed upstairs to talk to someone who might know where his medications might be. I felt as if both my dad and I were in a psychiatric ward trying to find the exit by getting more lost inside the building. Finally, we spoke to a doctor who informed us that we were in the wrong place. Yeah. I had a feeling. When it was clear my dad was officially talking nonsense, unaware of his incoherency, the doctor turned to talk to me instead.

I felt helpless and slightly embarrassed. The boa constrictor of anxiety had laced itself between my clammy fingers. We dropped off the wheelchair, as I reminded myself to take him to the Walgreens on 112th Street right by my college, so I shouldn't get lost.

You can do this, Ana, I imagined Will telling me. In my imagination, I nodded at him. And then I continued on in the jungle of streets. Lions roared, huge angry apes chased me, and a mountain lion was chilling in the backseat of the car. I could barely see the road because of the vines clouding my vision, but eventually we arrived at the Walgreens on 112th Street.

Safety. Oasis. Hopefully, this was the right place. Turned out it was.

As soon as my dad took a seat in the waiting area, he snapped out of his incoherency and realized his behavior. "I'm so sorry, Anaregina. I don't know what's wrong with me."

I felt so angry. Not at him exactly but at the entire situation. "It's okay, Papi," I said. Always a brave face. That's one thing I hate about cancer—the way it makes you act fake for the sake of your loved ones when deep down, you're pissed as hell.

After some new trouble involving insurance and extended release and blah, blah, blah, my mother informed us that we didn't really need to get it, so we left the pharmacy, and I drove my dad home, close to exploding from stress all over again.

***

Later that night, I invited Ted and Barney over. Just because I needed my friends. Barney arrived at the same time I got to my house after dropping my dad off at the hospital. I broke down in his arms, and he called me Miss Waterfalls. At least I laughed. Instantly, I felt better now that he was here. Ted was kind enough to bring me the most delicious spicy chicken sandwich from a fast food restaurant. I hadn't eaten in hours and tore into that thing. We talked and laughed until I finally calmed down.

After the boys left, I noticed something off about my brother, Adam, who was on house arrest for the time being, a thick black bracelet hugging his ankle. I suspected he was definitely on something, I just wasn't sure what. Hours later, I heard him and my mother screaming at each other so loudly I could feel the wall shake. The boa constrictor of anxiety finally bit me in the throat. Apparently, he took some of my dad's medication, painkillers probably. My mom says it was alcohol but I don't remember honestly.

Part of me wanted to grab a kitchen knife and slice my arm open just to get them to stop screaming. I imagined myself telling Tyronne about it, then Will, then decided against it. They continued to scream, scream, scream, scream, scream, and scream. I'd never felt more powerless in my entire life. I couldn't breathe. I wanted to call my dad but I knew I shouldn't. The empty, Hallmark birthday card resting on the kitchen counter seemed to mock me. It was close to midnight and my temples felt like they were going to explode. My heart began racing faster than the speed of light. I felt as if I didn't act now, I would literally stop breathing.

I grabbed my phone and ran outside to breathe. I ran, and ran, and ran, and ran until I could finally feel oxygen entering my lungs and decongesting my brain again. When I arrived at the lake by my house, the ripples of water illuminated by the moon worked hard to kill the boa constrictor of anxiety.

I called Will. "Hello," I said, my voice sounding terse.

"Hey, baby, what's up?" His tone was sweet and caring. I could take an eternal swim in it.

"Let me tell you about Adam's twenty-third birthday today."

CHAPTER 31
The Forty Minute Text

I received the text on Wednesday. I read it and completely dismissed it. I glanced at it again on Thursday and took a screenshot of it at 4:27 AM.

Dad
4/09/2015 Thu

Good morning my dear
and lovely daughter Anaregina.
I hope you have a wonderful day,
full of blessings and opening
roads to fulfill your destiny
of creating great things for
the benefit of yourself and
Humanity. Remember
Love is the fuel for these kind
Of endeavors and you are a
Lake of infinite love with all
These tributary rivers
Emptying their waters on
Lake Anaregina, the Rogelio
River, the Xiomaras River, the
Adam River and many more
(you know). Big kiss and a
bear hug.

Love, Dad

Answering the text felt as daunting as studying for a statistics final. I was procrastinating, yes. I was procrastinating my answer so much so when I arrived to the hospital the next day to see my dad, I still hadn't replied. I saw it as a deed, as a sentence. I did not let myself feel the emotion behind the text. I felt like a cold asshole.

"Did you get my text?" Dad asked. He was lying down on the white hospital bed, his body less of a man's now and more the withering body of a skeleton.

I glanced up from my phone. I was probably Snapchatting Will or something. I met his hollow gaze, his tired eyes filled with his love for me. "Yes, I did," I said solemnly. Adam was in the chair next to me, his lion tattoo ferociously climbing his tricep, frozen on his arm. Before my dad could utter another word I said, "I'm sorry, Papá, I did read it, but I didn't have enough time to reply everything I wanted to say to that message. But I will reply tonight."

"It took me forty minutes to write that text," he laughed humorlessly. "It's never been that difficult for me to type out a text in my entire life," he slowly spoke to Adam and me. Silence devoured the room.

CHAPTER 32
The Secret Battle

I wish I could fight the fight for you
I'd swallow the pain
I'd bathe in the misery
I don't care

Give me your cancer
Be free for a while
Breathe through my lungs

I'll dress in full armor
Use love as my sword
Use strength as my shield
I'll obliterate every malignant cell

Please, please, please
I'll eat all the pain
I'll drink all your poison
I won't fight in vain

I don't care
I love you
I love you
I love you Dad

I wish I could fight the fight for you

By the time I finished reading the last line, my dad was fast asleep in the eternally white hospital bed. The dance continued. In the hospital. Out the hospital. In the hospital. Out the hospital. In the hospital. Out the hospital. One day, in the middle of driving to the hospital, my dad received a phone call from Rafael, the other man. He called him "Papo," and by the familiarity and intimacy infused in his tone, I felt like I was listening to a conversation I should not be listening to. They spoke in Spanish, however, to me it felt like I was listening to a language I'd never heard before. Here on the other line was the portal to my dad's lifelong inner conflict, my dad's secret battle.

To be openly gay or not to be openly gay.

"Papo," my dad said again (I'd never heard him say "Papo" before), "I don't think I can keep going on like this." Urgency and the sound of tears being held back filled the dashboard. I couldn't even imagine what Rafael must have been feeling on the other side. For some reason, I couldn't hear the tune of my dad's final melodies of goodbye. Instead, I heard a telenovela of two secret gay lovers, one of them with two children and a wife, and the nosy daughter was listening in to one of their secret passionate conversations. He continued to speak in that unfamiliar, urgent, passionate tone. I spoke to him in my mind…

It's okay.

It's okay that your gay, or bi, or whatever.

I don't care. I don't care how long you kept this a secret for.

I don't judge you, Dad. I cannot and will not judge you.

I didn't judge you when I found out you got molested by a priest when you were a small, innocent child. I didn't judge you when a short time afterwards you took interest in boys instead of girls and your mom shunned you for it, and your parents died unaware of a whole other part of you, you didn't dare explore. I didn't judge you when I found out you had a phase as a sex addict. I am not judging you now.

But Dad wasn't listening to me. He told Rafael he loved him and hung up.

***

It was another hot April day, and I was stressed about passing my finals for World History and Humanities class. Both only had one midterm and one final. Ha, lucky me, right? The stress over my finals was blowing out of proportion. The day I took my history final, I took a crumb of Clonazepam just so I could breathe through the test. I was stressed beyond imagination, even though it ended up being easy. I made the single, hot soccer mom who juggled a job and three kids look like she was at fucking Disney World. Jodie (the real love of my life who sleeps with me every night) had now contracted breast cancer, the money I'd saved to go to Germany had gone to her surgery and to pay fucked up Alienna Health Insurance.

Obviously, I only regretted the latter. Meanwhile, my dad was getting eaten alive by cancer. To say he was all bones was not a hyperbole. I didn't see him for four days—FOUR WHOLE FUCKING DAYS—because my perfectionist ass CHOSE TO STUDY FOR FINALS INSTEAD. I chose studying for classes for my Associate of Arts degree over spending four more days with my dad who couldn't eat anymore unless someone was there feeding him. Now, I hated myself. I hated myself so fucking much, but I tucked the emotions behind my ear, aware that guilt would probably consume me next year.

One day, Rafael, my mom, and I were visiting my dad in the big, fancy hospital room (the big fancy ones are in the cancer unit which always made me think, Fuck you, Baptist, for making this so damned nice like if the hospital walls could speak, they'd say we look so goddamned nice with our pictures of beaches, because this will probably be the last beach you see in your life!). There I was eating a delicious Otis Spunkmeyer cookie, listening to the "adults" speak. I knew it was serious. I knew my dad felt uncomfortable with my presence. But I ate my cookie in whatever dress I wore that day and twirled my hair like an innocent seven-year-old kid who'd just walked into the room at the exact moment when her parents were deciding to end their "picture-perfect" marriage.

"Can you go buy me a cookie too, Anaregina?" my dad politely asked, as if I couldn't tell he was trying to get rid of me.

"Sure," I said, but I didn't hesitate to leave the room. I kept twirling my hair like a little clueless girl, as my dad began to tell my mom and Rafael the first of his goodbyes (my mom told me about this moment months later). He clasped Rafael's and my mom's hands together and told them to love and support each other. Rafael begged him to stop saying those things, to not give up, and "think of your grandchildren!"

But cancer isn't going to halt its destructive nature for my hypothetical children.

CHAPTER 33
Make a Wish

"Ana, are you listening?" Will asked, as we drove to Miami Beach. It was 10 PM, and because my curfew was 11:30 PM, Will was speeding.

Studying for finals was an escape for me… Now this was another escape for me… Fuck it, I needed this escape right now. Without even thinking twice about it, I reclined the passenger seat and undid the knot of my baby pink Forever 21 dress, slipping it off as elegantly and as teasingly as possible. Will stared at me in astonishment.

"Eyes on the road, babe," I said coyly, as my dress hit the floor.

"Oh, Ana…" He smiled, his lips salivating with lust. His eyes lingered on my now naked body, and I relished it. It was one of those rare days when you actually felt like the hottest thing on Earth. My makeup was on point, my curls were as luscious and bouncy as the model's in the TRESemmé commercials. For once, I'd succeeded at being sensuous and beautiful.

Will's hands lingered over my warm skin, and I basked in the naughtiness of being naked in his car, as we drove to the sexiest part of Miami: Downtown. I lightly moaned, enjoying the sound of it, as Will succeeded at having one hand on the wheel and the other in...well, you know. I loved seeing downtown's skyline lighting up over the bay, the building's lights, different shapes and sizes evoking freedom to me.

When we got to the parking lot of our destination, I slipped my dress back on, and just as if someone had randomly hit the back of my head with a brick, I suddenly thought about Ponyboy. "Thought about" was an understatement. Words were coming out of my boyfriend's mouth at the exact time I was seeing my ex-boyfriend's face. Holy shit, I thought. I wanted to go to the downtown and the beach late at night with Ponyboy so fucking bad.

Suddenly, I felt like a terrible human being. I hated myself.

Stop thinking of Ponyboy, Ana!

I stared at the car floor, trying to shake the image but when I looked up and met Will's deep brown eyes, they'd transmogrified into Ponyboy's.

Oh, my God, Ana…stop!

Finally, we arrived on Miami Beach, all the way to the edge of the ocean. There, I took my sandals off so I could feel each particle of sand underneath my feet. The shore teased my toes, and I giggled as cool water edged up and touched the tops of my calves. Looking at Will through my peripheral vision, I could tell the ocean was seducing him too. It was all so terribly romantic the way the full moon illuminated the ripples of the waves, the way they moved into each other in unique synchronization, like something unreal casting magic spells beneath the water.

"It's so beautiful," I said. Baby tears almost flooded my eyelids.

"I know," Will breathed by my cheek. He faced me and wrapped me in his arms. The moonlight made his face, nose, and teeth glow in a hauntingly gorgeous way. I was grateful that he was here, even though my brain kept betraying him.

"You look so beautiful, Ana," Will said in that I'm-a-musician-and-female-beauty-alone-can-hurt-me-like-I-want-it-to way.

"Thank you, you should see yourself." I smiled. "You're sparkling like Edward Cullen or something."

"Part of me is like, 'Fuck yeah, this is my hot ass girlfriend!' And then another part of me is like, 'I don't deserve her,' and yet another part is like, 'Shut up, Will.'" He paused, running his fingertips along my jawline. "It's so annoying having three trains of thought."

I smiled through my guilt, because all I could see were Ponyboy's ears. Ponyboy's nose. Ponyboy's smile wrapping around my arms and encircling itself around my chest. I'm sorry, Will. I'm sorry I can't stop thinking about him.

"Well, what are we waiting for?" I asked, glancing at the billowing white clouds behind the moon. I couldn't wait any longer. The ocean called to me. Come here, baby, she cooed at me. I stripped down to nothing and literally ran right into her. I'd never felt so free, insane, and magical in my life.

"Is it cold?" Will asked from fifteen feet away, glee pouring from his voice.

"Not really, just come in, you have to feel this!" I yelled, drinking in her salty scent, as I admired her cool, black mountains gently swaying me back and forth. After a couple minutes of hesitation, Will stripped down buck-naked and joined me. But guess who my mind went back to? Yes, the Ponyboy fantasy that never happened.

"I'm so fucking cold!" Will squirmed. The sound of the ocean's waves broke around him, soothing me.

"Pansy," I laughed. Her mysterious blackness frightened me. Who knew what was lurking in her darkness? I climbed on to Will's back and felt safe, like a human being from the beginning of time, like this was how nature intended us to be. Naked with nature. And aware that we may have to swim for our lives at any moment.

"Fuck," Will deadpanned.

"What?" I squealed. Was it a shark, a fucking shark?

"There's two guys over there…" He pointed to the entrance of the beach where a patch of tall grass grew next to a trail. Two humanoid shadows stood out in front of the glossy strip of hotels and restaurants.

"Ugh, fuck." This was worse than sharks. Will stood in front of me to block their view, since now I was feeling all awkward about being bare-breasted and bare-butted. "Can you go get my clothes, please?" I begged. He went off to retrieve my dress, while I stared at the sky and the stars dotted all over it, hypnotized by the way they gossiped over my deepest secret, twinkling and laughing at me. "Maybe they're leaving," I murmured hopefully.

"It looks like they're coming closer, Ana," he said, halfway out of the water.

He was right. They were, and the moment was over. Damn it, couldn't we have a single moment of pure freedom anywhere in this world without getting caught by police or my dad? I walked towards the shore backwards, so the men couldn't see my boobs. Although, I'd been told that I have really nice nipples. Still, because…strangers. I kissed the ocean goodbye and waded towards Will. He greeted me at the shoreline with my dress.

"Maybe the towel would be better," I said.

He handed me my towel and was pleased to dry off as well. Meanwhile, I relished the feeling of wet hair and wet skin in the cool night. I like to think that wet hair exudes a sexier version of myself. I dried myself off and slipped back into my dress, not even bothering with the underwear, because sex was on the menu, and eating out was for dessert. Unfortunately, the dessert part got interrupted by some stranger taking a long walk on the beach about ten feet across from us. Stranger, if you are reading this, I am the girl you saw on Miami Beach that night getting head from her boyfriend.

"Eh, better him than a cop." Will shrugged.

Well, yes, however…I am not happy whenever I am interrupted mid-orgasm.

"Yeah, we don't have much luck with those." I giggled. Although the element of getting caught here was even more exciting than the parking lot of the park by my house. Once the people had passed, we started having sex next to one of those lifeguard cabins and had to stop after another minute, because another couple started strolling towards us. I sighed. Interrupted again! Ugh! It was bad enough we had to use a fucking condom.

Think of the positive, Ana.

The view. The full moon, the water, the billions of stars. All my bad feelings melted away to the grains of sand. I felt rejuvenated. And look at that, I was not thinking of Ponyboy anymore!

"We should go. It's getting pretty late," I said, checking my phone. I put on my sandals and rattled the towel in the wind to get rid of the sand. Will reached for my hand, and I stared longingly at the view. I didn't want to tear away from it, but alas, it was time. As we walked, I got the perception that the ocean got me. She knew, she understood…

Minutes later, when we reached the parking lot illuminated by lamp posts, we spotted a shooting star high above the neon lights of Miami Beach, and I shrieked. I could not believe it. "Make a wish," I said, feeling like I'd just recited the line of a corny romance movie.

Will closed his eyes and thought of something. I hope it isn't about me.

Because even then, like the stubborn sand stuck between my damp toes, I still couldn't stop wishing for Ponyboy. I wished for the fourteen-year-old boy who'd spent an hour with me at Barnes and Noble searching for a dime because we were missing ten cents to buy me a chocolate chip cookie. I wished for the past to stay in my present. I wished the future could go exactly how I wanted it to. I wished…

But the things I really wanted were exactly what I could not have.

CHAPTER 34
Love is God

I was wearing the same seafoam dress my dad said I couldn't wear when I went to visit Adam in jail for the first time. Fuck, this is hard to write, but it's crucial. It's so fucking crucial, despite the pain that comes with writing it.

"I am going to put on some healing music," Mom declared. She lay on her stomach stretched out next to me, while I lay on my stomach too between my parents.

"Okay." The sound of my dad's voice sounded so healthy all of a sudden.

My brother walked into their bedroom, his thick eyebrows reaching the top of his forehead, and he looked as though he was going to lift some heavy weights. Mom was entranced with her cell phone, searching for the perfect YouTube mix. I was calm, because I could feel my dad's calmness. He said nothing. My brother made himself comfortable, as he curled up on the white bed with us. It was the closest we had ever been with each other in years.

I looked at my dad. No, I did not look at my dad. I felt my dad. I could feel the malignant cells inside of him packing their bags, taking a vacation, as the rest of his cells danced to a melody I could not hear, but I could feel. He didn't say a word. His eyes remained closed, as my mom played the Tibetan healing music, which consisted of ladies rubbing metal bowls creating an unearthly, god-like sound. I was transfixed, even the cells in my body were at peace.

All these months the cancer had been attacking my father, but in this moment, my dad's entire body and face emanated pure bliss. Wow, is this really the power of the music? I asked myself.

Happiness flooded my veins, as I watched my dad's lips curve into a peaceful smile.

My brother murmured some words to my mom, but I only heard the sound of his voice. Mom reset the healing bowls song while she replied to Adam, but again her words didn't translate in my mind. They only sounded like harmony. I wasn't thinking anything as this moment was happening. My subconscious was recording this perfect moment to write about it later.

Surprisingly, I felt no pain. The stillness of my father's presence was my only focus. I can feel his love flooding my room now, as it did that night. I couldn't help but rejoice the moment and stare at the image of my dad lying in bed completely silent. My mother and brother continued to speak, their voices full of joy, wholeness, togetherness. I refuse to use the word love, because one simple word could not do it justice.

Imagine the most soothing sound you've ever heard multiplied times infinity, then give it the shape of a feeling so warm, this feeling takes form. Now, break the feeling into shards of light, let it expand inside you, as it bursts at all your seams. You feel as if though you could blind the sun, with all your light and humble power.

My father spoke the most soothing words I'd ever heard come out of my dad's mouth, as if each syllable was a ray of light that stabbed my heart in the most beautiful way possible. The melody of the music had a vivacious effect, like I could see the vibrations of the bowls echoing in the empty space inside the room and all around me. My dad was on a completely different level. I cannot fully comprehend how. I only have the privilege of witnessing. He floated, as we lied around him like sea lions basking in the sun on a glacier. His nose a small mountain of abundant life, his eyebrows a calm sea dispersing to the tips of his eyelids, where the water evaporated casting a glow that traveled to his upturned lips carved out of perfectly smooth marble stone. Each vein of the marble rippled in every wrinkle on his face, in a way that made wrinkles seem like crevices to an undiscovered mine rich with gold.

Words slipped from his mouth, the first drops of rain that surprise your warm skin. "God is in the room," he finally spoke. "God is in the room."

CHAPTER 35
So Much for "The Gay Rights Campaign"

God dammit, I had a feeling this wasn't going to be good.

"Come sit over here," Leslie told me, her tone warning of really bad news. We sat outside the office where we sometimes debriefed after work, where the smell of cigarettes haunts you like a shitty break-up.

"I tried the best I could today," I said. I was referring to making ten dollars in the most difficult site to make quota which was downtown, where one encountered more homeless people than people willing to give you money for gay rights.

"I know, baby girl," she said in her raspy, sultry Leslie voice. We sat criss-cross applesauce, and I noticed she was avoiding eye contact with me. "Don't worry about it."

An awkward silence hung in the air. Um, okay…

"Have you found out anything about my proposal?" I asked.

She stared at the floor, her face squinting with discomfort. Dude, what the fuck without that proposal I can't work in the summer three days a week instead of the required minimum of five. Isn't taking care of your parent with terminal cancer a valid excuse?

"Yeah, about that. Okay, look, this isn't because you are a bad canvasser, because we both know that you are a good one, but lately with what's happening in your life…" Now, she looked me in the eyes.

My stomach sank.

"I decided not to submit the proposal," she said.

My stomach sank even further than I thought it could. "So, because of my situation with my dad having cancer and me having to help take care of him, it's not worth finding out if I can work three days a week instead of five?" I said in disbelief.

Her gaze remained glued to the floor. I couldn't believe this. "Ana, we've been seeing you get so sad for the past couple of months. You didn't make up the days you didn't work, and—"

"I was in the hospital seeing my dad," I interjected, a tiny quiver in my voice.

"You've been getting here late," she paused, "I…I know there's a good reason. It's just… You've also been on standards for the last couple of weeks, and the truth about proposals is that they are for people who are usually really, really good, like surpassing quota, you know?"

No, I didn't know. I knew that Zoe, our prior director/boss, said I could get one for sure. My stomach sank to the core of Earth, as Leslie's eyes started to get watery. Now, it all made sense.

"But you know, Ana, if you say the following words…" She gave me a wink-wink type of look. I quit. That was the answer. Those were the words she wanted to hear. "Then, I won't have to fire you, and when you're ready to come back, I could easily submit a proposal saying you were absent taking care of your dad." She gave me a feign, sympathetic smile, and like a Muggle underneath a spell, the words rolled out of my mouth automatically.

"I quit," I said, feeling the tears fight my eyelids. What the fuck was happening right now? I didn't want to quit my job, but it seemed I didn't have a choice.

"And look, Ana, as your friend, I think you should spend as much time as you can with your dad. You know, just talk to him, ask him anything you want to know."

"Uh-huh," I said, still in shock. Some of my coworkers walked by me, and I had to avert my gaze from them. I hated to think that they knew this was going to happen. Today. Right now. It felt like all my friendships had been ripped apart all at once. I wanted to leave right now. Leslie's last words echoed in my brain and made me feel like I'd swallowed the aftertaste of vomit.

Monica exited through the office door, and my robot self gave Leslie a light hug, as she said goodbye. I definitely did not have a crush on her anymore. I strolled to Monica, trying to process what had just unfolded.

"What happened?" she asked, as we turned away from the blue office building.

"That's what I'm trying to figure out," I said.

"What?" She shot me a puzzled look. Suddenly, the shock was over, and I started to feel fucking furious.

"Leslie made me quit, so she wouldn't have to fire me." I smiled, disdain on my cheeks. It was this moment when I began the habit of getting mani-pedis in an attempt to stop a meltdown, but nonetheless, I came home and fell apart on Adam's bed, sobbing as though the love of my life had just dumped me.

You should spend as much time as you can with your dad…
Her words haunted me for days.

CHAPTER 36
Airsoft

"I'm going airsofting with James now," I told Will over the phone.

"Yeah, that's fine," he muttered.

It's obviously not fine. "Are you sure? He said you could come too," I insisted.

"No, Ana. I'm not going."

"Alright, babe," I gave up trying. Of course he wasn't going to go. James would be there. James invited me. And he was pretty jealous of James.

I was only asking Will to be the "good girlfriend" I was. We hung up, and then I strolled to my living room and glanced at myself in the mirror. I wore a shimmery silver top with giant red lips on it and black jeans with leather strips on the side (I needed to look tough). This was way too glamorous for airsoft, but I had no other options. It was my only long-sleeved shirt.

Outside banana *banana emoji* James texted me.

Okie! I replied.

I entered my parents' room where both my mom and dad were sleeping and said goodbye. As always, I looked my dad in the eyes, avoiding looking at his cancer-ridden body. The tension stored in my neck and shoulders felt exhausting, but I paid no attention to it. It wasn't like I had cancer. As I locked the door, I said goodbye to Jodie and Tuti. A smile emerged on my face from the moment I opened the car door.

"Banana!" James exclaimed in a cheery, funny voice. He was in the passenger seat. Both he and his friend were in full-fledged camo gear, equipped with airsoft equipment consisting of huge, matte black guns.

"James Rat!" I tried to match his tone, though I could hear the sadness behind my voice.

"Banana, may I introduce you to my best friend, Joe."

"Ello, mate!" Joe shouted in a British accent as he turned the corner.

"Hi, I'm Ana." I shied into the backseat. It was a gorgeous, sunny day, the kind of day that made me appreciate me living in Miami. Joe and James kept switching the radio station, as I envisioned what running around in a field shooting each other with BB guns would be like.

"Are you okay with this being your gun?" James showed me a metal BB gun about three feet in length. How was I supposed to know anything about it?

"Um. Yeah, it's fine," I said. All of a sudden, I found myself swarmed with the electrifying feeling that I was about to embark on an adventure. I indulged in the feeling even more when the song "Shut Up and Dance" came on the radio.

Oh, don't you dare look back
Just keep your eyes on me
I said you're holding back
She said shut up and dance with me
This woman is my destiny
She said oh oh oh
Shut up and dance with me

Happiness! Yes! The upbeat melody of the song crept into my earholes and soothed the pain in my body. Finally. Yes. But then…Joe switched the station to some country song. No! No! Fuck. ANA, SAY SOMETHING NOW, DAMN IT.

"Wait, I was listening to that," I said in a low, whiny voice.

"Oh, sorry, madam," he said, switching the station back to the song.

The chemical, physical, kryptonite
Helpless to the bass and the fading light
Oh we were bound to get together
Bound to get together
She took my arm
I don't know how it happened
We took the floor and she said
Oh don't you dare look back
Just keep your eyes on me
I said you're holding back
She said shut up and dance with me
This woman is my destiny
She said oh oh oh
Shut up and dance with me

I felt so happy, I even started dancing in the backseat, despite my shyness. I would do anything to cling to a sliver of joy at this point. Fifteen minutes later, we arrived at the airsoft field, a vast, green empty field filled with tents and people wearing camo, touching their big, fake guns. Quietly, I stood next to James, as he introduced me to some of his buddies. Out here, I noticed that Joe was actually really cute. He had light green eyes and curly brown hair. He gave me a light pat on the head, as if I was a cat, and I smiled.

"Okay, we're next," James announced. Butterflies howled in my stomach. You got this, Ana!

Surprisingly, I felt prepared. James taught me and two other girl-friends of his (who I liked) how to work the guns and the basic rules. Shoot other people. Don't get shot. His ex fuck buddy was there, and she looked as though she'd stepped out of an action movie and was preparing for her next murder scene. I liked that she, too, was an English major, though I didn't enjoy the glare she gave me when she first met me.

You're overanalyzing her, Ana, I told myself. That could just be her resting face.

We stepped into the "battlefield" where paintball fights apparently also took place. The I-have-to-pee-but-not-really feeling settled in, as we waited by the gate covered in a black mesh material. I was placed on James's team.

"Okay, it's time to go in," George (another one of James's buddies) announced.

Oh, my God. Oh, my God. Oh, my God.

"Okay!" I gulped. We stepped through the gate and went by another wall covered in black mesh material where the actual battlefield was revealed. I secured the sweaty protective mask over my face and wiped my clammy hands on my jeans while holding onto my gun. My heart pounded inside my chest like a starving prisoner. I remained on my side, and Johnavan, James's other friend, strolled to the other. I became hyperaware, as adrenaline coursed through my body, and my last thought left me. This was what it's like to be in an actual real life video game!

"Go!" A tall man standing behind the wall instructed.

Bang! Bang! Bang!

The BB bullets went off in all directions. I instinctively crouched down and hid behind a pile of hay and remained that way until I felt safe enough to hide behind a tall patch of grass ten feet in front of me. James's ex fuck buddy fearlessly crept to the front of our side, as she shot around at everybody. She got shot in the leg and raised her hand in defeat. I made sure nobody was looking, as I slithered my way into a wooden cavern with two small holes for windows, occasionally peering up to look for my enemies.

I panted like a homeless dog in the desert. So, this was war? You just hide the whole time? No. It couldn't be. I stomped my way out of the cavern and revealed myself to the other side, as I began to shoot at our opponents. I didn't get anyone, but I felt cool as hell. The sharp, loud sound of the BBs flying out of my weapon each chanted, "You're a badass, Ana, you're a badass, Ana!"

Once I realized I was shooting at hay, I fired my gun a little higher. I adjusted my aim again, as I watched James tag some short bearded guy who looked straight out of a war movie. I'm going to shoot the guy next to him!

Ow. Ow! Ow! Ow!

A stinging sensation burned on my neck an inch next to where an Adam's apple is on a guy. Damn it, I'd been shot. I raised my both my hands up and walked to the sidelines with the rest of my teammates that had been shot. I felt so relieved to be out. My breathing slowed down, and I lightly touched my neck where I was shot. A bump had already formed. It was like there was a little crater in there.

Who the fuck did this? I didn't even see who did it!

"Don't look at it, Ana," James said when we were back underneath the tents.

"Why not?" I asked. Now that the adrenaline wore off, it hurt just to turn my neck.

"Trust me, if you look at it, you'll freak out. It looks worse than it actually is."

"Am I bleeding?" I asked.

"Yeah, a little bit," he admitted. Yes! I was a badass. Yup, this moment right here defined my doubt of whether or not I, Anaregina Frias, could sum up to badass material.

Joe scrunched his face as he looked at my neck, and asked me, "Do you want to go for round two?"

I shook my head. No, my faux war days were over. It was time for my rest with the girls now. The guys went for round two, while I sat with Kaybis and Aleida. I found out that they went to Ferguson High School, and James's ex, Miley, came up in the conversation. In my head, James's unrequited love for her knocked on the door of my mind. Shhh, it's a secret. We continued to make small talk and before we knew it, the guys were back. Joe had been shot in the forehead, but it just looked like a red mosquito bite. He was dressed in armor from head to toe.

"James," I say as soon as I see him. "I'm starving!"

"Me too, Banana. Let's go eat burgers. They're cooking some over there." He pointed at a barbeque stand fifteen feet away. The scent of cooked meat wafted through the thick air, the sun boiled my skin, so I rolled up my sleeves, mentally fighting with myself about whether I should go for round three. My phone rang. I automatically assumed it was Will. But it was Adam's name on the screen.

Strange, he rarely called. I answered the phone. The tone of his voice set the dormant butterflies in my stomach ablaze.

"Hey, you have to get here right now. Like right now."

"Why, what's happening?" I cupped my phone to my ear with both hands. James looked at me like an alert watch dog.

"It's Jodie. Her thing came off of her wound, and she's bleeding all over the house. You need to come right now."

"Okay. I'm on my way. Bye."

We hung up on the phone, and James sprang into action driving me home. It felt like I was a character in a movie or book where only shitty bad things happen to the main character. Even the weather seemed darker, cloudier. How fitting for the dark twist.

"Don't worry, Ana-Banana, she's going to be fine," he reassured me. Happy pop tunes filled the car, but I didn't believe a word of hope anymore.

"Yep," I said, inhaling a breath of air. James's musky scent made its way in there, and despite the putrid tinge of sweat, it was a reassuring smell. "Thanks for taking me back home."

"Not a problem. Let me know how everything goes with her."

"I will." I leaned over to give him a quick cheek kiss, as he wrapped his warm, hairy arms around me. For a fleeting moment, everything felt safe, and then I stepped out of the car door and walked home.

Home. The place I dreaded to be in the most. Home, the place that now felt like a hospital in disguise. Home, a shelter that inhabited not a happy, beautiful family, but a sad, tired family getting up close and personal with the shackles of an incurable disease. To my relief, the Jodie thing was a lie manifested by Adam to get me to come home quicker. To my horror, I had other news waiting to be delivered.

My mother's eyes were red and swollen. "Papá said he doesn't want to live anymore," she laid it on me.

"What?" I said, as waves of shock rippled through me.

"He said he wants to leave as soon as Jane and Petra return to Mexico next Wednesday," she muttered. The sadness in her voice alone was enough to make me want to get shot in the throat by the airsoft BB gun ten times over again. I couldn't believe what I was hearing. I literally couldn't believe it. Knots upon knots of stress formed inside my entire body. My heart and mind spoke to each other in foreign languages trying desperately to process the news delivered to me.

I wanted to throw up. Down. Around. Everywhere. No. No, absolutely not. He couldn't just decide to die next Wednesday, such a trivial fucking day. I rushed to my room and picked up the copy, You Can Heal Your Life by Louise L. Hay, a self-help book that Papá had lent me, advised me to read. I said hello to my visiting aunts, as the image of Will telling me he wanted to kill himself in Lafayette rendered in my mind like a movie. I was overcome with anxiety then because I really thought he was going to do it.

It's just a feeling. He's voicing a feeling, just like Will did that night. It's okay. It's just a feeling, I told myself over and over again. There was more adrenaline in me now than before getting shot by a tiny plastic bullet going 75 miles per hour. But I couldn't cry. Not yet. I needed to be calm. I needed to face this. I wanted to fix this. I couldn't give up, he couldn't give up. I sat upright on my bed and started flipping the pages of the book to the end where Louise L. Hay explained her cancer story. I found the page, doggy-eared it and went to my parents' bed where my dad was lying.

This time, I couldn't focus only on his eyes. This time, I saw him as a whole. I saw him dying. His droopy skin was clinging onto his skeleton for dear life. His eyes seemed to be sinking into his eye sockets, preparing themselves for the arrival of my greatest fear. I cringed.

"Hola, Papá," I said, covering up my wound with my hair, as I didn't want to worry him.

"Hola, Anaregina," he croaked. He could barely speak. I distinctly heard the lack of saliva in his voice.

"Do you want water?" I asked, eyeing the green sponge tube thing to get him water.

"No, no," he protested. The air felt dense with tension.

"Okay," I said, feeling surprisingly calm.

Tears began overflowing from his eyes.

"Mama told me that you don't want to keep on living anymore…" I said. My words did not feel like my own. I felt like a younger, calmer version of myself. Like an innocent little girl asking her father to please stay, because there was so much more to see, and it was much too early to leave it all behind.

"I'm so sorry. I'm so, so sorry, Anaregina," my dad repeated over and over again, incessant tears streaming down his face. This was just a feeling. This was just how he feels, he's not dying yet. He's not going to die.

"Don't be sorry, Papá, you have nothing to be sorry about. Please don't say you're sorry, because none of this is your fault," I insisted. His contorted face relaxed a little bit, as I sat in the corner of the warm, white bed.

"I just feel like I've disappointed you, Adam, and Mama."

"No, you haven't disappointed me. You haven't disappointed any of us," I said. The anxiety to read the excerpt of the book was biting me behind my head, crawling around my ears. He needed to hear this already. "I'm going to read you this part of the book where Louise L. Hay shares her story of how she overcame cancer. Do you remember it?"

He nodded, eyes wide open, pupils slightly dilated. Every part of him was visibly tense. I reached for his hand for a moment, inhaled a deep breath, and exhaled. I ignored my dad looking like a small, scared child instead of my fifty-eight-year-old father who once took me to the rocks of the mountains in Acapulco when I was a mere baby, and his arms were my home, my stronghold.

I opened up to page 199 and cleared my throat. My dad smiled. I felt better.

"Then one day I was diagnosed as having cancer. With my background of being raped at five and having been a battered child, it was no wonder I manifested cancer in the vaginal area. Like anyone else who has just been told they have cancer, I went into total panic. Yet because of all my work with the clients, I knew that mental healing worked, and here I was with a chance to prove it to myself. After all, I had written the book on mental patterns, and I knew cancer is a disease of deep resentment that has been held for a long time until it literally eats away at the body. I had been refusing to be willing to dissolve all the anger and resentment at them over my childhood. There was no time to waste, I had a lot of work to do," I paused and glanced at my dad. He was beginning to look sleepy, which I took as a good sign.

"The word INCURABLE, which is so frightening to so many people, means to me that this particular condition cannot be cured by any outer means and that we must go within to find the cure. If I had an operation to get rid of the cancer and did not clear the mental pattern that created it, then the doctors would just keep cutting Louise until there was no more Louise to cut," I paused. My intestines did a somersault.

I continued reading, "I didn't like that idea. If I had the operation…" I stopped. My dad's hand felt cold and weak, and his eyelids were drooping. I should've just let him sleep. I skimmed the rest of the page and felt empowered, as I read the last paragraph.

"I did not have an operation. However, as a result of all the thorough mental and physical cleansing, six months after my diagnosis I was able to get the medical profession to agree with what I already knew, that I no longer had even a trace of cancer! Now I knew from personal experience that disease can be healed, if we are willing to change the way we think and believe and act! Sometimes what seems to be a big tragedy turns out to become the greatest good in our lives," I paused as my dad slowly spoke through the crack of his lips.

"Thank you, Anaregina. I love you so much." A glimmer of hope flashed in his face but sleep quickly guided him back to peace. It'll be okay. It'll be okay.

And for once, I believed myself.

CHAPTER 37
Last Goodbye

Wednesday, May 13th, 2015.

In the past couple of days, I'd finished reading You Can Heal Your Life and Siddhartha. I hadn't left my house in days. I hadn't shaved my legs in weeks. My aunts were staying at my house for another week. I was lying down on my oatmeal-colored couch in my living room, never noticing that hours had passed of me staring up at the ceiling. Another dimension could have been unfolding before my eyes, and I would not have noticed. I felt my phone vibrating on my thigh. I checked the text.

Y mi platano? My dad texted me wanting his banana.

Fuck! I'm supposed to feed him breakfast. As guilty as I felt, I didn't have enough energy to get up and feed him. I didn't have enough energy to do anything, in fact. Except read and make art. Perhaps God sent an angel that day to make me get off my ass and make him a bowl of oatmeal. I chopped off the banana slices as thinly and swiftly as possible and put them in another small bowl. Then, I walked to his room.

"I'm sorry I took so long, Papá," I said, barely recognizing my own voice from how deep in thought I was minutes ago. I read a bit of anger in his face, but it faded faster than a shooting star. I wished things could be different right now, but the wishing had no use. I had to use my strength right now. Just try and make him laugh, Ana.

"Can I have the oatmeal first?" he asked.

"Before the water?"

"Water first, then oatmeal."

"Okay, Papi." I picked up the tube attached to the sponge on his bedside and dipped it into the glass of water, then stuck it in my dad's mouth. He bit onto it, absorbing all the water. After a couple of sips, he stopped me with his hand, and I reached out for the oatmeal. It was still warm, thank God. I swirled it around so it cooled down a little more then made a happy face out of it with the fork.

"Look, Papá, smile. I made a happy face out of oatmeal. See, I can turn anything into art!" I laughed. Where was this joy coming from? I had no idea, but it made my dad chuckle and my heart soar.

"You are more than you think you are," he said quietly as he placed his hand over mine. I cherished the warmth of it, and I observed every wrinkle, every spot like I was going to have a test on it the next day.

"Thank you, Papá," I said. I'll never forget those words.

He had only enough energy left to give me the tiniest of smiles in response. But I cherished it. I continued to feed him until he stopped me with his hand again. I patiently waited for him to finish chewing his last bite before he finally spoke to me.

"Have you finished my letter yet?" he asked.

"Almost," I said agonizingly. I had written my dad a eulogy, the most painful thing I'd ever had to write.

"I'm waiting for it," he said calmly. A spasm of pain shot throughout his body, and he curled to the side in fetal position.

I sighed. "I know you are, Papi. I'm going to finish it right now," I promised, although a part of me refused to. Time, however, wasn't on my side. I waited until he closed his eyes so I could slip into my room and face the last piece of artwork I knew I'd ever give to my dad. A giant green poster board folded to look like a card that said, "I love you Papá," in blue-painted cursive letters with my goodbye pasted inside. I decorated it with blue-painted fish because of our love of the ocean.

The last thing I needed to do was tape the pictures from the family album and give it to him. I taped them inside the card and on the back. It was alleviating to see the photos of my dad when he was young and healthy. There I was in front of him at the fifth grade dance in my sparkly pink dress, embarrassed that both my parents came to see me. There I was opening the Snoopy gift-wrapped box containing my dad's sixth birthday present to me, a Dalmatian puppy named Snoopy. I felt like I was suspended in the air, teetering between intense calm and intense anticipation of pain. I finally finished posting the pictures, but I added even more details with a silver Sharpie, by filling it with stars, smiley faces, hearts, and endless "We love you's."

Not too long ago, I had seen Tyronne and was caught in the throes of being mentally distracted with thoughts of breaking up with Will and seeing Ponyboy. Tyronne had told me, "Stop focusing on them right now. You need to focus on your dad, sweetie. He's not going to leave until he gets your goodbye."

"Yeah, but is it really possible to plan and know exactly when you're going to die?" I asked him.

"My mom did," he replied.

I got home that day and went straight to work on this card. Now, I was finally finished with it. Now it was time to read my final goodbye to him. But I kept thinking there would be at least the rest of the summer with him. I hoped so. I really fucking hoped so. I gathered the strength to get off my ass and slip into his room again. Petra was in there with him, and once she saw the card in my hand, she left to give us time alone, smiling and reaching for my hand as she left the room.

"Okay, Papá, I finished it," I said with a smile.

"Good." He smiled back, faint but happy. "I've been waiting."

"I know, I'm sorry."

"It's okay, Anaregina."

"Thank you, Papá," I said.

He grabbed my hand and held it like it was a cold, frightened kitten. "I love it," he said, admiring the front.

"Thank you," I said, feeling like if I didn't start reading right now then I was going to implode. I felt like if I read it to him, then that would be it. It would be over. Goodbye would really be goodbye, and then he would die. As I sat next to him, he turned his head to face me. I made an effort not to cry right now, as I cleared my throat:

"To: The Most Wonderful, M a g n i f i c e n t, Extraordinary, Fabulous, Awesome, Amazing, Strong, Courageous, Impressive, Good-Looking, Awe-Inspiring, S t u n n i n g, Excellent, Divine, Beautiful, Charismatic, FUNNY, Adventurous, Thoughtful, INTELLIGENT, Heroic, Insightful, Lionhearted, Sweetest, Wisest Person I Know," I read.

Twice I swallowed away my urge to cry.

"I love you. I love you, Dad. I love you so much. I can't even express it. I am so grateful to be your daughter to share our blood and our memories. I will make you so proud. I will be the best goddamned writer I'll ever know. I'll write so much and so well that I'll be the next sensation or at least a woman who followed her heart and turned her dreams into goals, and then ultimately her reality. I can do it. I am destined for great things, like you said. I plan on showing you that. I know I have shown you that already. You are so wonderful, Papá. I forgive you for anything you feel like you went wrong with me or Mamá or Adam. You did the best you could and I know that. I know that with my heart and soul. I just really hate having to see you go so soon. It's really difficult to imagine my life without you, but I will be happy that you lived and loved and gave me your presence. Thank you for everything. Thank you for giving me the gift of life and raising me. Thank you for giving me the most perfect childhood anyone could have ever asked for. For Perdy, for Snoopy, for allowing me to keep Jodie and all of our other pets we've had in our home. Thank you for providing me with a home, and food, and vacations to Mexico to see our beautiful family. Thank you for all the surprises/presents you would give me when I was little and you would come back from Teleplanet. Thank you for saving my life when I almost drowned in the pool when I was five. Thank you for being Santa Claus, and the leprechauns, and the Tooth Fairy. Nobody could have done that as well as you. Thank you for supporting me and believing in me and telling me that I am always enough. You have made me who I am. I would not be Anaregina Frias without you. Literally. I love you, Dad. I love your laugh and your smile and your whole soul and spirit. Thank you for opening up to me and trusting me with your life's story. I'll hear you in the old music I listen to, I'll see you when I close my eyes and think of you. El Principito, Pixie Stix, Cheerios, the movies we have seen, all of our words we've said will be in my heart. And believe me, Papá, I will have endless conversations with you throughout my life! You will always be in my heart and when my heart stops beating I will see you again. I'll tell you about my entire life's journey with Adam, and Mamá, and Perdy, and Abuelo Rogelio all present. We will all be there together coexisting between space and time, touring the magnificent mysteries of the Universe as we travel with the stars that once created us.

Thank you,

I will never stop learning from you and this entire experience.

Te quiero muchisisisisisisiisisisisisiisisisisisisisisisisisisisisisisisisisisi-
sisisisisisisisisisisisisiisisisisisisiisisisisisisiisisisisisisisisisisisisiisisisi
sisisisisisisisisisisisisisisisisisisisisisisisisisisisisisisisiisisisisisiisis
isiisisisssssssssssssssiiiiiiiiiiiissssssssssssssssiiiiiiiiiisisisisiiiiiiiiiiiiiiiiiiiiiiiii
ssssssssssssssssssssssiiiiiisisisisisiisisisisisiisisisisisiisisisisisisisiisisisisis
ssssiiiiisisisisisssssssssssiiisisisiisisisisisisisisisisisisisiisisisisisisisiisisisisiisiisisi
sisiissisisisiisisisisisisisisisisiissiisisisisisisisisisisisisisiisisisisisisiisisisisisisi
sisisisisisisisisiisisisisisiisisiisisisisisisssisisissisisisisisisisisisisisisisisissisi
sisisissisisisisisisisisisisisisisisisisisisisiisisisisisisiisisisisisisisisisisisisisi
sisisisisisisisisisisisisisisisisisisiisisisisisisisisisisisisisisisisisisisisisisisisis
ssssssssssssiiiiiiiiiiiiiiiissssssssssssssssssssssssssiiiiiiiiiiiiiiiiiiiiiiiiiiiiiiiiiiiiiiissss
ssssssssssssssssssiiiiiiiiiiiiiiiiiiiiiiiiiiiiiiiiiiiiiiiiiiiiiiiiiiiiiiiiiiiiiiiiiiiiiiiiiiiiiiiii
iiiiiiiiiiiiiiiiiiiiiiiiiiissssssssssssssssssssssiiiiiiiiiiiiiiiiiiiiiiiiiissssssssssssssssss
ssssiiiiiiiiiiiiiiiiiiiiiissssssssssssssssssssssssssssssssssisisisiiiiiiiiiiiiiiiiiiiiiiiissssssss
sssssssssiiiiiiiiiiiiiiiiiiiiiiiiissssssssssssssssssiiiiiiiiiiiiiiiiiiiiiiiiisssssssssssssssssiiiiiiiiiii
iiiisssssssssssiiiiiiiiiiiisisisisisisisiisisisisiiiiiiiiiiiiiiiiiiiiiiissssssssssssssssssssssssss
ssssssssssssssssssssssssssssssssssssssssssssssssssssssssssssssssssssssssssssss
ssssssssssssssssssssssssssssssssssssssssssssssssssssssssssssssssssssssssssssss
sssssssssssssssssssssssssiiiiiiiiiiiiiiiiiiiiiiiiiiiiiiiiiiiiiiiiiiiiiiiiiiiiiiiiiiiiiiiiiiiiii
iiiiiiiiiiiiiiiiiiiiiiiiiiiiiiiiiiiiiiiiiiiiiiiiiiiiiiiiiiiiiiiiiiiissssssssssssssssssssssssssss
ssssssssssssiiiiiiiiiiiiiiiiiiiiiiiiiiiiiiiiiiiiiiiiiiissssssssssssssssiiiiiiiiiiiiiiiiiiiiiiiiiiiiiiiiiii
iiiiiiiiiiiiiiiiiiisisisisisimossssssssssssssssssssssssssssssssssssssssssssssssss

ssssssssssssssssssssss

iiiiiiiiiiiiiiiILOVEYOUiiiiiiiiiiiiiiiiiiiiiiiiiiiiiiiiiiiiii
iiiiiiiiiiiiiiiILOVEYOUiiiiiiiiiiiiiiiiiiiiiiiiiiiiiiiiiiiiiii

ssiiiiiiiiiiiiiiiiiiiiiiiiiiiloveyouiiiiiiiiiiiiiiiiiiiisssssssssssssssssiiiiiiiiiiiiiiiiiiiiiiiii
iiiiiloveyouiiiiiiiiiiiiiiiiiiiisssssssssssssssssssssssiiiiiiiiiiiiiiiiiloveyouiiiiiiiiiiiiiiii
iiiiiiiiiiiiisssssssssssiiiiiiiiiiiiiiiiiiiiiiiiiiiiiloveyouiiiiiiiiiiiiiiiiiiiiiiiiisssssssssssss
sssssssssssssssiiiiiiiiloveyouiiiiiiiiiiiiiiiiiiiiiiiiiiiiiiiiiiiiiiiissiiiiiiiiiiiiiiiiiiiiiiiiiiiii
iloveyouiiiiiiiiiiiiiiiiiiiiiiiiiiiiiiiiiiiiiisssssssssssssssssssssssssssssssssssiiiiiiiiiiiiiiiiii
iiiiiiiiiiiiiiiiiiiiiiiiiiiiiiiiiiiiiloveyouiiiiiiiiiiiiiiiiiiiiiiiiiiiiiiiiiiiiiiiiiiiissssssssssssssssss
sssssssssssssssssssssiiiiiiiiiiiiiiiiiiloveyouiiiiiiiiiiiiiiiiiiiiiiiiiiiiiiiiiiiiiiiiiiiiiiiiiiiiiiiiii
iiiiiiiissssssssssssssssssssssssssssssssssssssssssssssiiiiiiiiiiiiiiiiiiiiiiiiiiiiiiiiiiiiiiiilov
eyouiiiiiiiiiiiiiiiiiiiiiiiiiiiisssssssssssssssssssssssssssssssssssssssssssssssssssssiiii
iiiiiiiiloveyouiiiiiiiiiiiiiiiiiiiiiiiiiiiiiiiiiiiiiiiissssssssssssssssssssssssssssssssssssssssss
sssssssssssssssssssssiiiiiiiiloveyouiiiiiiiiiiiiiiiiiiiiiiiiiiiiiiiissssssssssssssssssssssssssssss
sssssssssssssssssssssssssssssssssssssiiiiiiiiiiiiiiiiiiiloveoyuiiiiiiiiiiiiisssssssssssssssss
ssssssssssssssssssssssssssssssssssssssssssssssssssssssssiiiiiloveyouiiiiissssssssssssss
sssssssssssssssssssssssssssssssssssssssssssssssssssssssssssssiILOVEYOU!iisss
ssssssssssssssssssssssssssssssssssssssssssssssssssssssssssssssssssssssssssssssss
sssssssssssssssssssssssssssssssssssssssisisisisisisisisisisisisisisisisisisisiisisismo,

Anaregina Frias."

By the end, we were both in tears. I waited for words to come out of my dad's mouth, but he didn't have enough energy to say anything other than, "I love you so much."

So he communicated with his soul instead. He raised his hand up, and I clasped his hand with my own. We held it there for a couple of seconds. All the love I could ever possibly feel from him, with him, for him, became eternally sealed in that ineffable moment. He promised me he would watch over me from the stars. And I believed him.

CHAPTER 38
The Beginning

"Anaregina, wake up." Adam nudged me on the shoulder. The mechanic could not be here already. Last night, I faintly remembered Adam telling me the car mechanic was coming today while I researched bladder cancer, texted my friends, and continued telling Papá everything I was grateful for even as he slept.

I made a grunting noise. "No, Adam." I was not waking up for the car mechanic right now.

"Wake up, it's Papá." His words seeped into my consciousness.

My eyes flitted open immediately. I shuffled out of bed in what felt like fast and slow motion at once. As I was walking to his bedroom, my aunt, Petra, gently stopped me halfway, big tears in her almond eyes.

"Your dad is not okay, sweetie," she said. Her tone made my heart sink. I walked into the bedroom, and suddenly, I was hyperaware.

This is it.

He was lying on the hospice bed, his face sinking almost imperceptibly to the back of his head, his eyes small beads, open but no longer really watching. He opened and closed his mouth, taking in gasps of air and exhaling wheezing grunts. The image of a fish out of water surfaced in my brain.

This was not my dad anymore.

A short, blonde nurse stood over him, checking his vitals. Jane and Adam perched on the bed next to him, as Petra and I loomed over him at the foot of his hospice bed. Mom was at work, helping people with their problems, unaware of the current status of the man she loved. I was frozen, watching my dad behave like a fish out of the ocean. Wheezing. Gasping. Inhaling. Exhaling. Every breath shorter, every gasp softer.

Jane stroked his forehead and his hair.

I held my dad's hand. It was so weak and so frail and so cold. And then it hit me.

This really is it.

My dad is dyi—

The thought would not finish itself in my mind. I was interrupted by a sensation I'd never felt before. Watching the nurse place the stethoscope over my dad's heart, I waited. She waited. All of a sudden, I felt my dad's hand tense and it began to quiver, and I felt an energy I had never felt before. This was his soul taking over. I squeezed and concentrated on his hands.

Here is all my energy, Dad. Here is the best of me, here is all my happiness, all my love, all my gratitude. Everything. Everything. Here it is. All of it. All of it. The quivering stopped. I lifted my head up.

The word "Falleció" escaped the nurse's lips.

Dead.

Dead. Dead. Dead. The word seemed tangible, like I could catch it in the air before it floated to the sky. She checked the time on her watch. "A las doce y media," she said. 12:30 PM. I was still holding onto his hand. Tears streamed down my cheeks, but they did not feel like they belonged to me. Jane gently closed his hands. Adam placed his hand on his chest.

"Are you sure?" he asked the nurse. "I still feel something," he said confidently.

"Yes," she said in a serious, slightly awkward tone.

I watched as the muscles of my dad's face instantly relaxed. He looks so peaceful, as though he had been carved out of beautiful marble. In almost a wavelike motion, the rest of his muscles did the same. No one spoke. Petra sat crying, and I could sense Adam's state of denial. My attention fixated on my dad's body. It began to tense up just as quickly as it had relaxed moments ago. I was still holding his hand.

Then, it dawned on me.

This was not my dad anymore. I was holding a dead body.

This was his body. But he was not here.

Tears gushed down to my throat, and while I was aware of what had just happened, I couldn't believe it. I felt like I was dreaming. Floating, in fact.

I too was no longer here.

***

You are above the relief of his pain and the torment of your sorrow. You are watching over this event of your life in the clouds, as you eat popcorn and feel sorry for the girl crying over her dad's body. You still haven't let go of his tense hand. You wait until the nurse, Petra, Jane, and Adam trickle out of the room so that you can speak to him. You repeat over and over again that you love him so much. You watch in amazement as his lips barely turn up to a tiny smile, revealing a small white line of teeth. You question your sanity. You remind him again how fucking grateful you are for him. You continue to tell him all of the things you had started to tell him last night, the things that you wanted to wait for when you were married and with kids. You say, "Dad, in eighth grade I used to sneak out into Kallusa Elementary School with Ponyboy." You wonder how that is relevant, and you try and think of more memories that you want to share that you want to say thank you for. No specific memory comes to mind. You are overwhelmed with love, gratitude and some kind of beautiful sorrow you still cannot understand. You can feel that he is at peace now. You forget to give him one last hug, and then you ask your brother if he wants to have a moment with him. He says yes, but you cannot tear the gaze off of your father's body. You do it anyway. You already let go of his hand. You think of your mom. Driving home from work, and how she has no idea. Pain flushes over you. You sit down on the couch with your aunts and the nurse and watch in awe as they could still manage a conversation with each other. You feel perverse enjoyment that they too are crying. You ask them if they want to have a moment with your dad, and they shake their heads no.

"I was speaking to him in my head, mi cielo," Jane says.

Her warmth exudes from her features, and you are wrapped in her love for a moment. Your other aunt's love too. You continue to feel so sorry for yourself, as you eat popcorn and watch the girl's mother arrive home. You find out she already knows the news, and she sees your father's body too. You cannot read any emotion on her face other than a calm peace. You watch as the people who collect dead bodies enter your home and ask you to not be in the room where your father is. You may not be holding your dad's hand anymore, but you know deep down you still have not let go. Your tears are relentless, you want to scream loud enough so that people in China could hear you. You watch as the two stocky men stroll your dad, who is now wrapped in a white blanket, to your front door. They speak to your mom and your bother, and you take this opportunity to touch your dad's toes. You say in the softest voice you can muster that you love him so much. You don't want him to go. In your head, you ask the man who is putting your dad's body in the trunk of the white hospice van to please be gentle with him. The men are serious and to the point. You feel guilty for finding the younger man's muscular calves attractive. You feel May's heat sting your skin, and you feel angry that the day is so beautiful. You feel an emptiness akin to a hollow cave encapsulate your heart, as the van turns on and starts to drive. Your brother has his arm draped over your shoulder. He squeezes you, as you both watch the van turn around the corner. It's the last time you'll ever see your dad. Your stomach becomes a deep void you've never known before. You remember the time you were five years old and you were watching your dad fix the sprinklers and petting your Dalmatian. You ran up to your dad and gave him a big bear hug and strolled into the house where Mom and Adam were. You told Dad that when you die you want this exact moment to be your heaven and he smiles at you.

You cannot stop crying. You feel sorry for yourself again as you watch the bagels your aunts brought you, but you cannot eat them. Petra tells you really should, and you refuse. How could you possibly eat anything at this moment? You feel as if though you cannot breathe. You grab your phone and run outside. You run, run, run until you could breathe again, and you wait until you catch your breath. You call Will. He answers right away. You are both in so much shock. He hands the phone to his little five-year-old sister and your heart warms up for a moment at the sound of her sweet, quivery voice. You are sitting on your rock by the lake, and you watch in amazement as a beautiful, foreign-looking duck swims towards a regular-looking duck and her two baby ducks. A peaceful energy washes over you, and for one second, you feel as if you are yourself again, as if you've floated back down into your body. The beautiful duck gracefully swims away from the mom duck and her baby ducks. You are telling this to Will with a smile on your face. He tells you he's on his way to see you.

"Meet me at my park," you tell him. You hang up.

You run to the hill that overlooks your elementary school, your childhood. It's exactly where you want to be. Will told Ted and Barney and they arrive first. They envelop you in a trio hug, and you feel their love fill the void that is your stomach. You've imagined this moment in your head over one hundred times, and now that it is here, it feels strange and dreamlike. Will hugs you, and in that moment, you tell yourself that just for being here for me, I'd marry him. He notices your legs, and you feel embarrassed that you haven't shaved your legs in two weeks. Your friends drive you home, and the plan that you are going to your best friend's pool has been made. You feel as though the whole world knows your dad died on Thursday, May 14th at 12:30 PM. You feel as though you have to inform the whole world, maybe then you'll believe it, maybe then you'll float back into your body. You have no idea but for the next couple of your days you're about to receive the most amount of chocolate chip cookies and flowers you've ever received in your life. You are in the shower, shaving your legs, and for the first time you realize how skinny you look and enjoy the momentary pleasure of it. You think of how it's been about two hours since your dad died, and you feel like punching the wall as hard as you can. You think of how that would make your mom feel so you decide against it.

You drink one of your dad's protein milk drinks from the hospital. You cherish every vanilla drop of it. For one moment you feel as if though you've accepted your dad's death. You float away even further now, maybe you are eating popcorn in outer space as you watch your body go to Rachel's pool and laugh and forget and have fun. You are with your friends and as you feel their love, it's like your dad hasn't died. You feel like yourself a little bit as you swim in the pool, and smile as you tell your dad, "We are both free now."

You feel as if that is the sole truth, yet when you look at your phone and feel the physicality of it, you are confused that you will never call or text your dad again. You are angry that Will has resigned himself to be alone, you are surprised that his attitude is grim and depressing in contrast to yours. Your brother hasn't left your side. You, Adam, Rachel, Barney, Ted, Will, Saul, Marie, and Adam's friend from rehab all go to eat at Denny's together. You order a steak, and for the first time in days, you can finally taste the flavor in food again. You talk to Rachel in the bathroom, you feel as if she is speaking to you without really saying any words. Denny's is nice. Ted drives you home. There is an unspoken agreement that he is sleeping over. You both go back to your rock, back to the peaceful strip of water you claim as your own and gaze at the moon which has a rainbow halo around it. You've never seen that before. You feel reassured that everything is going to be okay. A part of you misses your first love and you wonder aloud why things ended the way they did and why you didn't get back together with him. Ted talks about the irrational nature of love. You are tired, you both walk home. You think of how strong Hazel is for already having gone through this, even though you know you are okay, as you are still watching the scenes of this day unfold. It's already May 15th, and you feel comfort as you continue the conversation with Ted about your dad or the universe or love or whatever it is you're talking about. You survived today you think, as sleep finally takes you in and holds your hands. You are free of your mind, of your emotions, of your body.

You are dreaming, sound asleep, completely unaware of what the Universe has in store for you the next day. I am watching you. I am here. *It's okay.*

I am *always* here.

EPILOGUE

"Right over there," I pointed to the light brown building bearing the sign: Green Office Building.

"Alright, I'll park over here," Jacob said, turning the car around.

"We have a couple of minutes before my therapy starts," I told him, unwrapping my delicious chicken sandwich.

"Finish your sandwich!" Jacob urged, nudging my shoulder.

"I know! I've been talking this whole time!" I whined, taking a bite and savoring the melted cheese and juicy tomato swirling in my mouth.

"You know, Ana…you were right."

"About what?"

"What I've been through this year in the Marines is no match to what you've gone through. I'm sorry if I made it seem like I had it worse."

I smiled at him. What else could I say? I'd said pretty much everything. There was almost no need for today's therapy session. He leaned over and gave me a hug. I hugged him back and chuckled. "I told you so."

He shook his head slowly in disbelief. "You really have grown up to be a strong ass woman. I guess I missed my chance."

"Yeah. You did." I chuckled. But it was still nice to have Jacob as a friend. I glanced at the time. The bright sun burned my eyes, as it made its way down the sky, leaving room for the stars to come out and play.

"Thank you, Jacob," I said, opening the car door, still feeling his embrace lingering on my skin.

"No, Ana. Thank you. You just put my life into perspective."

I smiled and exited the car, carrying his compliment all the way to the stairs of the therapy office along with a four letter word I spelled over and over again between each step—hope.

"The Lonely Cockroach"

by Rogelio Frias

Once upon a time, there was a garden full of tropical plants and fruit trees by a house, and inside one of these fruit trees, there lived a little cockroach. The little cockroach loved to grow vegetation and watch the flowers bloom and turn into fruit (in case you didn't know, almost all flowers bloom into fruit). She loved to eat the mangos, oranges, and avocados that grew in the beautiful garden. We might say the little cockroach was very happy, but this would be a lie, because the truth was—she was very lonely. Of the four hundred or so eggs that her mother had laid, hers was the only one to survive. She had no sisters or brothers with which to play, and because mother roaches lay eggs then leave them, she didn't have her mother or father either.

One day, the lonely cockroach decided it was time to make some friends so she wouldn't have to feel like the only cockroach in such a large garden. In plain daylight, she set out to look for friends—a big mistake, since roaches tend to come out at night, although she didn't know at the time. She crawled up the orange tree and saw a colorful bird picking at one of the juicy oranges, with green and yellow feathers all over its body. When it saw the lonely cockroach, it stopped eating and stared at it.

"Who are you?" the roach asked.

"I'm a parakeet from the Amazon," the bird replied.

"What are you doing in this garden?" the cockroach asked.

"I'm eating an orange, because I love them so. My owner used to feed them to me when I lived in her cage."

"What's a cage?" the roach asked.

"It's a box you cannot get out, cannot fly, and you can only eat and sleep. It's verrrry boring. One day, when my owner opened the cage, I flew out. He'd forgotten to trim my wings this time, so I took the chance."

"So, your owner didn't love you?" the little cockroach asked.

"At first when he took me home, he loved me a lot. He would talk to me and show me how to talk. He would repeat words over and over so that

I could learn them. He would take me out of the cage, put me on his shoulder, and scratch my head. I was very happy, but over time, when he noticed I wasn't repeating words as quickly as he would've liked, he got tired and didn't pay attention to me anymore. He left me long periods of time in the cage and wouldn't take me out anymore. He would only come by to give me food and water, clean my prison, and I noticed that these tasks would bother him, which is why I escaped."

"Well, now that you are free, do you want to be my friend?" the little roach asked.

The parrot thought about this a moment then replied, "But you don't have green and yellow feathers like I do. You don't have a beak like me either, and I don't think you can squawk as loudly as I can."

"No, I can't do the things that you do."

"Then we can't be friends," said the parrot sadly, flying off the branch.

Too bad, thought the little roach. I thought we might've been good friends.

She climbed down the orange tree and went up the wooden fence next to the garden. Along the way, she ran into a gray rat running along the fence, a little ball of dog kibble between its teeth. The little roach had to shout so that the rat wouldn't run him over. "STOOOPPPP!" she screamed.

The rat seemed surprised and exclaimed, "Why are you stopping me? Don't you know that we rats are always running to keep from getting caught?"

"No, I didn't, but had I not shouted, you would've run me over. Some of my legs or Antennae would've been broken!"

"Well, what do you want? Tell me quickly. I'm in a big hurry. I have to eat and feed my children, eat and feed my children again, and once that's done, have children again, and feed those too."

"Wow, you're so busy! No wonder you're running so much."

"I repeat, what is it you want? Tell me already," the rat asked.

"Would you like to be my friend?" the little cockroach said quickly for fear of being run over by the rat.

"No, I cannot. I already told you everything I have to do, eat and feed my children, eat and feed my children. I don't have time for such nonsense, so please get out of my way."

The cockroach moved out of the way, and the rat ran to her den to eat and feed her children. "What a pity the rat could not be my friend," the little roach said. "I'll keep looking for new friends."

She climbed down the fence and came to the back terrace of the house where a large white dog with black spots slept peacefully. The little cockroach was very curious to see this great animal and decided to tickle his nose with one of her Antenna. When the dog felt tickled, he leaped up and started barking which scared the lonely little roach.

"Shut up, please. You will break my ears. You bark very strongly."

The dog was surprised to see that the cockroach answered him rather than run away. "Why aren't you running away? Aren't you afraid of me?"

"No, I am not afraid. Your loud barking hurts my ears. Why should I be afraid of you?"

"Because I am the caretaker of this house, and it is my job to scare strangers like you so they stay away."

"That's your job?"

"Yes."

"Why do you take care of this house?" the little roach asked.

"Haven't you heard that dog is man's best friend?"

"No," replied the cockroach. "Well, those living in this house are humans—a man, a woman, and a small child."

"Then, they are your best friends?"

"Yes," answered the dog.

"Then you know how to be a friend!"

"Of course!"

"What is it like having a friend?" the little roach asked.

"Well, every time I see them even through the glass doors, it gives me great joy. I wag my tail from side to side to let them know how happy I am to see them. If they come into the courtyard, that makes me happier, as I can approach them, and they caress my head, pet me, and talk to me. They also are happy to see me, but not always. Sometimes they are upset or angry and only come out to fill my plate with food."

"How do you feel when that happens?"

"I stop wagging my tail and hang my head. I don't know if they are angry at me, but that does not matter because they are my masters, and I still love them."

"Then you can be my friend!" the little roach said happily.

"Hmm, I don't know," the dog said. "Can you caress my head?"

"No."

"Can you scratch behind my ears?"

"No."

"Can you play fetch with me?"

"No."

"Can you feed me?"

"No."

"Then I don't think we can be friends. You don't do any of the things that my humans do."

"I could keep you company and talk to you here in the garden."

"That's true. Sometimes I feel lonely, but then you might distract me from my job, and I wouldn't be able to watch the house. No, I definitely can't be your friend. Now, go, I must keep watch."

"But you were asleep when I tickled your nose."

"That's true, but my excellent sense of smell and hearing warns me anytime something foreign is near the house. So, go find someone else."

The little cockroach left the dog sadly and found a small hole in the wall of the house. She was curious and went through it, finding herself inside the house. It was dark and humid, as she walked around for a while unable to see very well. She saw a ray of light and upon getting closer, saw it was another hole in the wall though which she could pass easily. She entered the indentation and discovered a beautiful place—a bedroom with a wooden floor, shimmering and clean. On the walls were drawings of unicorns, clouds, the sun, hills with green pastures, sheep, cows, and children playing with hoops. There were many toys on the floor—dolls, balls, colored and numbered cubes. In the middle of the room was a pretty little girl with hair black as night and eyes as big as the moon.

The 10-month-old baby was seated on a pink blanket, chewing on a plastic ring even though she had no teeth. The little cockroach approached her very slowly. She was afraid of the baby making a loud noise same way the dog had. When the baby saw the little roach, she stopped chewing the plastic ring, smiled, and extended her hand to grab her. The little cockroach had to leap away so that the baby's hand wouldn't crush her. Nonetheless, she remained watching the baby, hypnotized watching those large eyes full of spark and innocence.

Same way she'd done with the other creatures, the little roach asked the baby if she wanted to be her friend, but the baby just kept smiling without answering the question. The little roach crept closer and climbed onto the baby's bare foot, making the baby laugh even harder. This made the lonely cockroach smile and laugh too. How fun it was to be with such an adorable creature!

Suddenly, she heard a noise—the baby's mother's footsteps, and her voice—"Ana, my love, what is making you laugh so hard?"

Though the bedroom door, the little roach saw a young woman, tall with the same eyes as her daughter, and she ran to hide behind her baby. The little girl stopped laughing and smiled at her mother. "Oh, what a smiley little girl! You're so happy, my little heart!" the mother said to Baby Ana, kneeling and giving her kisses on her forehead.

"Well, my love, I'll let you play while I go back to work." When the mother left the room, the little cockroach came out of hiding from behind the baby, and when little Ana saw her, she smiled again.

The little roach climbed onto her foot, as Ana began smiling and cracking up once again. What a joy it was to be with this pretty little girl. In her heart, the little cockroach knew that now she had a playmate. After a while, she heard the baby's mother's footsteps, as she called out, "It's time for your bath!"

The little roach once again ran to the small hole in the wall where she could watch the mother hold her baby in her arms and take her from the room. At last she was happy! Finally, she had someone to play with. Several days went by, and every day, the little roach would climb out of her hiding spot to play with little Ana. She knew that, even though they couldn't speak to each other, their hearts were intertwined through play and laughter.

One day, while both playing and laughing, the little roach didn't hear the mother's footsteps coming into the room, and upon seeing the roach near her baby screamed louder than the dog had with her barks. So acute was the little roach's hearing, the screams hurt her ears as though someone had pierced her eardrums with a needle.

"Ayyyy! How horrible! A roach!" While the mother screamed, she picked up the baby and tried forcefully stepping on and squashing the little roach.

The roach would shift from side to side trying not to get stepped on, as the footsteps would come awfully close. Finally, she ran to her small hole in the wall to hide, watching as the mother breathed with difficulty after stomping so hard against the wood floor.

Upon hearing her mother scream, Ana became frightened and cried out. The little roach didn't know what was happening. She'd never seen her friend cry before and felt great pain in her heart, so much that she began crying too.

Several days went by, and Ana hadn't come back to the room. The little roach would patiently wait for her every afternoon, hoping she'd be alone so she could play with her. It never happened. One morning, two men wearing uniforms and name tags on their shirts came into Ana's room and began making tiny holes in the wall through which they'd push small hoses that would squirt white foam. The interior of the walls began to fill with foam, and the little roach, being curious and all, got close to the foam. One of her Antennas touched it. Nothing happened, so she bravely walked over the foam.

The little roach began feeling a strange sensation. Suddenly, she felt very sleepy. She couldn't walk anymore, and her eyes were closing despite wanting to stay awake. How strange that now she couldn't move her feet nor her Antenna, even though she no longer wanted to be on top of the foam.

Thoughts came to her mind, recalling all the afternoons spent laughing with her little friend, Ana, and something strange happened. The little roach could see her own body immobile in the foam, but in that moment, she realized she could pass through the walls into the baby's room, floating through the air, and something even more surprising occurred—traveling through the walls into the room where the uniformed men were, she could reach the spot where her friend was without any problem.

There she found Ana next to her mother, still biting the plastic ring. Upon seeing the little roach, Ana once again smiled the same way she had every afternoon when the little roach had come to play with her. The lonely little roach climbed up to the baby's bare foot, and as always, Ana cracked up from the tickling sensation the little roach's feet were causing. Surprised, the baby's mother turned to see what was making her laugh so much, but this time the little roach wasn't scared—she was having more fun than ever before.

She saw how the mother's eyes filled with maternal love upon seeing her daughter happy. Now the little roach was very happy indeed. She could be with her friend forever now, and they could play together without ever worrying about anything separating them ever again.

A Chapter for Rafael

You barely know who I am, and I barely know who you are. But I love you and accept you with my entire heart and soul, not only because of how much you loved my dad, albeit yes, that has a lot to do with it, but for your existence. You've shown me a dimension to love that's been blurred into so many lies and misconceptions that I could only imagine the resilience you have gained from my dad's love. We may not know who our hearts are, but we are continually loved by the same heart every waking moment of our lives. Even if you've moved on, we will eternally be connected by that same love—my dad's heart. And the grand truth is that it isn't just my dad's love that connects you and me, but God's love that connects every single being on this planet. It's not a matter of making marriage legal or ensuring job equality in the workplace, it's only a matter of waking up. Thank you. I am awake, and I love you.

ACKNOWLEDGMENTS

I was nineteen and I was canvassing for GRC when some dude pissed me off because he told me he didn't care about gay rights. I walked into Starbucks and saw a sign that was advertising a course for first-time authors, taught by Gaby Triana. I took the course. It was fabulous. Then two years later Gaby became my editor. Thank you for being such a kind, compassionate editor, Gaby, and for opening this door for me.

Around a year later, I met my first reader, also coincidentally at Starbucks. He became the reason I decided to keep at it in spite of a lieu of rejections from literary agents. Thank you, DC. I thought of you every time I wanted to secretly give up. You reminded me of the healing power of literature, and you gave me the opportunity to be the healer. Thank you. Thank you. Our dads are definitely proud of us.

I feel grateful for every single person in Always. Every. Single. Person. (you know who you are).

I'm grateful for my fourth-grade teacher, Debbie Terreros, for introducing me to the sacred craft of writing, and for being the first teacher to believe in me.

I'm grateful for my mom, my dad, my brother, my grandmother, my aunts, my uncles, my cousins, and my friends from Mexico. I love you. Always.

I'm grateful for Micaela Diaz who gave me comforting words of advice when I felt like no one would read it. She told me, "Always will reach the people it's meant to reach". Thank you. I love you.

For Chelsea Garcia, who talks to me as if though I'm already some big shot bestselling author/ filmmaker living it up in LA. THANK YOU. I love you.

For Claudia Suero, who feels like my soul sister and artist companion. YOU HAVE SO MUCH TALENT AND I CANNOT WAIT FOR THE WORLD TO SEE IT. I believe in you just as much as you believe in me. Our conversations inspire and nurture me so much. T h a n k y o u. I love you.

For Marialaura Suero, you're the first person to read "A Girl I Loved in Mexico" and I am so grateful we share the love of literature. Your voice is as rare and unique as your soul. You blow me away with your wisdom, soul sister. Thank you. I love you.

For the authors/memoirists who have inspired my writing: Elizabeth Gilbert, Cheryl Strayed, Amanda Palmer, Lena Dunham, David Sedaris, Laura Vaisman, and Porochista Khakpour just to name a few. You're all so phenomenal to me.

And Rupi Kaur…I went to your show at Olympia Theatre in Miami, FL and decided on that day I, too, would be up on that stage reciting my work. You are a force to be reckoned with, and you inspired me to self-publish my very first baby! Thank you, girl.

Last but not least, thank you Franz-Joseph Castillo.

I have no idea what the future holds but ever since I met you, I haven't been the same. I've felt unstoppable. I'm making my wildest dream come true, and I have a best friend who is doing the same thing (well right now you're playing a video game…which sounds pretty annoying…so many explosions…). Anyway, you are my twin flame. You are a star in the making, my love. You are golden, as you are. I love you. I'm here for you. Forever and always. I love you.

Thank you.
I love you.
Always, always,
always.

ABOUT THE AUTHOR

Anaregina Frias is an author, poet, actress, filmmaker, and proud dog mom. A strong proponent of self love and spiritual growth, Ana writes to heal her wounds. She shares her writing with the world in hopes that it can also help her readers heal. You can catch her on Instagram (@author.anaregina.frias) where she uses her platform to attest to the true merit and strength of vulnerability. She currently lives with her dog, Jodie, in Miami, FL, where she was born and raised.

Always